MORAVIAN FAMILIES OF GRACEHAM, MARYLAND

The
Families Belonging to the Moravian
Community and Congregation at
Graceham in Maryland and
Some of Their
Neighbors

1750–1871

Henry James Young

HERITAGE BOOKS
2019

HERITAGE BOOKS
AN IMPRINT OF HERITAGE BOOKS, INC.

Books, CDs, and more—Worldwide

For our listing of thousands of titles see our website
at
www.HeritageBooks.com

A Facsimile Reprint
Published 2019 by
HERITAGE BOOKS, INC.
Publishing Division
5810 Ruatan Street
Berwyn Heights, Md. 20740

Originally published 1942

International Standard Book Numbers
Paperbound: 978-1-888265-87-3
Clothbound: 978-0-7884-9080-4

CONTENTS

PREFACE V

ABBREVIATIONS USED VI

ALPHABETICAL LISTING OF FAMILIES ... 1

SOME NEGRO BAPTISMS 122

PREFACE

It is a matter of great regret to the translator and editor that his entrance into the United States Army will make it impossible to add a bit of polish to this account before releasing his notes for typing. It was originally his intention to make a literal translation of the whole of the register; but the appalling magnitude of the task, together with the fact that practically all of the non-genealogical material is embodied in Oerter's History of Graceham, served to dissuade him.

In view of the fact that this is in the nature of an abstract, arranged alphabetically by family groups, an indication of the source of each entry is given: e.g. 2:147 means Volume II, page 147, in the photostat copies of the Register that are to be found in the custody of the pastor loci and at the Maryland Historical Society. The original registers have been sent to the Moravian Archives at Bethlehem, Pennsylvania.

The coöperation of the pastor and of the Maryland Historical Society are much appreciated.

Henry James Young

York, Pennsylvania
February 16, 1942

ABBREVIATIONS USED

Ja	January
F	February
Mr	March
Ap	April
My	May
Je	June
Jl	July
Ag	August
S	September
O	October
N	November
D	December

ACKER, Mary Magdalena married Jacob Hahn.
ADAM, Jacob married Eve Elizabeth Miller.
    Issue: Eva Maria (1:149), born N 18, 1835; baptized D 13, 1835.
ADAMS, James married Elizabeth _____.
    Issue: Cynthia married Conrad Lammerson.
ADELSPERGER, See Armsperger
ADLESPERGER, Catharine married John Hahn.
ALBAUGH, Andrew H. married N 22, 1860 Miranda Priscilla Clem (2:156).
ALLENDAR, Mary Ann married William M. Flatt.
AMBROSE, Amanda C. married Washington A. Reidenour.
AMBROSE, Hannah married George Stokes.
AMBROSE, John of Harbaugh's Valley married Jl 26, 1877 Amanda Smith (2:163).
AMBROSE, Mary married William Delaplane.
AMBROSE, Sophia married Peter Schober.
ANDERS, Samuel married Anna _____.
    Issue: Effie Orelia (2:69), born D 2, 1871; baptized F 15, 1876.
ANDERSEN, Johann married Elisabeth _____.
    Issue: Maria (1:184), born O 23, 1797; baptized D 10, 1797.
ANDERSON, Thompson, near Otterbein Chapel, married Mr 3, 1870 Susan Warn
    (2:160).
APPLE, Susanna Magdalena married Isaac Hankey.
ARMSPERGER or ADELSPURGER, William married Hannah Hughes.
    Issue: Mary Emma Jane (1:102), born S 20, 1842; baptized D 4, 1842.
        William Alvin (2:115), born Ag 15, 1846; baptized D 6, 1846.
ARNOLD, Ursula Barbara married John Frederick Schlegel.
ARTHUR, Maranda V. married James A. McGuigan.
ARTHUR, Margaret married Timothy Cox.
ARTHUR, Sarah married William Stull.

BACHMAN, Henry T. of Nazareth (2:156) married O 28, 1860 Sarah Ellen Gernand
    of Graceham (2:34), dau. of John Jacob Gernand and Syvilla (Wilhide); born
    Ag 7, 1839; baptized Ag 25, 1839.
    Issue: Clara Rebecca (2:244); born F 2, 1865; died Ag 14, 1868; buried at
        Graceham Ag 15, 1868.
        Joseph Chester (2:62), born Je 5, 1868; baptized Jl 26, 1868.
        Helen (2:64), born F 22, 1870; baptized Ap 10, 1870.
BACHMAN, U. C. married M. A. _____.
    Issue: Sarah Jane (2:54), born S 17, 1859; baptized O 16, 1859.
BAILY, William, innkeeper, married Phoebe (or Peppina) Salome _____.
    Issue: Edward (1:196), born Ap 2, 1801; baptized Jl 27, 1803.
        Mary Elisa (1:196), born Mr 28, 1803; baptized Jl 27, 1803.
        Jacobus Terbit (1:208), born O 30, 1807; baptized Ap 3, 1809.
BAKER, Mary A. married David A. Martin.
BECKER, Anna Dorothea (2:240), born O 20, 1800; died F 26, 1865; buried at
    Creagerstown F 28, 1865.
BECKER, George married Anna Barbara Ewald.
    Issue: Maria Magdalene (2:121), born O 10, 1855; baptized My 6, 1856.
        Anna Elizabeth (2:124), born Ag 2, 1858; baptized Mr 30, 1859.
        Augustus Henry (2:125), born Ja 16, 1862; baptized Mr 24, 1862.
BAKER, Henry Augustus married Mary Elizabeth Crouse.
    Issue: Mary Ann (2:130), born O 24, 1869; baptized O 24, 1869.
BECKER, John Frederick, breeches-maker, married Anna Elizabeth Schneider.
    Issue: Anna Theodora married John Jacob Gernand.
BALTZELL, Lawrence (1:85, 2:226), born Ag 10, 1803; married Ja 19, 1830
    Susan Hahn, daughter of Jacob Hahn and Maria (Acker). He was the son of
    Jacob Baltzell and Charlotte (Christ); died Jl 12, 1855, buried at Mechan-
    icstown Jl 14.
    Issue: Sarah Ann Catharine (1:106), born Ja 2, 1844, baptized Ap 14, 1844.

1

BANKS, Thomas W. married Hannah Maria Irvin.
Issue: Anna Maria (2:113), born Mr 6, 1846, baptized O 14, 1846.
BÄR, Eva married Martin Bohr.
BÄR, Maria married Michael Bohr.
BARKMANN, Christina married Jacob Biggs.
BARTON, _____ married Lewis Troxel.
BARTON, Mary Margaret married William N. Fogle.
BASSFORD, Louisa married Edward Gernand.
BASTIAN, Catharine married Samuel Dorf.
BATTHAUER, Andreas (1:91, 1:107), Probationer Mr 6, 1764, Communicant Ap 16,
    1766; married Hannah _____ (1:91, 1:107, 1:229), who was born in Hesse-
    Cassel Ap 3, 1733, Probationer Mr 6, 1764, Communicant Ap 16, 1766, died O
    8, 1771 at 1 a.m. and buried O 9.
BAUER, Susanna married John George Beierle.
BAUERSACHS, Lydia married Frederic Young.
BAUMAN, Elizabeth married Abraham Snyder.
BAUMGÄRTNER, Elizabeth married Jonathan Weller.
BAXTER, Joseph died Je 26, 1870, aged 24-6-28, buried at Stone Church,
    Mechanicstown Je 27 (2:246).
BEATTY, Lewis A. (2:227), born Mr 20, 1782, died Ap 9, 1856, buried in
    Mechanicstown Ap 11, 1856.
BECK, Daniel of Lockland, Ohio (2:161), aged 27, married first S 7, 1871
    Frances Dorsey, dau. of Owen and Hetty Dorsey of Graceham.
BECK, Gerhard married Lydia Lieberknight.
Issue: William Henry (2:113), baptized F 9, 1845.
BECK, The Reverend John Martin married Anna Johanna Grube, dau. of Bernhard
    Adam Grube.
Issue: John (1:172b), born 2:30 a.m. Je 16, 1791, baptized Je 19, 1791.
    Benigna Louisa (1:244,178), born 3 a.m. Je 16, 1794, baptized 1st
        Sunday after Trinity, buried in the churchyard Ag 22, 1794; cause
        of death: eye-cough-cold complex with convulsions.
    Johanna Elisabeth (1:182), born 5 p.m. My 31, 1796, baptized Je 5,
        1796.
BEIERLE, Frederick (2:145), married D 23, 1828 Sabina Herbach (1:201),
    daughter of Christian and Maria Elisabeth (Williar) Herbach, who was born
    N 10, 1805, baptized N 28, 1805.
Issue: Samuel Nicholas (1:142), born D 18, 1831; baptized Ap 1, 1832.
BEYERLE, Jacob (Lutheran elder); his eldest daughter Maria Magdalena married
    Paul Süss.
BEIERLE, John George son of Jacob and Maria Dorothea Beierle married Susanna
    Bauer.
Issue: Maria Barbara (1:186), born N 8, 1798, baptized N 23, 1798.
    Elisabeth (1:196), baptized O 5, 1803.
    Jacob (1:205, born F 18, 1808, baptized Mr 1, 1808.
    Rebecca married Peter Wile.
BEIERLE, John married Susanna Miller.
Issue: Anna Margareta (1:94), born Ja 7, 1838, baptized My 6, 1838.
    John Miller (1:98), born O 3, 1839, baptized Ja 25, 1840.
    Laura Emma (1:110), born Je 21, 1844, baptized S 29, 1844.
    Lewis Americus (2:114), born My 28, 1846, baptized Jl 19, 1846.
BEIER[LE], Philip Jacob married Elisabeth Bippus (1:152).
BEIERLE, Magdalena married Solomon Valentine.
BEIERLE, Maria married Thomas Ogle.
BEIERLE, Susan married Jacob Matthews.
BEKKENBACH, _____ married James Gammel.
BENHOFF, John married Sarah Müller.
Issue: Sophia (1:218), born Je 10, 1815, baptized F 8, 1816.
BENNER, Nancy married Philip Young.

BENNER, Thomas Leander (member of no church) married Mary Catharine _____ (Methodist).
Issue: Margaret Ellen (2:131), baptized D 18, 1870.
BENSER, Barbara married Richard Lammerson.
BERG, Elizabeth married Daniel Staub.
BERNHARD, George Peter married Catharina Dieter.
Issue: Joseph (1:267), born Ja 5, 1799, baptized Je 11, 1799 by Schlegel on a trip to Cumberland and Bedford.
BERNHART, _____ (1:87) married Mary Gilbert daughter of John and Elizabeth Gilbert and later wife of Peter Finnegan.
BERRY, James married Peggi Trebe.
Issue: Jacobus (1:197), born O 12, 1803, baptized D 18, 1803.
BERTS, Sarah married Henry Favorite.
BICKLE (or BIKLE), Christian Emmanuel married Barbara Fichter.
Issue: Ludwig Albrecht (1:148), born N 6, 1834, baptized Ja 17, 1835.
Carl August (1:151), born Jl 3, 1836, baptized O 17, 1836.
Wilhelm Emanuel (1:97), born N 3, 1838, baptized Mr 31, 1839.
BIGGS, Amanda married Elias Groff.
BIGGS, Benjamin, Esquire, married Elisa Ohler.
Issue: Amanda (1:197), born My 4, 1803, baptized D 11, 1803.
BIGGS, Catharine married Jacob Cookerly.
BIGGS, Catharine married John Knauff.
BIGGS, Frederick married Maria _____.
Issue: Frederick Willson (1:221), born Mr 11, 1818, baptized O 29, 1818.
BIGGS, Jacob (2:242), born Mr 11, 1788, died My 6, 1866, buried in the family cemetery My 8.
BIGGS, Jacob, farmer, married Christina Barkmann.
Issue: Zacharias (1:196), born Ap 15, 1803, baptized Je 5, 1803.
BIGGS, Jacob (1:86) son of Jacob and Eve Biggs, married Je 2, 1831 Maria Troxel, daughter of John and Elisabeth (Dodero) Troxel.
BIGGS, John, farmer and store-keeper, married Priscilla Wilson.
Issue: Elisabeth (1:191), born My 5, 1801, baptized My 20, 1801.
Carolina (1:196), born S 18, 1803, baptized S 25, 1803.
BIGGS, John Jacob (2:225), born O 4, 1847, died D 14, 1854, buried in the family cemetery.
BIGGS, Joseph Wilson, M.D. (2:246), married Juliana Orr; he died Ag 3, 1870, aged 71-10-13, buried at Stone Church, Mechanicstown, Ag 4.
Issue: Arminius Augustus (1:141), born Mr 4, 1831, baptized Ap 14, 1831.
Carline Marcella (1:95), born D 10, 1837, baptized Ag 21, 1838.
BIGGS, Mary C. married John S. Irons.
BIGGS, Susan M. married John Knauff.
BIGGS, Thomas Wilson, born N 13, 1828, died D 22, 1875 after a lingering illness brought on principally by hard drinking; buried at Mechanicstown D 24, 1875.
BINKELE, Johan Adam (1:91), Probationer O 16, 1773, married Magdalena (1:91), Probationer O 16, 1773.
Issue: John Jacob (1:160), born Ja 23, 1767, baptized Ja 27, 1767.
John (1:161), born in the evening F 12, 1768, baptized F 15, 1768.
John Petrus (1:162), born S 15, 1770 (in the morning), baptized S 17, 1770.
John Jacob (1:164), born 8 a.m. Ag 1, 1772, baptized Ag 2, 1772.
Elizabeth (1:165), born N 25, 1774 (4 a.m.), baptized N 27, 1774.
BINKELE, Peter married Margaret _____.
Issue: Elizabeth (1:126,232), born D 19, 1749, died Ja 23, 1780, married John George Harbaugh.
Anna Maria (1:158), born Ag 29, 1764, early in the morning; baptized S 2, 1764.
Jacob (1:160), born in the morning O 8, 1767, baptized on the Anniversary of the congregation.

3

BIPPUS, Christine married John Umbach.
BIPPUS, Elisabeth married Philip Jacob Beierle.
BIRCH, Sarah Ann married Henry Eaton.
BISSINGER, Maria Magdalena married Jacob Snyder.
BLACK, Henry married Elizabeth Lot.
  Issue: Margaret Magdalena (1:147), born N 23, 1833, baptized Ag 7, 1834.
BLACK, John (1:89) married Ag 7, 1838 Hannah C. Perry.
BLAZE, John, schoolmaster, married Barbara _____.
  Issue: Joshua (1:190), born Ja 25, 1800, baptized N 30, 1800.
BLECH, The Reverend Carl Gottlieb married Maria Warner.
  Issue: Ernst Friedrich (1:202), born My 18, 1806, baptized My 18, 1806.
    Nathan Warner (1:206,264), born Jl 15, 1808, baptized Jl 17, 1808,
      died Ja 14, 1815 and buried Ja 15..
    Carolina Sophia (1:211), born N 5, 1810, baptized N 11, 1810.
    Phoebe Anna (1:215), born Jl 18, 1813, baptized Jl 25, 1813.
    Maria Elisabeth (1:219), born Je 11, 1816, baptized Je 16, 1816.
    Edward Julius (1:111, 266), born Ap 24, 1819, baptized Ap 24, 1819,
      died Ap 24, 1819 and buried Ap 25.
BLICKENSDERFER, Jesse married Jane W. Rondthaler.
  Issue: Grace Margaret (2:66), born Ja 16, 1872, baptized Mr 17, 1872.
BLUMENSTEIN, Catharine married George Rausch.
BOBLETS, Caroline married Enos Cover.
BOBLETS, Ephraim (1:90) married Mr 20, 1842 Caroline Emilie Gernand (1:113),
  daughter of William and Anna Elizabeth (Johnson) Gernand, who was born Je
  26, 1820 and baptized Jl 28, 1820.
BOBLETS, Jacob of Frederick County (2:149) married F 8, 1846 Josephine Eliza
  Gernand (2:290,6), daughter of Jacob and Anna Theodora (Becker) Gernand,
  of Graceham, who was born Ag 12, 1825, baptized S 4, 1825, admitted to
  Communion O 8, 1839.
  Issue: Eugene Jacob (2:43), born D 21, 1846, baptized F 28, 1847.
    William Henry (2:45), born Ja 7, 1849, baptized Mr 18, 1849.
    Alice Caroline (2:46), born Mr 19, 1851, baptized Ag 8, 1851.
    Ida Angelica (2:48), born F 7, 1853, baptized My 28, 1854.
    Edgar Ephraim (2:123), born N 30, 1856, baptized S 7, 1858.
BÖCKEL, Tobias married Maria Elisabeth Dock (1:260), who was born Mr 24,
  1720 in Bissweilen, Alsace; later wife of George Glatt; she died O 4, 1804
  and was buried O 5.
  Issue: None ?
BOHR, Martin married Eva Bär.
  Issue: John (1:267), born My 26, 1797, baptized Je 10, 1799 by Schlegel on
    a trip to Cumberland and Bedford.
BOHR, Michael son of Nicolaus and Magaretha (Colmer) Bohr married Maria Bär
  Issue: William (1:267), born N 24, 1798, baptized Je 10, 1799 by Schlegel
    on a trip to Cumberland and Bedford.
BÖHRING or BÖHRINGER, Andreas married firstly _____ (name not given) and
  had by this marriage.
  Issue: Eva Elisabetha (1:156), born F 2, 1760, baptized Jl 28, 1760.
He married secondly Eva Rosina Kertscher daughter of Andreas and Dorothea
Kertscher and had by this marriage the following
  Issue: John Andrew (1:156), born N 22, 1760, baptized D 7, 1760.
    Lawrence (1:156), born N 8, 1761, baptized N 15, 1761.
    George Henry (1:157), born 11 p.m. N 2, 1762, baptized N 7, 1762.
    John (1:226,158), born 8 p.m. My 24, 1764, baptized Je 3, 1764,
      died Jl 28, 1767 and buried in the churchyard.
    Matthaeus (1:159), born Jl 19, 1765, baptized Jl 21, 1765.
    Dorothea (1:160), born Ap 11, 1767, baptized Ap 26, 1767.
    John (1:161), born in the evening O 26, 1768, baptized O 30, 1768.
    Anna Johanna (1:162), born 11-12 p.m. S 17, 1770, baptized O 7,
      1770.

4

Anna Rosina (1:163), born 3 a.m. O 5, 1771, baptized O 6, 1771.
Maria Elisabeth (1:164), born towards evening Ja 30, 1773, baptized
F 2, 1773.
BOLLER, Amanda O. married Theodore L. Nale.
BOLLER, Benjamin Hieronymus (2:29), son of William Henry and Anna Maria
(Meffert) Boller, born My 2, 1836, baptized Je 12, 1836, married Anna
_____.
Issue: Harold Ellsworth (2:57), born D 5, 1861, baptized Ja 27, 1862.
William Llewellyn (2:59), born N 6, 1863, baptized N 23, 1863.
BOLLER, Charles Frederick (2:1), son of John and Catharine (Reidenauer)
Boller, born Ja 30, 1823, baptized F 9, 1823. By Rachel Meffert (1:222)
daughter of John and Catharine (Eyler) Meffert, born Mr 3, 1819, baptized
Mr 21, 1819, had an illegitimate son Charles Frederick (1:105), born O 1,
1843, baptized O 9, 1843.
BOLLER, David (1:202), born Ag 11, 1806, baptized Ag 31, 1806, married
Harriet Feezer or Feiser.
Issue: Margareth Elisabeth (1:104), born Je 28, 1841, baptized S 5, 1841.
Beatus (2:217), died 1846 or 1847.
Ellen Maria (2:112), born Jl 4, 1844, baptized Ap 6, 1845.
BOLLER, Edward (no church) married Margaret Savilla Troxel (Reformed).
Issue: Clarence Grayson (2:131), born S 15, 1870, baptized Mr 22, 1871.
Franklin Guy (2:133), born S 22, 1873, baptized F 1, 1875.
BOLLER, Elizabeth married William Stimmel.
BOLLER, Elizabeth married Michael Irons.
BOLLER, Elizabeth married (1) Philip Woodring, (2) John Harbaugh.
BOLLER, Ellen E. (daughter of Israel Boller) married Franklin D. Zentz.
BOLLER, Henry Alexander (2:10), born Ap 14, 1827, baptized Je 4, 1827,
married Cassandra Matilda Hahn.
Issue: John Henry (2:48,223), born My 22, 1853, baptized Jl 17, 1853, died
Ag 15, 1853, buried Ag 16.
Isaiah Washington (2:49), born Ag 13, 1854, baptized Ag 27, 1854.
America Victoria (2:125), born Ag 31, 1861, baptized N 11, 1861.
BOLLER, Israel (2:22, 294), son of John Boller and Catharine (Reidenauer),
born O 4, 1832, baptized O 26, 1832, married Savilla Harbaugh (1:95)
daughter of Henry Harbaugh and Martha Ann (Young), who was born Ap 15,
1838, baptized Je 30, 1838.
Issue: Mary Catharine Elizabeth (2:53), born Je 15, 1858, baptized Ag 29,
1858.
Martha Delilah (2:55,240), born O 15, 1860, baptized D 30, 1860,
died D 6, 1864 and buried at Graceham D 7.
Sarah Ellen (2:58), born S 3, 1862, baptized O 12, 1862.
Georgianna Susan (2:60), born F 19, 1865, baptized My 14, 1865.
Harry Reuben (2:62), born D 18, 1866, baptized Ap 14, 1867.
Samuel Ephraim (2:65), born 1870, baptized O 23, 1870.
Emma Sophia (2:65,246), born My 29, 1870, baptized O 23, 1870, died
My 15, 1871, buried at Graceham My 16.
Charles Nelson Bachman (2:67), born Je 18, 1872, baptized N 21,
1872.
Chloe Daisy Key (2:68), born Jl 22, 1875, baptized N 14, 1875.
BOLLER, John R., farmer (1:133, 2:256,286), son of Philip William Boller,
farmer, and Catharina (Lanius), born Jl 16, 1796 in Northampton Co., Pa.,
married (1) N 21, 1820 Catharine Reidenauer (2:221,286), daughter of Jacob
Reidenauer, joiner in Mechanicstown and Maria (Schmidt), who was born Je
19, 1803 in Frederick County, died S 23, 1851 and buried S 25. Both were
admitted to Communion O 8, 1820.
Issue of this marriage:
Elisabeth (1:80,117), born at Graceham F 9, 1822, baptized F 13,
1822, died F 14, 1822 and buried F 15.
Charles Frederick (2:1), born Ja 30, 1823, baptized F 9, 1823.

5

Maria Emilia (2:5), born D 7, 1824, baptized Ja 13, 1835, married
William Sipes; she died Jl 26, 1862.
Henry Alexander (2:10), (2:293 says Henry Augustus), born Ap 14,
1827, baptized Je 4, 1827, Communicant 1843, married Cassander
Matilda Hahn.
William Owen (2:17,294), born Ap 13, 1830 in Frederick County,
baptized My 30, 1830.
Israel (2:22,294), born O 4, 1832, baptized O 26, 1832, married
Savilla Harbaugh.
Sophia Theresa (2:26), born N 19, 1834, baptized Ja 1, 1835, mar-
ried Ephraim W. Gilbert.
Sabina Matilda (2:31), born Jl 25, 1837, baptized O 1, 1837.
Sarah Caroline (2:34), born N 25, 1839, baptized D 31, 1839, mar-
ried Joshua Gilbert.
John Adam (2:39,216), born Mr 17, 1842, baptized Ap 10, 1742, died
O 7, 1844, buried O 8. His age was 2-6-21.
Anna Catharine (2:41,216), born Ja 31, 1844, baptized F 14, 1844,
died Jl 22, 1844, buried Jl 23. Her age was 0-5-23.
Susan (2:45), born My 4, 1846, baptized Je 20, 1846, married Wesley
Dubel.

Married (2) F 21, 1852 (2:152) Maria Wilhide (1:201; 2:295), daughter of Frederick Wilhide and Catharina (Peitzel), who was born D
23, 1805, baptized Ja 5, 1806, Communicant Ag 13, 1823. He died
S 30, 1880 and was buried at Graceham O 2, 1880.
BOLLER, Phillip William (2:146,218,291), son of Henry Boller and Maria
Elizabeth (Jenner), born Mr 6, 1766 at Appenheim in the Palatinate;
admitted to Communion at Lititz Ag 13, 1788; married (1) Ap 9, 1794 at
Bethlehem Catharine Lanius (2:189), born in York County, Pennsylvania F
10, 1767, died Mr 11, 1824, buried Mr 13. Issue of this marriage follows:
Mary Magdalena (2:195), born F 22, 1795, married George Hoffman,
died S 12, 1828 aged 33-6-21.
John R. (1:133, 2:256,286), born Jl 16, 1796, married (1) Catharine
Reidenauer and (2) Maria Wilhide; he died S 30, 1880, buried at
Graceham O 2, 1880.
Carl Friedrich (1:262), born Ja 7, 1800 in Pennsylvania, died S 18,
1807 of convulsions, buried S 20.
Sarah (2:287), born My 3, 1802, married Benjamin Süss.
David (1:202), born Ag 11, 1806, baptized Ag 31, 1806, married
Harriet Feezer.
William Henry (1:204), born O 23, 1807, baptized Ja 3, 1808.
Catharine (1:211), born Ja 19, 1811, baptized Ap 15, 1811, married
William Stark.
another son.
another daughter.

Married (2) in 1824 Susanna Nitschman (2:203), born O 29, 1786 in
Adams County, Pennsylvania, died Mr 15, 1833 of dropsy, buried Mr
16.
Married (3) Ag 8, 1833 (2:146) Gertraut Williar (2:209), daughter
of Andreas Williar and Margaretha (Herbach), and formerly wife of
Jacob Reidenauer; she was born N 10, 1784, baptized N 15, 1784,
died Je 11, 1835 of consumption, buried Je 13. Philip William
Boller died D 9, 1848, buried D 10.
BOLLER, Sabina married Ezra Young.
BOLLER, Theodore Leander (2:157,31), son of William Henry Boller and Anna
Maria (Meffert), born Ap 1, 1838, baptized My 13, 1838, married Ja 1, 1863
Ann Elizabeth Dorsey.
Issue: Orpha Alice (2:127), born S 25, 1863, baptized Je 5, 1864.

Harry Greely (2:244), born N 13, 1865, died Ag 5, 1868, buried at Graceham Ag 6.

BOLLER, William Henry (2:147,289), son of Philip William Boller and Catharina (Lanius), born O 23, 1807, Communicant Ap 15, 1824, married Ap 10, 1834 Anna Maria Meffert (1:214, 2:240,289), daughter of John Meffert and Catherina (Eyler), who was born Mr 18, 1813, baptized Ap 3, 1813, Communicant at Lititz 1830, died Mr 6, 1865, buried at Graceham Mr 7.
Issue: Daniel Josias (2:26), born O 26, 1834, baptized N 13, 1834.
Benjamin Hieronimus (2:29), born My 2, 1836, baptized Je 12, 1836, married Anna _____.
Theodore Leander (2:31), born Ap 1, 1838, baptized My 13, 1838, married Ann Elizabeth Dorsey.
Lewis Edward (2:38), born S 13, 1840, baptized O 18, 1840.
Amanda Orphy (2:40), born D 9, 1842, baptized Ja 29, 1843.

BORN, Jacob, farmer and joiner (1:108,128), son of Daniel Born; Communicant Ap 1, 1790, married (1) S 1, 1789 Anna Margaret Weller (1:92,108,161,258), eldest daughter of John Weller and Maria Barbara (Krieger), who was born Ag 18, 1769 at 1 p.m. near Graceham, baptized Ag 20, 1769, Probationer O 11, 1789, Communicant Ap 1, 1790, died S 1, 1800, buried S 3. The issue of this marriage follows:
John (1:170b), born My 15, 1790, baptized My 20, 1790, married Margaret Fröhlich.
Margaret (1:173b), born Ag 9, 1791, baptized Ag 14, 1791, married John Smith; she died F 25, 1823.
Maria (1:176), born 11 p.m. Ja 6, 1793, baptized Ja 13, 1793, married John Wilhide.
Elizabeth (1:179), born 2 a.m. Ja 28, 1795, baptized F 1, 1795.
Sarah (1:263,182), born N 17, 1796 at 2 a.m., baptized N 27, 1796, died Mr 8, 1810 of an ardent nerve fever; buried Mr 11.
Rosina (1:186), born D 9, 1798, baptized D 16, 1798, married George Weddel.
Catharine (1:190,258), born 12:30 a.m. Jl 30, 1800, baptized Jl 30, 1799 [sic], died N 5, 1800, buried N 6.

He married (2) Christina Böckel; the issue of this marriage follows:
Daniel (1:194,259), born Jl 17, 1802, baptized Jl 23, 1802, died Ag 6, 1802, buried Ag 8.
Friedrich Jacob (1:199,262), born N 21, 1804, baptized D 2, 1804, drowned in a spring near home N 8, 1808, buried N 10.
Salome Theresia (1:202), born O 4, 1806, baptized O 26, 1806.
Lydia (1:205), born Mr 21, 1808, baptized Mr 27, 1808.
Joseph (1:210), born My 13, 1810, baptized My 27, 1810.

BORN, John (1:131,170b), born in Frederick County My 15, 1790, son of Jacob Born and Anna Margaret (Weller), married Ja 11, 1814 Margaret Fröhlich daughter of Heinrich Fröhlich and Margaretha (Wilhide), who was born in Frederick County. He was baptized My 20, 1790.

BOUSER, David.
Issue: David A. L. (2:250), born Ag 4, 1876, died O 9, 1876, buried in Reformed Cemetery, Sabillasville, O 10.

BOWERS, Jonathan (1:83), son of Frederick Bowers and Elizabeth (Kurtz), married N 22, 1827 Rebecca Derr daughter of John Derr and Elizabeth (Brim).

BOYER, Benjamin Franklin (Lutheran) married Cornelia Ann Elizabeth Harbaugh.
Issue: Emma Missouri (2:64,131), born O 20, 1858, baptized My 2, 1870.
John Hampton (2:64,131), born Ag 24, 1860, baptized My 2, 1870.

BRANDENBURG, Samuel married Magdalena _____.
Issue: Hannah (1:88) married (1) George Wile; (2) George Colliflower.

7

BRANNER, Michael married Anne Feezer.
  Issue: Samuel Kelly (2:112), born Ja 16, 1845, baptized Mr 2, 1845.
BREITBARTH, Maria Elizabeth married Erdman, Sebastian.
BRIM, Elizabeth married John Derr.
BROWN, Amy married John C. Weller.
BROWN, Anna Barbara married Simon Augustus Weller.
BROWN, David, sadler in Mechanicstown, married Elizabeth Kamp.
  Issue: William Wallis (1:79,113), born Mr 16, 1820 in Mechanicstown,
    baptized S 21, 1820, died S 24, 1820 and buried S 25.
    Henrieta (1:118), born Jl 29, 1821, baptized Jl 15, 1822.
BROWN, George (2:159), married Mr 14, 1867 Mary Ann Geesey.
BROWN, Ignatius married Elizabeth McFee.
  Issue: Jeremiah (1:84) married Mary Ann Flauth.
    William (1:86) married Elizabeth Fox.
BROWN, Jeremiah (1:84), son of Ignatius Brown and Elizabeth (McFee) married
  My 29, 1828 Mary Ann Flautt daughter of Jacob Flautt and Emilia (Wolf).
BROWN, John (1:89), son of [Mathias?] and Barbara Brown, married S 29, 1839
  Magdalena Demuth daughter of Henry and Ann Maria Demuth.
BROWN, Joseph (2:243), son of Mathias and Barbara Brown, born Ag 28, 1808,
  died Jl 22, 1866, buried Jl 23 at Apple's Church, married Elizabeth Demuth
  Issue: Amy (1:146), born Jl 3, 1833, baptized S 25, 1833.
    Anna Barbara (1;148), born D 6, 1834, baptized Ap 29, 1835.
BROWN, Lydia Ann married William Leidy.
BROWN, Mathias married Barbara _____.
  Issue: [John (1:89), married Magdalena Demuth ?].
    Joseph married Elizabeth Demuth.
BROWN, Susan married David Harbaugh.
BROWN, Susan married Henry Weddell.
BROWN, Susanna married Daniel Gordon.
BROWN, William (1:86), son of Ignatius Brown and Elisabeth (McFee), married
  S 13, 1830 Elizabeth Fox daughter of George and Ann Elizabeth Fox.
BROWN, William. By Ann Margaret Moser (1:213), daughter of Leonard Moser
  and Lydia Anna (Wolfart), who was born My 15, 1812 and baptized Ag 2,
  1812, had in illegitimate son William Henry (1:148), born N 8, 1832,
  baptized D 10, 1834.
BROWN, William (2:156), married My 1, 1859 Mary E. Carmack.
BRUIN, John George.
  Issue: George (1:267), baptized Je 11, 1799 by Schlegel on a trip to
    Cumberland and Bedford.
BRUNNER, Peter, farmer in the mountains (1:125,79,91,108), born Rothberg,
  Alsace Ja 12, 1740, son of Georg Brunner and Apollonia (Melcher), both of
  Ratte [?], in Zweibrücken; married Ap 16, 1764 (1) Dorothea Lochman
  (1:244,91,108), daughter of Jacob Lochman and Elizabeth (Haffner), born Jl
  12, 1743 in Lancaster, Pennsylvania. Both were Probationers O 12, 1766;
  both were Communicants O 7, 1769, and both were readmitted N 13, 1785
  after five years exclusion. Dorothea died N 20, 1794 and was buried in a
  private burial ground in the Mountains N 22. They had, in all, eleven
  children, four of which survived him, five survived her. They had twenty-
  seven grandchildren and twenty-four great-grandchildren. Their issue, in
  part, follows:
    Maria Elisabeth (1:159,226), born D 31, 1764, baptized Ja 3, 1765,
      died Ap 19, 1766 and buried in the churchyard Ap 21.
    Jacob (1:160), born Mr 18, 1766, baptized Mr 23, 1766.
    Anna Barbara (1:160), born 3 a.m. S 16, 1767, baptized S 20, 1767.
    Henry (1:162,232), born N 10, 1769 at 2 p.m., baptized N 12, 1769,
      died Je 11, 1781 and buried on his father's farm.
    Petrus (1:163), born S 26, 1771, baptized S 29, 1771.
    George (1:163,230), born S 26, 1771 at 7 p.m., baptized S 19, 1771,
      died O 29, 1772 and buried in the Churchyard N 1.

8

Elizabeth (1:165), born Ap 10, 1774, baptized Ap 17, 1774.
John (1:166), born S 10, 1776, baptized S 18, 1776.
Margaret (1:167), born Ja 31, 1779, baptized Mr 14, 1779.
He married (2) (1:79) in Ag, 1796 Anna Elizabeth Haber, formerly
wife of _____ Schmidt. Peter Brunner died Mr 19, 1821, buried
Mr 21 (not in the churchyard).
BUCH (?), Susanna married Emanuel Feizer.
BUCHMEYER, John Henry married Rachel Theresa Ziegler.
Issue: John Frederick (2:7), born N 27, 1825, baptized Ap 15, 1826.
Ann Maria Elisabeth (2:15), born S 11, 1829, baptized S 20, 1829.
Theresia Sophia (2:21), born F 5, 1832, baptized Mr 5, 1832.
Henry Orville (2:31), born S 29, 1837, baptized N 19, 1837.
Clementina Leonora (2:34), born S 24, 1839, baptized O 20, 1839.
BÜHLER, Maria, married (1) ____ Spieker; (2) Daniel Protzman.
BUHRMAN, [Henry[1]] died [Je 9, 1901, aged 82-5-28[1]]; married Charlotte
Matilda Fahs (2:4), born My 24, 1824, baptized Je 27, 1824, dau. of Henry
Fahs and Sophia Frederica (Rudolphi), died [Je 29, 1897, aged 73-1-5[1]].
Issue: Sophia Catory (2:223), born Mr 1, 1852, died S 26, 1853, buried at
Fox's Church S 27.
BUHRMAN, Levi (2:153) married D 27, 1853 Cornelia Augusta Fahs (2:9), daugh-
ter of Henry Fahs and Sophia Frederica (Rudolphi), who was born O 23,
1826, baptized D 25, 1826.
BURCH, William married Martha Hewett.
Issue: Thomas Henry (1:101), born Ja 22, 1842, baptized in Mr, 1842.
Mary Elisabeth (1:110), born Jl 6, 1844, baptized O 2, 1844.
BUSH, Charles Michael (2:231), born Ap 8, 1858, died S 5, 1858, buried S 6
at Apple's Church.
BUSH, David (1:84), son of George Bush and Elizabeth (Crall), married Jl 24,
1828 Rebecca Curfman, daughter of Peter and Susan Curfman.
BUSH, George married Elizabeth Krall (2:18,19), who was baptized O 8, 1830,
died D 26, 1848(?) and buried at Mechanicstown.
Issue: David (1:84) married Rebecca Curfman.
Maria married Nathanael Weller.
BUSH, John married D 10, 1782 Anna Elizabeth Stauffer (2:192,3) who was born
Ap 6, 1760 at Skipack, baptized Ap 11, 1824, died F 20, 1826, buried near
her residence, beside her husband on F 22. She lived to see eight grand-
children.
Issue: Maria Catharina (1:191, 2:217), born Mr 26, 1784, baptized My 25,
1801, married John Jacob Krieger, died Je 10, 1847.
son.
son.
BUSH, John (2:218), died O 4, 1849, aged about 60, buried O 6.
BUSH, Margaret married Michael Dorsey.
BUSH, Mary E. married William Miller.
BUSK, Mary Ann married John Miller.
BUSSE, Matilda Caroline married Ambrose Rondthaler.
BUTLER, Adam married Caty Snog.
Issue: Anna (1:199), born S 19, 1804, baptized N 5, 1804.
BUTLER, Sally married Stephen Hedges.
BUTLER, Susanna married John Daniel.
BUTLER, Susanna married Daniel Jodum.

CAMPLANE, Harriet Ann married Henry Heffner.
CARE, Martha married George Devilbiss, junior.

----

[1] Data here bracketed are from tombstones in the Lutheran Cemetery at
Foxville.

CARLLY, Reuben married Barbara Zollinger.
Issue: Mary Herbert (1:116), born Jl 28, 1820, baptized My 6, 1821.
Zephaniah Herbert (1:116), born Jl 28, 1820, baptized My 6, 1821.
John Zollinger (1:120), born F 15, 1823, baptized Ap 20, 1823.
Reuben Bates (1:122), born S 28, 1824, baptized Ag 9, 1826.
CARMACK, Ephraim (1:87) married Mr 7, 1833 Mary Kuhn daughter of Henry and Elizabeth Kuhn.
CARMACK, Mary E. married William Brown.
CAROTHERS, James married Elisabeth _____.
Issue: William (1:218), born Mr 2, 1815, baptized O 15, 1815.
CARSEN, Maria married Henry Rodeneiser.
CARSON, John Thomas (2:245) married Isabella Weller; he died Ja 22, 1870, aged about 32, and was buried at Graceham.
Issue: Ella Susan (2:60), born My 18, 1865, baptized O 8, 1865.
Charles Edward (2:62), born O 6, 1866, baptized Ag 4, 1867.
Emma Catharine (2:64), born S 22, 1869, baptized Ja 17, 1870.
CARSON, Martha married William Esterlein.
CARTY, Mary married David Shealer.
CHRIST, Charlotte married Jacob Baltzell.
CHRIST, Israel son of Jacob and Christina (Leinbach) Christ. By Rachel Meffert (1:222) daughter of John and Catharine (Eyler) Meffert, born Mr 3, 1819, baptized Mr 21, 1819, had an illegitimate son Israel (1:95), born S 1, 1838, baptized N 25, 1838.
CHRIST, Jacob, gunstock-maker (1:130), of Graceham, married Mr 14, 1809 Christina Leinbach (2:214), 1:174), daughter of Christian and Anna Rosina (Pauss) Leinbach, born F 24, 1787, baptized Mr 4, 1787, died My 23, 1842, buried My 25, 1842.
Issue: John Rudolph (1:209), born O 11, 1809, baptized N 12, 1809.
Anna Sophia (1:213), born Ja 27, 1812, baptized Mr 1, 1812.
William henry (1:215), born N 24, 1813, baptized D 5, 1813.
Israel (1:218), born D 29, 1815, baptized F 25, 1816.
Anna Juliana (1:221), born Ja 16, 1818, baptized My 11, 1818, married George Hosler..
Maria Elizabeth (1:113), born Ag 2, 1820, baptized S 7, 1820.
Charlotte Emilia (1:119), born O 12, 1822, baptized D 1, 1822.
Rebecca Louisa (2:6), born Ap 18, 1825, baptized My 23, 1825.
Henrietta Angelica (2:11), born Ag 27, 1827, baptized O 14, 1827.
CLABAUGH, _____ married Eliza Jane Süss (1:118; 2:255), daughter of Samuel and Maria (Stotz) Süss, born Ja 2, 1822, died N 5, 1879, buried at Grceham N 7, 1879.
CLEM, Josephine Matilda married Samuel S. Rogers.
CLEM, Mary C. married Jacob F. Krieger.
CLEM, Miranda Priscilla married Andrew H. Albaugh.
CLEM, Sarah Ann E. married Grafton H. Craver.
CLEMAN, Margaret had an illegitimate daughter by Jacob Rothrock.
CLEMANN, Margaretha, widow (1:91), Probationer Mr 6, 1764.
CLIFTON, Harry G., Lutheran (2:161), residing at the Ridge, son of George and Mary Clifton, married O 5, 1871 at the age of 28 Ann Eliza Haley (Dunker) daughter of Lawrence and Elizabeth (Harbaugh) Haley at the Ridge, aged 25 when married.
CLOSE, William (2:199), died Jl 6, 1831 of erysipelas at the age of 21, buried Jl 7, 1831.
COLE, Charlotte married Peter Heffner.
COLLIFLOWER (sometimes Garenflor, Kollerflauer, KöllnFlohr, etc.)
COLLIFLOWER, Bernard (2:152,16) son of John and Matilda (Wilhide) Colliflower, born Ja 10, 1830, baptized Mr 21, 1830, died [Je 5, 1901], married Mr 24, 1853 Mary Emeline Gernand (2:23) daughter of John Jacob and Sybilla (Wilhide) Gernand, born F 10, 1833, baptized Mr 17, 1833, died [N 12, 1906].

Issue: William Henry (2:48), born Ja 29, 1854, baptized Ap 23, 1854, married Belva A. E. Cramer, died F 8, 1877.
    James Albert (2:50), born Je 26, 1856, baptized Ag 13, 1856.
    Allen Eugene (2:55), born S 4, 1859, baptized O 30, 1859, died [My 26, 1888].
    Laura Emeline (2:254,56), born O 27, 1861, baptized Ja 12, 1862, died My 20, 1879, buried at Graceham My 22, 1879.
    Addison Harvey (2:68), born Je 12, 1875, baptized O 10, 1875, died [Ja 30, 1894].
COLLIFLOWER, Catharine married John Gerreth.
COLLIFLOWER, Elizabeth married Joseph Gerreth.
COLLIFLOWER, Franklin Amadeus (2:47), born N 21, 1852, baptized F 13, 1853, married Martha Miller.
Issue: Charles Maurice (2:73), born Ag 31, 1880, baptized O 2, 1880.
COLLIFLOWER, George (1:131), married My 31, 1812 Elizabeth Stauffer (1:176) daughter of Christian and Barbara (Weller) Stauffer, born in Frederick County Ag 31, 1792, baptized Mr 3, 1792.
Issue: Joseph (1:214), born Ja 19, 1813, baptized F 26, 1813.
    William Michael (1:217), born Ap 26, 1815, baptized My 29, 1815.
    John Christian (1:117), born Ap 20, 1821, baptized Ag 7, 1821.
    George Jerome (1:120), born O 11, 1823, baptized N 4, 1823.
    James (1:135), born F 18, 1827, baptized My 15, 1827.
COLLIFLOWER, George (1:88), son of Michael and Susan (Snyder) Colliflower, married Mr 28, 1834 Hannah Brandenburg (previously married to _____ Wile), daughter of Samuel and Magdalena Brandenburg.
COLLIFLOWER, Jago (2:160, 1:110), son of John and Matilda (Wilhide) Colliflower, born Je 3, 1844, baptized Je 24, 1844, died [Ja 17, 1914], married D 26, 1869 Agnes C. Weller, born [S 17, 1843].
Issue: Harry Luther (2:65), born N 3, 1870, baptized D 4, 1870, died [F 14, 1888].
    Bertha May (2:69), born Ja 18, 1876, baptized Ap 30, 1876.
    John Robert (2:7), born O 22, 1877, baptized My 19, 1878.
    William Leslie (2:72), born N 21, 1879, baptized My 20, 1880.
COLLIFLOWER, John, farmer (2:143,286), born in Washington County Jl 10, 1799, married F 17, 1825 Matilda Wilhide (2:249,286) daughter of John and Maria Barbara (Weller) Wilhide, born in Frederick County Ap 9, 1805, died D 21, 1875, buried at Graceham D 23, 1875, Communicant Ag 13, 1823; he died [O 5, 1882], Communicant Ap 3, 1828.
Issue: Michael Joseph (2:7), born Ja 1, 1826, baptized Ja 25, 1826, married Harriet Elizabeth Shuff.
    Bernard (2:16), born Ja 10, 1830, baptized Mr 21, 1830, married Mary Emeline Gernand.
    Samuel (2:21), born Mr 30, 1832, baptized Ap 4, 1832.
    Susan Elisabeth (2:27), born N 23, 1834, baptized Mr 11, 1835, married John T. [or F.] Fogle.
    Mary Jane (2:30), born Mr 27, 1837, baptized My 15, 1837.
    John Tilghman (1:100), born S 26, 1840, baptized Ja 19, 1841.
    Jago (1:110), born Je 3, 1844, baptized Je 24, 1844, died [17th of Ja, 1914], married Agnes C. Weller.
    Harriet Elizabeth (2:46,232), born Jl 2, 1850, baptized Ag 18, 1850, died My 7, 1859, buried at Graceham My 8, 1859.
COLLIFLOWER, John Tilghman (2:158) son of John and Matilda (Wilhide) Colliflower, married D 13, 1863 Mary Isabella Hesser.
Issue: Elmer Edwin (2:60), born D 18, 1864, baptized Mr 5, 1865.
    Leila Catharine (2:243,62), born N 30, 1866, baptized Mr 31, 1867, died S 11, 1867 and buried same day at Graceham.
    Laura Mary (2:63), born S 1, 1868, baptized S 8, 1868.
    Clarence Wilson (2:65), born Jl 19, 1871, baptized S 24, 1871.
    Joseph Howard (2:67), born Mr 3, 1874, baptized My 10, 1874.

11

Lloyd Ross (2:70), born Ag 19, 1877, baptized D 16, 1877.
COLLIFLOWER, Michael married Susanna Snyder (2:227); she was born D 8, 1763, died Je 29, 1856 and buried Jl 1, 1856.
Issue: Anna Mary (1:205), born My 10, 1807, baptized Mr 1, 1808, married William Hancock.
George married Hannah Brandenburg.
COLLIFLOWER, Michael Joseph (2:150,7) son of John and Matilda (Wilhide) Colliflower, born Ja 1, 1826, died [D 2, 1901], married N 29, 1849 to Harriet Elizabeth Shuff who was born [Mr 23, 1828] and died [O 17, 1891].
Issue: Sophia Elizabeth (2:46), born S 26, 1850, baptized N 24, 1850, married Samuel J. Troxel.
Franklin Amadeus (2:47), born N 21, 1852, baptized F 13, 1853, married Martha Miller.
Mary Jane (2:50), born N 24, 1854, baptized Ap 22, 1855.
Sarah Ellen (2:52), born S 27, 1857, baptized D 27, 1857.
Molly Florence (2:54), born My 14, 1859, baptized Je 29, 1859, married Frederick Fisher.
Charles Milton (2:234,56), born Ja 22, 1861, baptized Mr 3, 1861, died Ag 3, 1861, buried at Graceham Ag 4, 1861.
George Washington (2:58), born Jl 5, 1862, baptized Ja 18, 1863.
Emma Rebecca (2:61), born Je 25, 1865, baptized Ag 5, 1866.
Jesse Edgar (2:66), born Ag 24, 1871, baptized D 3, 1871.
COLLIFLOWER, Susanna married Jacob Doil.
COLLIFLOWER, William Henry (2:162,253,48), son of Bernard and Mary Emeline (Gernand) Colliflower of Graceham, born Ja 29, 1854, baptized _____, died F 8, 1877 and was buried F 10, 1877 at Graceham; he married Mr 8, 1875 Belva A. E. Cramer of Graceham.
Issue: Roy Frisby (2:69), born Ap 21, 1876, baptized Jl 9, 1876.
CÖLLN, Anna married Isaac Renatus Harry.
COLMER, Margaretha married Nicholas Bohr.
COOKERLY, Jacob married Catharine Biggs.
Issue: Prudence (1:195), born D 9, 1802, baptized Mr 20, 1803.
COOKERLY, John of Creagerstown married Margaretha Schmidt daughter of _____ and Catharina Schmidt
Issue: Keti (1:202), born F 20, 1806, baptized Mr 30, 1806.
COONS - See Kuhns
COOPER, Richard married Cecilia _____.
Issue: Elizabeth (2:118), born D 8, 1852, baptized Ja 1, 1853.
CORBAN, William A. married Henrietta H. Scott.
Issue: Albert Scott (2:223), born Je 12, 1853, died F 15, 1854, buried F 16, 1854 at Mechanicstown.
COVER, Cyrus (1:139) son of Jacob and Margaret (Stimmel) Cover, born Ag 2, 1829, baptized O 25, 1829; he married Henrietta Leidy.
Issue: Alvin (2:119), born Ja 9, 1854, baptized Ja 17, 1854.
COVER (KOBER), _____ married John Witmer.
COVER, Daniel (1:89) son of John and Elisabeth (Ott) Cover, married Je 2, 1839 Catharine Heffner daughter of Peter and Charlotte (Cole) Heffner; she was previously married to _____ Renner.
COVER, Daniel married Lydia _____.
Issue: Jason Jerome (1:120), born F 5, 1823, baptized Je 25, 1823.
Opten Aquilla (1:122), born Mr 18, 1826, baptized Ap 30, 1826.
COVER, Elizabeth married Nicholas Lingefelder.
COVER, Enos of Mechanicstown married Susan Gilbert (2:221) who died Ag 21, 1852 and was buried at Mechanicstown Ag 22, 1852.
Issue: Caroline Grizelda (2:219), born N 11, 1848, died D 28, 1849, buried at Mechanicstown D 29, 1849.
COVER, Enos (2:153) married O 6, 1853 Caroline Boblets.
COVER, Enos of Mech[anicstow]n.
Issue: Lela Kate (2:123), born Jl 14, 1858, baptized O 12, 1858.

12

COVER, Jacob of near Mechanicstown married Margaret Stimmel.
Issue: Cyrus (1:139), born Ag 2, 1829, baptized O 25, 1829, married Henrietta Leidy.
Margaret (1:142), born Ag 12, 1831, baptized D 26, 1831.
Jerome (1:146), born Ag 30, 1833, baptized N 3, 1833.
twins (Appollonia (1:95), born Je 12, 1838, baptized Jl 22, 1838.
(Adeline (1:95), born Je 12, 1838, baptized Jl 22, 1838.
COVER, John son of _____ and Mary Cover married Elisabeth Ott.
Issue: Levi Constantine (1:141), born Jl 5, 1829, baptized S 6, 1831.
Daniel (1:89) married Catharine Heffner.
William (1:87) married Lucinda Heyne.
COVER, Joseph, tanner (1:131) of Mechanicstown, born in Frederick County, married Ap 7, 1816 Susanna Koch (1:180) daughter of Georg and Maria (Duckness) Koch, who was born in Frederick County My 2, 1795 and was baptized Je 14, 1795.
Issue: Anna Rebecca (1:220), born Ja 11, 1817, baptized Ap 6, 1817.
Susanna (1:112), born F 29, 1820, baptized Ap 30, 1820.
Joseph hanson (1:118), born F 28, 1822, baptized Ap 28, 1822.
George Alfred (1:121), born Je 1, 1824, baptized N 21, 1824.
Wesley Alexander (1:122; 2:194), born Mr 4, 1826, baptized Ap 30, 1826, died Ag 30, 1827, buried Ag 31, 1827.
Levi (2:13), born Ag 18, 1828, baptized D 28, 1828.
Erastus (2:20), born Jl 12, 1831, baptized Ag 7, 1831.
COVER, Mary Ann had an illegitimate daughter by Frederic Miller.
COVER, William married Elizabeth Seiffert.
Issue: Mary Amanda (1:144), born N 15, 1831, baptized S 2, 1832, married George R. Kuhn.
COVER, William (1:87) son of John and Elisabeth (Ott) Cover, married Mr 8, 1832, Lucinda Heyne daughter of Henry and Elizabeth Heyne.
Issue: Anne Elisabeth (1:146), born Ag 4, 1833, baptized O 12, 1833.
COVER, William (2:152) of Mechanicstown married Ap 15, 1852 Virginia Gilbert of Mechanicstown.
COX, Timothy married Margaret Arthur.
Issue: Isabella Blakford (1:197), born N 1, 1789, baptized D 28, 1803.
Jane Ege (1:197), born S 2, 1803, baptized D 28, 1803.
Abigail (1:260), died O 25, 1802, buried O 26, 1802.
CRABBS, Amanda married Jacob Levi Firor.
CRABBS, Henry (2:243) born Ap 28, 1843, died D 11, 1866, buried at Mechanicstown D 12, 1866.
CRAMER, Belva A. E. married William Henry Colliflower.
CRAMER, William married Sarah _____.
Issue: Infant daughter (2:231), born D 29, 1858, died same day, buried D 30, 1858.
CRAVER, Grafton H. (2:156) married Sarah Ann E. Clem Mr 15, 1860.
CRAWFORD, Jonathan, tailor, married Anna Woodring.
Issue: Rebecca (1:114), born S 8, 1820, baptized N 22, 1820.
CREEGER, CREAGER, etc. - See KRIEGER
CRISE, Jacob (1:86) son of Peter Crise, married Je 30, 1831 Magdalena Hoover daughter of Christian and Magdalena Hoover.
CROLL, Heinrich married Magdalena _____.
Issue: Lydia (1:185), born N 9, 1797, baptized F 18, 1798.
CROUSE, Ephraim married _____ Weller.
Issue: John Calvin (2:221), died Ag 28, 1852, buried at Mechanicstown Ag 30, 1852.
Thomas Michael (2:222), died Je 7, 1853 aged 0-9-10, buried Je 8, 1853 at Mechanicstown.
CROUSE, Frederick married Elizabeth _____.
Issue: Laura Catharine (2:129), born Jl 18, 1866, baptized O 21, 1866.
CROUSE, Mary Elizabeth married Henry Augustus Baker.

13

CROUSE, Sarah M. married Daniel Ed. Martin.
CRUM, Margaret married David Valentine.
CRYAN, Angelina married Henry W. Weichsel.
CUNNINGHAM, Sarah Jane married John Wilson.
CURFMAN, Peter married Susan _____.
   Issue: Rebecca (1:84), married David Bush.
CURTIS - See KOTTER

DANIEL, John, laborer, married Susanna Butler.
   Issue: Elisabeth (1:191), born Ja 20, 1801, baptized Ap 30, 1801.
DAMUTH, Minerva Florentina (2:243), born F 1, 1841, died Je 22, 1866, buried
   at Apple's Church Je 24, 1866.
DAVIS, James married Elizabeth Miller.
   Issue: Sophia (1:138), born Ja 8, 1829, baptized Ag 3, 1829.
DAVIS, John J. (1:90) of Frederick County, married Ag 24, 1843 Rose L.
   Nelson of Baltimore County.
DAYHOFF, Abraham married Elizabeth Dörr (2:227) who was born Ja 21, 1791,
   died Je 17, 1856, buried at Apple's Church Je 18, 1856.
DAYHOFF (DEHUFF), Peter.
   Issue: John William (2:238), born N 20, 1860, died S 27, 1863, buried at
      Apple's Church S 28, 1863.
DEAFFENDAHL, Samuel married Elizabeth _____ (2:233) who was born Ap 23,
   1822, died Jl 17, 1861 and who was buried at Mech[anics]town.
DEAR, Sarah married John More.
DEBERRY, ____ married Mary Ann Williar.
   Issue: Barbara Harriet Miranda (2:117), born Mr 19, 1850, baptized Jl 14,
      1850.
DEBERRY, John W. (2:162) married D 31, 1874 Sophia Martin.
DEBERRY, William (1:90) married Ag 30, 1844 Mary Ann Houcks.
DEHUFF, ____ married Mary Jane Warner.
DEHUFF, Anna Maria married Philip Rice.
DELAPLANE, Joshua married Mary _____.
   Issue: Margaret Sophia (1:89), married Andrew Earhart.
DELAPLANE, Wesley (2:155,25,294), son of William and Salome (Süss) Dela-
   plane, was born F 13, 1834, baptized Mr 10, 1834, married Mr 15, 1859
   Sevilla Catharine Krieger (2:37) daughter of James and Elizabeth (Weller)
   Krieger, who was born Ag 10, 1840 and was baptized S 6, 1840.
   Issue: Ellen Salome (2:55), born D 11, 1859, baptized F 22, 1860.
      Caroline Cornelia (2:57), born Ap 19, 1862, baptized Jl 6, 1862.
      Sophia Elizabeth (2:244,59), born Ja 2, 1864, baptized Mr 24, 1864,
         died Ag 19, 1868, buried Ag 20, 1868 at Graceham.
      Edwin Siess (2:61), born Je 4, 1866, baptized S 9, 1866.
      Emma Rose (2:244,62), born N 11, 1867, baptized F 6, 1868, died Mr
         16, 1868, buried Mr 17, 1868 at Graceham.
      Mary May (2:64), born Ja 5, 1870, baptized Ap 10, 1870.
      James Llewellyn (2:67), born O 6, 1872, baptized N 27, 1872.
DELAPLANE, William (2:146,210,30) son of William and Mary (Ambrose) Dela-
   plane, was born S 19, 1807, baptized on his deathbed Ap 1, 1837, died of
   consumption My 9, 1837, buried My 11, 1837; he married Ap 9, 1833 Salome
   Süss (1:210) daughter of Godfrey and Anna Maria (Krämer) Süss, who was
   born Je 17, 1810 and baptized Jl 15, 1810; she later married Parmenio
   Renatus Harry.
   Issue: Wesley, born F 13, 1834, baptized Mr 10, 1834, married Sevilla
      Catharine Krieger.
DELFY, Catharine married Henry Wilhide.
DEMUTH, Christopher married Anna Elizabeth _____.
   Issue: Anna Maria married Christian William Laembke.
DEMUTH, Elizabeth married Joseph Brown.

14

DEMUTH, Henry, farmer, married Anna Maria Monn.
Issue: Samuel (1:213), born O 12, 1811, baptized My 17, 1812.
Anna Sophia (1:114), born S 5, 1820, baptized O 7, 1820.
Magdalena (1:89) married John Brown.
DEMUTH, Johann married Catharina _____.
Issue: Sophia Theresia (1:184), born Ag 23, 1797 at 11:45 p.m.; baptized
Ag 27, 1797.
DENS, Betse married William Green.
DERR (DÖRR), Elizabeth married Abraham Dayhoff.
DERR, John married Elizbeth Brim.
Issue: Rebecca married Jonathan Bowers.
DERR, Mannie married William Edward Late.
DERR, Mary Ann married Jacob Frederick.
DERR, Rebecca married Jonathan Bowers.
DERR, Sophia married Daniel Stauffer.
DEVILBISS, Casper (1:167b) son of George and Elizabeth (Ogle) Devilbiss was
born D 25, 1787, baptized F 3, 1788, married Anna Maria _____.
Issue: Jeremias (1:211), born D 15, 1810, baptized D 17, 1810.
DEVILBISS, George (1:264), a friend and regular visitor for many years; died
Jl 28, 1813, buried Jl 31, 1813; married in 1772 Elizabeth Ogle (1:254-
255), born Jl 26, 1752 at Wilmington, Delaware; she was well cared for by
her parents; she died My 2, 1800 of slow consumption, of which she was
sick ten years; buried in the churchyard My 4, 1800.
Issue: Caspar (1:233, 1:169), born My 3, 1782; baptized Je 20, 1782; died
Mr 7, 1783; buried at Graceham Mr 8, 1783.
Rebecca (1:171), born Ja 14, 1784, baptized Mr 7, 1784.
Elisabeth (1:173), second daughter, baptized Ap 16, 1786.
Caspar (1:167b); born D 25, 1787 at 9:10 a.m., baptized F 3, 1788.
Jacob (1:244, 1:170b), born Ap 4, 1790 at 6-7 p.m., baptized My 2,
1790; died S 9, 1794, buried in the churchyard S 10, 1794; mar-
ried Anna Maria _____.
3 sons.
1 daughter.
DEVILBISS, George, junior, married Elizabeth _____.
Issue: John (1:189), baptized Ap 23, 1800.
DEVILBISS, George, junior, farmer, married Martha Care.
Issue: Elizabeth (1:194), born F 2, 1802, baptized Jl 11, 1802.
Rebecca (1:198), baptized S 29, 1804.
DEVILBISS, Irving (2:151) married My 25, 1851 Elizabeth Domer.
DEVIS, Philippina (or Phoebe) married John Jacob Metz.
DEWALD, Magdalena married John Zoller.
DICK, Susanna married William Mumford.
DIELFORTER, Maria Catharina married (1) Engelhard Süssman and (2) Jacob
Lochman.
DIETER, Catharina married George Peter Bernhard.
DINDEMANG, Susanna married Berez Schils.
DITNERMESSER, Maria married Samuel Leinbach.
DIXON, Mary married William Weller.
DOCK, Maria Catharine married John George Süss.
DOCK, Maria Elisabeth married Tobias Böckel.
DOCK, Maria Elizabeth married (1) George Glatt and (2) Tobias Böckel.
DODERO, Elizabeth married John Troxel.
DOFFLER, George (1:85) son of George and Catharine Doffler, married Ag 5,
1830 Mary Ann Harbaugh daughter of Yost and Elizabeth Harbaugh.
DOIL, Jacob, at the Furnace, married Susanna Colliflower.
Issue: Michael Colliflower (1:116), born Mr 12, 1821, baptized Ap 23,
1821.
Susanna (1:120), born Jl 26, 1823, baptized O 1, 1823.
Henry (1:122), born O 27, 1825, baptized Ap 25, 1826.

DOMER, Elizabeth married Irving Devilbiss.
DOMER, William married Anne Eichelberger.
    Issue: Ellen Catharine (2:119), born Jl 28, 1852, baptized Mr 3, 1853.
DORF, Elizabeth married Matthew Seiphert.
DORF, Samuel, tailor, married Catharine Bastian.
    Issue: Elias (1:194), born Je 21, 1802, baptized Jl 11, 1802.
DORSEY, Ann Elizabeth married Theodore Leander Boller.
DORSEY, Charles A. (no church), born [1845]; died [1913]; married Anna
    Milinda Gaugh (Lutheran) who was born [1844] and died [1903].
    Issue: Walter Reed (2:132), born N 20, 1871; baptized Mr 4, 1872; died
        [1929].
        William Clay (2:247,132), born Ja 19, 1874; baptized Ja 27, 1874;
        died F 6, 1874; buried at Graceham F 8, 1874.
DORSEY, Harriet Elizabeth married William G. Shafer.
DORSEY, John (1:88), son of Michael and Elisabeth Dorsey, married Anna
    Barbara Eyler (1:214) daughter of Adam and Maria (Meier) Eyler, born D 29,
    1812; baptized Ap 18, 1813.
    Issue: John Adam (1:103), born Ja 30, 1840; baptized Ja 21, 1843.
        Allen (1:103), born Ap 10, 1842, baptized Ja 21, 1843.
    The above John Dorsey and Anna Barbara Eyler were married Je 12, 1834.
DORSEY, Michael married Elizabeth _____.
    Issue: Harriet married William Wilhide.
DORSEY, Michael married Margaret Bush.
    Issue: William Henry (1:105), born O 31, 1840; baptized O 1, 1842.
DORSEY, Owen, born [Mr 29, 1817]; died [S 2, 1883]; married Hetty _____,
    who was born [N 3, 1819]; died [F 17, 1904].
    Issue: Mary Amanda (2:62), born D 25, 1853; baptized Ap 5, 1868.
        Frances (2:161), married Daniel Beck.
DORSEY, Owen.
    Issue: Flora Mozelle (2:61), born Jl 8, 1850, baptized Mr 25, 1866; mar-
        ried Aloysius Walter.
DOTTEROW, Sophia married Henry Krieger.
DOYLE, Samuel.
    Issue: Amy married Emanuel Martin.
DRACHSEL, Maria Ellen (1:217), illegitimate daughter of Elias Drachsel and
    Sarah Seiffert, was born Je 15, 1812 and was baptized Ap 24, 1815. Maria
    Schenkel was this child's foster-mother.
DRAWL, Joseph married Bridget _____.
    Issue: Samuel (1:267), born Mr 7, 1799; baptized Je 8, 1799 by Schlegel on
        a trip to Cumberland and Bedford.
DUBEL, Benjamin married Elizabeth Reidenauer.
    Issue: Henry (1:184), born S 24, 1797; baptized N 14, 1797.
        Barbara (1:196), born My 28, 1803; baptized Je 26, 1803.
DUBEL, Wesley (2:160) married F 4, 1869 Susan Boller (2:45) daughter of John
    R. and Catharine (Reidenauer) Boller, born My 4, 1846; baptized Je 20,
    1846.
    Issue: Ellen Meda (2:64), born Ja 4, 1870; baptized Je 12, 1870.
DUNCAN (or DUNKIN), Sarah married Dr. Leander W. Goldsborough.
DURBIN, George or David D. (2:161), married My 19, 1870 Mary Margaret Engel
    (2:47) daughter of Nicholas and Eve (Gall) Engle, born D 28, 1851; bap-
    tized O 26, 1852.
    Issue: Charles Edward (2:247,65), born D 30, 1870; baptized Ag 24, 1871;
        died S 1, 1871; buried at Graceham S 3, 1871.
        Emma Rose (2:247,66), born Ag 26, 1872; baptized S 1, 1872; died S
        1, 1872; buried at Graceham S 2, 1872.
        Anna May (2:66), born Ag 26, 1872, baptized S 1, 1872.
        Lewis Francis (2:69), born O 5, 1876; baptized F 12, 1877.
        Robert Milton (2:71), born F 20, 1879; baptized Je 1, 1879.

DUSTMAN, Henry married Louisa Wilen.
Issue: Anna Catharina Friederica Micleta (1:97), born F 7, 1839; baptized Ap 7, 1839.
DWIER, John, blacksmith, married Hanna Shuff.
Issue: Jane (1:191), born O 22, 1799, baptized F 14, 1801.
Maria Catharina (1:191), born Ja 12, 1801; baptized F 14, 1801.
Thomas (1:195), baptized F 6, 1803.

EARHART, Andrew (1:89) son of William and margaret Earhart,married Ag 14, 1839 Margaret Sophia Delaplane daughter of Joshua and Mary Delaplane.
EARHART, Henriette (1:209), illegitimate daughter of William Earhart and Juliana Holtzman, was born Je 24, 1809 and was baptized O 1, 1809.
EARHART (EHRHARD), William married Margaret Holtzman.
Issue: Isabelle (1:120), born Ag 8, 1823; baptized O 1, 1823.
John Henry (1:144), born D 5, 1832; baptized D 6, 1832.
EATON, Edward married Sarah Schaeffer.
Issue: Mary Catharine (1:102), born My 11, 1838; baptized D 4, 1842.
EATON, Henry married Sarah Ann Birch.
Issue: Cornelia Rebecca (1:102), born S 17, 1842; baptized D 4, 1842.
EBERHARD, The Reverend Nicholas Henry (20 March 1723 - 18 April 1770).
The late brother Nicolaus Heinrich Eberhard was (according to his own account) born March 20, 1723 at Copenhagen, where his father was serving as surgeon in a regiment of grenadiers, and was brought up in the Lutheran religion; after a few years he with his parents moved to Helsinki, where his father was appointed customs collector. Here he persevered in his studies, and at the end of his school years, in June, 1741, went to the University of Copenhagen. From his youth he had felt the promptings of grace in his heart, and earnestly but vainly endeavored to free himself from sin and the world. After his return, in March, 1743, the suffering figure of the Savior vividly entered his heart and made him feel in an inexpressible way a forgiveness of sins and a simultaneous sundering of all the bonds of sin and the world, and his heart was set aflame with tender love. "My parents were alarmed by this change, so much so that my father absolutely ordered me out of the house. When this year (1744) passed I became tutor of the children of a nobleman in the country. I again experienced conflict in my heart, and found no rest until I resolved to leave, which the nobleman finally unwillingly permitted. Then in January, 1745, I went to Copenhagen to seek membership with the Moravians, of whom I had heard a short time before. I took the theological examination in November, 1746, not to become a minister (for my call to membership could not be gainsaid[2]) but because I believed it might be otherwise useful. Meantime my longing for the church[3] grew so great that I could no longer endure life in Copenhagen, and in April, 1747 decided to go to H[errn]haag[4] with three of the Brethren. I arrived there safely on May 16. I soon obtained permission to stay, and on July 7 arrived at the Seminarum at Lindheim, and in August at the Kinderanstalt at M[arien]born, and on August 30 was received as a member of the church[3], but because I delayed in seeking it and did not have the feeling that I was a poor sinner I could not appreciate the graciousness of this reception. I came to the children in October, and on January 2, 1748 for the first time received the Holy Supper with the Brethren. On September 15 I was made an acolyte, but in spite of all this grace my inward confusion continued, I had

---

[2] Denn mein Ruf zur Gem. war mir unwiedersprechl. ausgemacht.

[3] Gemeine.

[4] A Moravian settlement in the county in Büdingen from 1738 to 1750 (Hübners Reales Staats-Zeitungs- und Conversations-Lexicon, Leipzig, 1789)

no one in whom to confide or to whom I might tell my need. Often I thought of leaving, indeed, my spiritual confusion went so far that I thought there was no God and no Savior. Finally this thought got the upper hand, that the Savior through his love had drawn me unto himself and his church. My heart and spirit cleared; as a miserable sinner I had a perception of the wounds of Jesus. Meantime, in November, 1749 I had gone to Barby with the seminary, and there in August, 1751 I received my call to Pennsylvania. I travelled with Brothers Rundt and Bader from Barby to London, and with Brother Joseph's party to New York. On December 11 I arrived at Bethel. The year 1752 was a year of blessing to me. In this year I took over the book-keeping, with which the Savior graciously helped me, so that I was attached to the prayer company, the congregation and the young men's choir. On March 26, 1753 I was installed as Vorsteher of the Unmarried Brethren, on January 19, 1755 was ordained Diaconus at the Synod of Bethel. In February, 1756 I pursued my calling by travelling to Pachgatgoch, where I served the little group of Indians for one year nine months, and returned to Bethlehem in November, 1757. In April, 1758 I went to Lititz, to oversee the building of the choir houses and the Gemeinhaus. On September 18, 1763 I was made Diaconus of the congregation and helped by Brother Matthaeus. On February 21, 1764 I was married to Sarah van Vleck at Bethlehem, and returned to Lititz with her in April. In June, 1765 we were called to Oldmann's Creek in Jersey to serve the flock there. After serving this group with the Savior's gracious support for two years three months we went to Bethlehem by way of Philadelphia in December, 1767, whence we came to Manakosy in Maryland. Here the Saviour has blessed and guided us up to this time, and has given the people here much joy, but I pray for a special sense of his presence, with a thankful heart in the dust." On the night of April 3-4 he became feverish and developed severe pain in the chest; on the 8th he became so weak that his wife and the Brethren present thought him dead, but he came to and said "Oh, would that I had been able to go to the Savior." On the 10th Brother and Sister Powell reached us, having received news of his sickness; when they asked him whether to send for a doctor he replied, "No, the Savior will be my physician." The Savior was very near in order to receive him. On the 17th his gentle gaze seemed to show us that the illness had broken, but it soon appeared more evident that Our Best Friend would take his soul home; this occurred at 4 p.m. on the 18 April 1770, when Brother Powell gave him the last blessing. In the last year he often mentioned his desire to be set free and be with Christ, which came to pass. His age was 47 years 1 month. (1:227-228)

EBERMAN, Charlotte F. married Benjamin Ricksecker.
ECKER, Reuben married Sarah Kinsey.
    Issue: Laura L. married William E. Krieger.
ECKER, Sarah Elizabeth (2:243), born Jl 28, 1866; died Jl 31, 1866; buried at the Dunker Meeting House.
ECKERT, Peter of Middletown Valley married Catharina _____.
    Issue: Sarah Maria (2:23), born Mr 15, 1813; baptized Mr 31, 1833.
ECKMAN, _____ (1:84) married Jane Patterson (later the wife of Jacob Wise) daughter of John and Ann Patterson.
ECKMAN, Daniel (1:84) son of George and Sophia Eckman, married Ap 27, 1828 Anne Maria Wilson daughter of John and Sarah Jane (Cunningham) Wilson.
ECKMAN, George married Sophia Schley (1:204).
ECKMAN, John C. R. (1:90) married Je 15, 1842 Adeline Eyler.
EHRENSPERGER (or EHRENSPENER), Laurence (1:130) married Ap 23, 1811 Elisabeth Kuns daughter of Georg Kuns.
    Issue: William (1:213), born F 17, 1812; baptized Mr 1, 1812.
           Theresa (1:218), born Jl 21, 1815; baptized S 3, 1815.
EHRHARD, Polly married (1) _____ Matthews, and (2) Jonathan Shoff.

EIB, Andrew and wife Christina Margaret, Probationers O 8, 1769, Communicants N 2, 1775. (1:91,108)
EIB, Christina (1:227), born in Warwick Township, Lancaster County, Pennsylvania F 14, 1753; died Ja 5, 1769; buried in the churchyard Ja 7, 1769.
EIB, Johann Jacob (1:226) died Je 10, 1766 after 15 years of gout, aged 20-5-0; buried Je 11, 1766.
EICHELBERGER, _____ married Margaret Rebecca Fogle who later became the wife of Joseph H. W. Fick.
EICHELBERGER, Anne married William Domer.
EICHELBERGER, Harriet (2:225), died O 15, 1854; buried at Creagerstown O 17, 1854.
EICHELBERGER, Martin married Cassandra _____.
   Issue: Carrie Acton (2:241), born N 5, 1863; died Ap 22, 1865; buried at Cr[eagers]t[ow]n on Ap 23, 1865.
EICHELSBERGER, Samuel married Elizabeth _____ (2:226); she was born Ag 12, 1801; died Jl 28, 1855; buried at Creagerstown Jl 29, 1855.
EICHELSBERGER, Sophia married John P. Zimmerman.
EICHHOLTZ, Jesse married Lovinia Ann _____.
   Issue: John Samuel (2:124), born F 28, 1859; baptized Mr 18, 1860.
EICHHOLTZ, John (2:227), born D 31, 1799; died Ja 9, 1856; buried at Apple's Church Ja 11, 1856.
EICHHOLTZ, Samuel.
   Issue: Joanna (2:222), died Ap 29, 1853; buried at Apple's Church Ap 30, 1853. She was aged 4-5-28.
EICHHOLTZ, Samuel married Sarah _____.
   Issue: Emma Virginia (2:124), born Je 2, 1855; baptized Ap 15, 1860.
   William Isaiah (2:124), born Mr 22, 1858; baptized Ap 15, 1860.
EIGENBROD, Charlotte married John P. Fox.
EIGENBROD, Christian Henry, shoemaker (1:129,169; 2:205), born in Frederick County F 3, 1782; baptized F 10, 1782. He was the son of John Yost and Eva Maria (Schörer) Eigenbrod; he married at Graceham O 1, 1803 Margaret Eyler (1:170; 2:188) daughter of Jonas and Anna Regina (Herbach) Eyler, who was born in Frederick County Je 21, 1783; baptized Je 27, 1783; died of consumption Ag 31, 1823 and was buried S 2, 1823.
   Issue: Araminta (1:212), born O 16, 1811; baptized N 3, 1811; married George Smith.
   Priscilla (1:266,216), born O 16, 1814; baptized O 30, 1814; died Ag 27, 1819 of whooping cough; buried Ag 29, 1819.
He (Christian Henry Eigenbrod) married secondly on My 23, 1824 Rosina Höfer of Lititz. No issue. He died of an intestinal inflammation Ag 24, 1833; buried Ag 25, 1833.
EIGENBROD, John, blacksmith (1:128,166) son of John Yost and Eva Maria (Schörer) Eigenbrod; born My 16 1776 at Graceham; died [Ap 20, 1832]; buried at Apple's Church; he married Ap 22, 1800 Susanna Sänger who was born at "Liesland", Frederick County; died [Mr 21, 1862, aged 83-3-17]; buried at Apple's Church.
   Issue: Sophia (1:191), born Mr 19, 1801; baptized My 31, 1801.
   Susanna (1:114), born Ap 30, 1820; baptized O 7, 1820.
   Anna Catharine (1:88), married Joseph Witmer.
EIGENBROD, John Yost (1:233,107), born Schwarzenau in Wittgenstein on N 10, 1729; came to America 1748; Probationer 1758 at the Synod of Lebanon; Communicant My 22, 1763; died My 14, 1784; he was much hurt by a fall from a tree in 1771; from that time on he was not strong; he was in be three weeks with a bad chest cold before he died; he was buried My 16, 1784; he married in 1756 Eva Maria Schörer (1:91,107,262), Probationer O 24, 1762; Communicant My 22, 1763; due to weakness of age and a swelling in the legs and abdomen, she died Jl 3, 1809 and was buried Jl 4, 1809. Her age was 70-2-24.

Issue: Maria Barbara (2:211), born O 1, 1758; died Ap 22, 1840; married
John George Süss.
Elizabeth (1:156), born Mr 4, 1761; baptized Mr 19, 1761.
John Daniel (1:158), born 4 p.m. S 2, 1763; baptized S 4, 1763.
Juliana (2:12; 1:160), born F 12, 1766; baptized F 16, 1766; mar-
ried _____ Stotz.
Maria Magdalena (1:161), born O 16, 1768 in the morning.
Maria Sophia (1:162), born 8 a.m. Je 2, 1771; baptized Je 9, 1771;
married Peter Young.
Anna Rosina (1:165,230), born Ap 20, 1774 at 3 p.m.; baptized Ap
24, 1774; died Mr 28, 1775 and buried in the churchyard Mr 30,
1775.
John (1:166), born My 16, 1776 in the early morning; baptized My
19, 1776; married Susanna Sänger.
Margaret (1:167), born Mr 24, 1779; baptized Mr 28, 1779; died F
12, 1857; married Isaac Renatus Harry.
Christian Henry (1:169), born F 3, 1782; baptized F 10, 1782; died
Ag 24, 1833; married Margaret Eyler.
EIKER, David married Elizabeth Firor.
Issue: William Henry (1:143), born Je 17, 1832; baptized Jl 3, 1832.
ELDRIDGE, Ellis, laborer (1:83) married Ag 30, 1827 Mary Waldman (sister of
Thomas Waldman) (1:83,135); she was daughter of [Michael] Waldman, the
hero of the Revolution.
ELLENSPERGER, William married Hannah Hughes.
Issue: Elizabeth Ottilia (1:101), born My 5, 1841; baptized Ag 8, 1841.
ELSRODE, Catharine married Francis D. Hahn.
ENGEL, John Edward (2:46,162) son of Nicholas and Eva (Gall) Engel; born Je
18, 1849; baptized Ag 13, 1849; died [D 27, 1895]; married N 19, 1874 Anna
Maria Sweeney who died [Ag 8, 1935].
Issue: Charles Blackford (2:68,254), born Ag 19, 1875, baptized N 14,
1875; died Ja 22, 1879; buried at Graceham Ja 24, 1879.
William Nathaniel (2:70), born F 25, 1877; baptized Ag 6, 1877.
Howard Nicholas (2:71), born Ja 24, 1879; baptized Je 1, 1879.
ENGEL, Nicholas (2:149), born [N 9, 1816]; died [Je 18, 1901], married D 19,
1845 [Anna] Eva Gall, born [Je 16, 1826]; died [Ja 19, 1903].
Issue: Catharine Elizabeth (2:43), born D 19, 1846; baptized Ja 5, 1847.
John Edward (2:46), born Je 18, 1849; baptized Ag 13, 1849; married
Anna Maria Sweeney.
Mary Margaret (2:47), born D 28, 1851; baptized O 26, 1852; married
George D. Durbin.
William Henry (2:49,226), born My 12, 1854; baptized Mr 7, 1855;
died N 3, 1855; buried at Graceham N 5, 1855.
Ann Eliza (2:51,229), born S 20, 1856; baptized D 30, 1856; died S
6, 1857 and buried S 8, 1857.
Caroline Augusta (2:54), born O 21, 1858; baptized Ja 6, 1859;
married John H. Humerich.
Noah Joseph (2:55,233), born F 3, 1861; baptized F 17, 1861; died F
18, 1861 and buried at Graceham F 19, 1861.
Joseph Henry (2:57), born F 15, 1862; baptized Mr 24, 1862.
Sarah Malinda (2:61), born S 18, 1866; baptized D 13, 1866.
Emma Delavine (2:62,245), born Ap 14, 1869; baptized Jl 4, 1869;
died Ag 16, 1869 and buried at Graceham Ag 17, 1869.
Laura May (2:64,246), born Jl 28, 1870; baptized Ag 8, 1870; died
Ag 24, 1870 and buried at Graceham Ag 25, 1870.
ENGLER, Jane E. married John Henry Hoffman.
ERDMAN, Sebastian married Maria Elizabeth Breitbarth.
Issue: Martha Elisabeth (1:149), born Ag 7, 1835; baptized Ag 19, 1835.

ESTERLEIN, William (2:150), married in D, 1847 Martha Carson.
Issue: Scott (2:237), born F 18, 1861; died Ap 12, 1863; buried in John
Dorsey's Graveyard Ap 13.
Martha Adaline (2:239), born Je 12, 1863; died D 2, 1863; buried in
John Dorsey's Graveyard D 3, 1863.
ESTERLINE, Celestia Anna married Lemuel L. Wilhide.
EWALD, Anna Barbara married George Becker.
EYERLY, Elizabeth married John Peter Kluge.
EYLER, Aaron (1:90,114) of Frederick County, son of George and Elsie Anna
(Kauffman) Eyler; born S 28, 1820; baptized O 19, 1820; married N 23, 1844
Josephine Elizabeth Eyler (2:7) of Eyler's Valley, daughter of Captain
John and Rebecca (Harbaugh) Eyler; born N 8, 1825; baptized N 10, 1825.
Issue: Irwin (2:238), born N 1, 1844; died Jl 1, 1863 from effects of a
magazine explosion at Harper's Ferry while in the United States
service; buried Jl 9, 1863 at Mech[anics]t[ow]n.
EYLER, Adam, farmer (2:244), in the mountains, born Ag 16, 1787; died Ap 29,
1868; buried at Apple's Church Ap 30, 1868; married Maria Meier who died
[O 20, 1834, aged 50-9-9, according to her tombstone at Apple's Church].
Issue: [Zephaniah, born Je 25, 1811, according to tombstone at Apple's
Church]; died O 22, 1874.
Anna Barbara (1:214), born D 29, 1812; baptized Ap 18, 1813; mar-
ried John Dorsey.
Catharina (1:113), born Ap 26, 1819; baptized Je 25, 1820.
Cornelia Anne (1:137), born Je 25, 1828; baptized Ag 10, 1828.
EYLER, Adeline married John C. R. Eckman.
EYLER, Andrew Jackson (2:24,294), born Ag 15, 1833; he was son of Captain
John and Rebecca (Harbaugh) Eyler, and married Sarah _____.
Issue: Samuel Newton (2:127), born F 17, 1864; baptized My 10, 1864.
EYLER, Ann M. married John F. Gunder.
EYLER, Anna (or Nancy) married Elias Williar.
EYLER, Barbara Ann married Jacob Stitely.
EYLER (EILER), Benjamin (1:172) son of Jonas and Anna Regina (Harbaugh)
Eyler; born F 17, 1785; baptized F 22, 1785; married Barbara Schnierle.
Issue: Rachel (1:213), born Mr 14, 1812; baptized Ap 19, 1812.
Margaret (1:216), born Je 15, 1814; baptized Jl 3, 1814.
EYLER, Catharine married Jacob Reidenour.
EYLER, Charles married Mary Weller.
Issue: Joseph Albert (2:71), born F 8, 1879; baptized F 27, 1879.
EYLER, Charles A. married Charlotte Louisa Gurley (1:150) daughter of Thomas
and Amanda (Stoll) Gurley; she was born F 20, 1835 and was baptized Ap 3,
1836.
Issue: Edward Ross (2:130), born S 7, 1866; baptized Mr 19, 1869.
Charles Randolph (2:130), born Ap 29, 1868; baptized Mr 19, 1869.
EYLER, Eva married John Krieger.
EYLER, Frederick (2:232) or Eyler's Valley, born Ap 9, 1776; died My 3,
1859; buried at Graceham My 4, 1859; married Margaret Williar (1:170;
2:234,286), born S 11, 1783; baptized S 15, 1783; she was the daughter of
Andrew and Margaret (Harbaugh) Williar; she was a Communicant Ap 15, 1802;
died O 28, 1861 and was buried at Graceham O 29, 1861.
Issue: Horatio (1:211), born D 23, 1810; baptized D 27, 1810; died D 29,
1810 and was buried D 30, 1810.
Caroline (1:213), born Je 30, 1812; baptized Ag 20, 1812.
John Frederick (1:215), born Ja 30, 1814; baptized Ap 3, 1814.
Maria Catharine (1:218), born Ag 17, 1815; baptized O 15, 1815.
William (1:220), born Je 9, 1817; baptized Jl 27, 1817.
Charles Augustus (1:221), born Ag 30, 1818; baptized O 8, 1818.
Rebecca Anna (1:113), born My 18, 1820; baptized Je 25, 1820;
married Peter Marker.
Elizabeth (1:118), born Ap 23, 1822; baptized My 22, 1822.

21

Mary Jane (2:8,153,225), born Ag 17, 1826; baptized O 1, 1826; died Jl 30, 1854; married Cyrus C. Kuhn.

EYLER, George, weaver (1:130; 2:246,286), in the mountains, eldest son of Jonas and Anna Regina (Harbaugh) Eyler; born in Maryland F 6, 1782; a Communicant My 21, 1804; died Ap 10, 1871 and was buried at Mech[anics]-t[ow]n Stone Church; he married Ap 2, 1811 Elsie Anna Kauffmann (2:254, 286) daughter of George and Elsie Kauffmann, who was born Jl 20, 1784 in Maryland; a Communicant Ag 12, 1821; she died F 23, 1878 and was buried at Mech[anicstow]n F 26, 1878.
Issue: Lavinia (1:213), born Ja 6, 1812; baptized Ap 19, 1812; married Israel Williar.
    David (1:214), born F 22, 1813; baptized My 23, 1813.
    Judith (1:216), born O 6, 1814; baptized N 16, 1814.
    Margaret Anna (1:218), born Ja 2, 1816; baptized My 5, 1816.
    Perry (1:220), born My 24, 1817; baptized My 29, 1817.
    Benjamin (1:222), born Ja 16, 1819; baptized Ja 31, 1819.
    Aaron (1:114), born S 28, 1820; baptized O 19, 1820; married Josephine Eyler.
    Regina (1:118), born Mr 12, 1822; baptized My 12, 1822.
    Mary Amanda (2:3), born Ap 9, 1824; baptized My 11, 1824.
    Theresa (2:8), born Je 16, 1826; baptized S 17, 1826; married George Harvey Winters.
    Susanna (2:12), born Ag 1, 1828; baptized Ag 9, 1828.
    Harriet (2:20), born My 28, 1831; baptized Je 18, 1831.
He had 92 grandchildren and 24 great-grandchildren when he died.

EYLER, George F. (2:162), married at the age of 21 on D 21, 1871 Margaret Smith daughter of Joshua and Sophia (Stokes) Smith.
Issue: Frederick Washington (2:134), born Je 25, 1875; baptized F 15, 1876.

EYLER, Henry, farmer, in the mountains, married Elizabeth Luckenbach.
Issue: Joseph (1:219), born Je 10, 1816; baptized Jl 21, 1816.
    Elias (1:221), born Mr 31, 1818; baptized Ag 2, 1818.
    Henry (1:114), born Jl 27, 1820; baptized O 1, 1820.

EYLER, Jacob, hatter, in the mountains, married Margaret (or Rebecca) Luckenbach.
Issue: Isaac (1:217), born Ap 25, 1815; baptized Ap 28, 1815.
    Barbara (1:222), born F 18, 1819; baptized Ap 18, 1819.
    Soloman (1:115), born D 28, 1820; baptized F 12, 1821.
    Sarah, born Mr 12, 1809; died O 27, 1865; married Joseph Wilhide.

EYLER, John "of Rock Creek", farmer, (1:134,178; 2:286), residing on Rock Creek, in Pennsylvania, was born D 3, 1793 in Frederick County and was baptized Ja 26, 1794; Communicant Ag 13, 1819; he was the son of Jonas and Anna Regina (Herbach) Eyler; he married Ap 23, 1822 Catharine Klotz of Adams County.
Issue: Rebecca (2:3), born S 11, 1823; baptized O 17, 1823.
    Rachel (2:5), born O 29, 1824; baptized N 25, 1824
    Elizabeth (2:9), born S 24, 1826; baptized N 20, 1826.
    William (2:13,293), born O 22, 1828; baptized Ja 5, 1829.
    Margaret Catharine (2:28), born Je 23, 1835; baptized S 21, 1835.

EYLER, (Captain) John "of the mountain", farmer & Saw-miller (1:133; 2:243, 286) son of Frederick Eyler; he was born N 20, 1783 and resided in Eyler Valley; a Communicant D 14, 1820, died D 13, 1866 and was buried at Graceham D 16, 1866; he married D 14, 1820 Rebecca harbaugh (1:185; 2:256,286) daughter of Christian and Maria Elisabeth (Williar) Harbaugh; born F 12, 1798 in Frederick County and was baptized F 21, 1798; Communicant D 13, 1817; she died Ag 24, 1880 and was buried at Graceham Ag 26, 1880.
Issue: Mary Amanda (Catharine) (1:117), born Ag 29, 1821; baptized O 28, 1821; married David Harbaugh; she died [S 15, 1899].

22

John Cyrus (2:3,293), born D 3, 1823; baptized Mr 26, 1824; married
Cecilia Ann Elizabeth _____.
Josephine Elizabeth (2:7), born N 8, 1825; baptized N 10, 1825;
married Aaron Eyler.
Edwin Frederick (2:9,225,293), born D 18, 1826 in Frederick County;
baptized F 11, 1827; died F 7, 1855 and buried in Graceham F 9,
1855.
Charlotte Rebecca (2:13), born N 27, 1828; baptized F 1, 1829;
married John Adam Williard.
Martha Adeline (2:20,215), born F 12, 1831; baptized My 28, 1831;
died Ag 18, 1842; buried Ag 19, 1842.
Andrew Jackson (2:24,294), born Ag 15, 1833; baptized S 22, 1833;
married Sarah _____.
Lewis Francis (2:29), born O 4, 1836; baptized Ja 8, 1837.
Laura Jane (2:37), born N 23, 1839; baptized Mr 22, 1840; married
Milton Harbaugh.
EYLER, John Cyrus (2:3,293) son of John and Rebecca (Harbaugh) Eyler; born
in Frederick County D 3, 1823; baptized Mr 26, 1824; married Cecilia Ann
Elizabeth _____.
Issue: Charles Edward (2:54), born Ag 14, 1859; baptized S 24, 1859.
Viola Amanda (2:126), born D 5, 1861; baptized Ag 18, 1862.
Emma Claribell (2:127), born Mr 28, 1864; baptized My 10, 1864.
Mary Sophia (2:128), born O 25, 1865; baptized My 24, 1866.
EYLER, Jonas, farmer (2:191), who lived in the mountains, was born N 22,
1752 in Pennsylvania; died Ap 19, 1825 and was buried Ap 21, 1825; he
married Ap 24, 1781 Anna Regina Herbach (1:91,108,155; 2:219,292) daughter
of George and Catharina (Williar) Herbach; born F 12, 1759; baptized F 13,
1759; Probationer N 13, 1785; Communicant O 17, 1787; died [O 6, 1849] and
is buried at [Graceham].
Issue: George (1:169), born F 6, 1782; baptized Ap 12, 1782; married Elsie
Anna Kauffman.
Margaret (1:170), born Je 21, 1783; baptized Je 27, 1783; died Ag
31, 1823; married Christian Henry Eigenbrod.
Benjamin (1:172), born F 17, 1785 at 10-11 p.m.; baptized F 22,
1785; married Barbara Schnierle.
Samuel (1:174), born Ja 5, 1787 at 5:30 a.m.; baptized Ja 8, 1787;
married Maria Lewig.
Maria Barbara (1:168b), born Ja 17, 1789; baptized F 15, 1789;
married (1) DanielKrieger and (2) John Wilhide.
Catharine (1:173b), born Jl 4, 1791; baptized the 8th Sunday after
Trinity; died S 20, 1847; married John Meffert.
John (1:178), born D 3, 1793 at 10 a.m., baptized Ja 26, 1794; married Catharine Klotz.
Priscilla (1:181), born My 1, 1796 at 10 p.m., baptized Je 5, 1796;
married Jacob Hammer.
Amalia (1:265,185), born Je 22, 1798; baptized Jl 24, 1798; died My
12, 1817 of severe pains in head and chest, and was buried My 14,
1817.
Jonas Nathanael (1:194), born S 5, 1802; baptized S 9, 1802; married Sophia Theresa Moser.
EYLER, Jonas Nathanael, farmer & Day-laborer (2:144,194,286) son of Jonas
and Anna Regina (Herbach) Eyler; born S 5, 1802 in Frederick County;
baptized S 9, 1802; Communicant O 8, 1820; married Ap 2, 1826 Sophia
Theresa Moser (1:195) daughter of Leonard and Elisabeth (Schenkel) Moser;
born D 25, 1802 in Frederick County; baptized D 30, 1802; Communicant Ag
12, 1821.
Issue: Theodore Nathanael (2:9,293), born Mr 12, 1827; baptized Ap 13,
1827; married Caroline Wilhide.

Josiah (2:14), born Ja 7, 1829 in Frederick County; baptized F 15,
1829; married Urilla _____.
Anne Maria Ellen (2:19), born Mr 11, 1831; baptized My 12, 1831.
Martha Elizabeth (2:24,218), born S 4, 1833; baptized O 8, 1833;
died S 5, 1847; buried S 6, 1847.
Maria Catharine (2:29,211), born D 11, 1836; baptized D 27, 1836;
died Ag 23, 1838; buried Ag 24, 1838.
Raphael Randolph (2:37), born Mr 2, 1840; baptized My 31, 1840.
Prudence Agnes (2:39), born Ap 11, 1842; baptized My 11, 1842;
married Edward Owen Wilhide.
Frances Virginia (2:43), born O 4, 1845; baptized Ap 10, 1846.
EYLER, Joseph H. (2:156) married Je 3, 1860 Mary M. Wilhide.
Issue: Charles (2:71), born Mr 15, 1859; baptized Je 6, 1879.
Lucinda Kate (2:71), born My 19, 1869; baptized Je 6, 1879.
EYLER, Josiah (2:14) son of Jonas Nathanael and Sophia Theresa (Moser)
Eyler; born Ja 7, 1829; baptized F 15, 1829; married Urilla _____.
Issue: Caroline Prudence (2:240), born Mr 9, 1863; died D 27, 1864; buried
at Stone Church Mech[anicstow]n D 28, 1864.
EYLER, Magdalena married _____ Kauffman.
EYLER, Margaret Ann married Otto Cornelius Wilhide.
EYLER, Martha M. married Jacob Hetterly.
EYLER, Mary A. married John Weller.
EYLER, Mary L. married George W. Seips.
EYLER, Samuel (1:130,174) son of Jonas and Anna Regina (Herbach) Eyler; born
Ja 5, 1787; baptized Ja 8, 1787; married O 18, 1808 Maria Lewig (whose
father is dead and whose mother lives 50 miles from here).
Issue: Lydia (1:208), born Je 27, 1809; baptized Ag 10, 1809.
Maria (1:216), born Je 4, 1814; baptized Jl 26, 1814.
Anna (1:219,265), born Ag 3, 1816; baptized O 20, 1816; died My 12,
1818 of diarrhoea & vomiting; buried My 14, 1818.
EYLER, Solomon (2:153) married My 11, 1854 Susan Stitely.
EYLER, Susan married Jacob Ott.
EYLER, Susanna married Elias Harbaugh.
EYLER, Susanna married Joseph McClain.
EYLER, Theodore Nathanel (2:9,293) son of Jonas Nathanael and Sophia Theresa
(Moser) Eyler; born in Frederick County Mr 12, 1827; baptized Ap 13, 1827;
married Caroline Wilhide.
Issue: Franklin Pierce (2:48), born Ap 10, 1853; baptized Jl 31, 1853.
George Allen (2:52), born My 8, 1857; baptized N 18, 1857.
Charles Rudolph (2:57), born Mr 11, 1861; baptized F 11, 1862.
Anna Frances (2:58), born Je 1, 1863; baptized O 1, 1863.
Simon (2:60), born Ap 19, 1865; baptized F 26, 1866.
EYLER, Zephaniah (2:248), born [Je 25, 1811, (from his tombstone at Apple's
Church; doubtless Adam and Maria were his parents)]; died O 22, 1874 by
the accidental discharge of a gun; buried O 23, 1874 at Apple's Church.
EYSTER, Daniel married Magdalena Miller.
Issue: Elias (1:145), born Ap 24, 1833; baptized Je 2, 1833.
Daniel (1:149), born Je 28, 1835; baptized Ag 23, 1835.
Anna Barbara (1:152), born Je 27, 1837; baptized Jl 23, 1837.

FAHS, Abraham (1:129,264) son of Jacob Fahs (tinner) and Elisabeth (Köhler)
Fahs; born My 3, 1779 at York (or Heidelberg?); died Ag 14, 1813 of mental
illness and convulsions; buried Ag 16, 1813; married Ja 22, 1805 Elizabeth
Süss (1:129,131,172; 2:200) daughter of John George and Maria Barbara
(Eigenbrod) Süss; born in Frederick County My 25, 1785; baptized My 25,
1785; she married (2) Conrad Wilhide; she died Ag 30, 1832 (childbed);
buried Ag 31, 1832.
Issue: Cornelius (1:201), born O 18, 1805; baptized N 10, 1805.

Jacobus (i.e., James) (1:203; 2:209), born Ja 30, 1807; baptized F
22, 1807; died Jl 29, 1835 suddenly after a short illness; buried
Jl 30, 1835.
Jeremiah (1:206,262), born Jl 31, 1808; baptized Ag 1, 1808; died
Ag 3, 1808 of convulsions; buried Ag 4, 1808.
Arnold Richard (1:209), born S 20, 1809; baptized O 15, 1809;
married Julia Catharine Elizabeth Rösler.
Tobias (1:212), born S 2, 1811; baptized S 29, 1811; married Ara-
minta Williar.
FAHS, Arnold Richard (1:209) son of Abraham and Elizabeth (Süss) Fahs; born
S 20, 1809; baptized O 15, 1809; married Julia Catharine Elizabeth Rösler.
Issue: Eve Catharine Elizabeth (1:97), born F 18, 1839; baptized Ap 14,
1839.
FAHS, Henry, linen- and damask-weaver, married Anna Maria Hummer.
Issue: Lydia (1:261,198), born My 25, 1804; baptized My 27, 1804; drowned
in a tub of water Ag 2, 1805; buried Ag 4, 1805.
Zaccheus (1:202), born Ag 2, 1806; baptized Ag 10, 1806.
Lucinda (1:205), born F 26, 1808; baptized Ap 3, 1808.
FAHS, Henry, tailor, Mech't'n [Mechanicstown?] (2:286), born York Ag 12,
1798; Communicant D 17, 1814 Lititz; married Sophia Frederica Rudolphi
(2:286), born at Bethlehem Je 6, 1797; Communicant Ja 18, 18-- Bethlehem.
Issue: Emma Lavinia (1:118), born Ap 29, 1822; baptized My 9, 1822.
Charlotte Matilda (2:4), born My 24, 1824; baptized Je 27, 1824;
married [Henry] Buhrman.
Cornelia Augusta (2:9), born O 23, 1826; baptized D 25, 1826; mar-
ried Levi Buhrman.
Henry Clay (2:14,199), born D 25, 1828; baptized F 15, 1829; died N
28, 1830 of consumption, 11 months; buried N 30, 1830.
daughter, stillborn (2:198) S 19, 1830; buried S 20, 1830.
Edwin Emmanuel (2:21,202), born N 15, 1831; baptized D 26, 1831;
died F 16, 1833 of scarlet fever; buried F 17, 1833.
Allen Otto (2:25,294), born Ap 21, 1834; baptized Je 8, 1834.
William Hamilton (2:32), born Je 15, 1838; baptized Jl 22, 1838.
James Madison (2:32), born Je 15, 1838; baptized Jl 22, 1838.
Caroline Melinda (2:40,215), born Ag 22, 1742; baptized S 13, 1842;
died O 31, 1842, aged 0-2-9; buried N 1, 1842.
FAHS, Tobias (1:212) son of Abraham and Elizabeth (Süss) Fahs; born S 2,
1811; baptized S 29, 1811; married Araminta Williar (1:214) daughter of
Peter and Elizabeth (Müller) Williar; born S 20, 1812; baptized D 22,
1812.
Issue: Harriet Septimia (2:28), born O 18, 1833; baptized S 27, 1835.
James Abraham (2:28), born N 28, 1835; baptized Ja 17, 1836.
Victoria Elisabeth (2:31), born N 8, 1837; baptized Ja 21, 1838.
Julia Catharine (2:37), born N 13, 1839; baptized Jl 12, 1840.
FALDER, William (2:146), son of John and Hannah Falder; married Ap 12, 1832
Catharine Leinbach, daughter of Benjamin and Elizabeth Leinbach.
FAVORITE, Adeline married David Hubbard.
FAVORITE, Catharine, daughter of Frederick, married Greenbury Witmer.
FAVORITE, Christina married Jacob Gump.
FAVORITE, Frederick (Lutheran) (2:146), son of Henry and Sarah (Berts)
Favorite; married N 3, 1831 Rebecca Protzman (1:169b; 2:221,289), daughter
of Ludwig and Maria Elizabeth (Rauser) Protzman; born O 26, 1789; Communi-
cant O 8, 1820; she married (2) Andreas Williar; died N 7, 1852; buried N
8, 1852.
Issue: Abraham Isaiah (2:24), born Jl 25, 1833; baptized S 8, 1833.
FAVORITE, Henry married Margaretha _____.
Issue: Anna Miliana (1:218), born F 7, 1816; baptized Mr 24, 1816.

FAVORITE, Jacob (1:131), born in Frederick County; married N 3, 1812 Anna
  Catharina Gump, daughter of George and Anna Elisabeth (Frey) Gump; born in
  Frederick County F 27, 1792; baptized Mr 1, 1792.
  Issue: Ezra (1:215), born Ag 3, 1813; baptized S 9, 1813.
FAVORITE, Jacob, son of John and Elizabeth (Koller) Favorite; married D 11,
  1827 Catharine Mondshour, daughter of John and Sarah (Smith) Mondschauer.
  (1:83)
FAVORITE, John married Elisabeth Koller.
  Issue: Samuel (1:202), born Ag 4, 1804; baptized Mr 23, 1806.
    Jacob married Catharine Mondshauer.
FAVORITE, Joseph married Sarah Kuhn.
  Issue: Minerva Louisa (1:139), born Ap 1, 1830; baptized Je 9, 1830.
FAVORITE, Maria married Anthony Hildebeutel.
FAVORITE, Samuel married Mary Ann McGinness (or McInnes).
  Issue: Adeline Cecilia (1:144), born My 28, 1832; baptized O 8, 1832.
    Mary Ann (1:99), born Ap 29, 1840; baptized My 22, 1840.
FAVORITE, Sarah married Charles Williar.
FAVORITE, Sevilla (unmarried).
  Issue: William Robert (2:124), born O 23, 1858; baptized D 18, 1859.
FAVORITE, William married Catharine E. _____.
  Issue: Joseph Samuel (2:244), born Ja 9, 1865; died Ap 28, 1868; buried at
    Cr'town [Creagerstown?] Ap 29, 1868.
FAVORITE, William (Lutheran) married Lydia _____.
  Issue: Mary Ann Melissa (2:124), born S 26, 1859; baptized D 18, 1859.
FEEZER, Anne married Michael Branner.
FEEZER (or FEISER), Harriet married David Boller.
FEEZER, John Samuel (2:241), born Ja 9, 1847; died Jl 6, 1865; buried Jl 7,
  1865 at Mech'n [Mechanicstown?].
FEEZER, Levi (1:89) married S 6, 1838 Catharine Kessler.
FEIZER, Emanuel (1:90) married Mr 18[?], 1842 Susanna Buch (?).
FERNEY, Mary Catharine married Samuel Wilhide.
FETTER, Marcus married Elizabeth Harbaugh (1:111).
FEVER, John married Philippina Hekedorn.
  Issue: Maria Elizabeth (1;186); baptized Ja 23, 1799.
FICHTER, Barbara married Christian Emanuel Bickle.
FICK, Charles married Margaret _____.
  Issue: Emma May (2:135), born D 22, 1870; baptized Ag 20, 1876.
    Joseph Henry (2:135), born My 18, 1875; baptized Ag 20, 1876.
FICK, Daniel married Sophia Reecher (?).
  Issue: John Edward (1:96), born Jl 27, 1834; baptized Mr 10, 1839.
    Lucinda Eliza (1:96), born Mr 7, 1838; baptized Mr 10, 1839.
FICK, Daniel Elijah; born Ap 16, 1840; died O 25, 1863; buried at Graceham O
  27, 1863; (2:239).
FICK, James M. (single), died F 17, 1871, aged 42-6-12; buried at Graceham F
  19, 1871. (2:246).
FICK, Joseph.
  Issue: James Joseph (2:248), born My 4, 1873; died Mr 19, 1874; buried at
    Graceham Mr 20, 1874.
FICK, Joseph H. W. married Margaret Rebecca Fogle; she married previously
  _____ Eichelberger.
  Issue: Mary Virginia (2:129), born O 11, 1866 or S 12, 1866; baptized Ag
    11, 1867.
    Margaret Naomi Elizabeth (2:130), born F 25, 1869; baptized My 6,
    1869.
    Daniel Graceham Elijah (2:136), born D 28, 1878; baptized Je 1,
    1879.
FICK, Keziah Ann, born Mr 7, 1798; died My 16, 1869; buried at Graceham My
  17, 1869. (2:245).
FIESER, _____ (1:94) married Barbara Bikle.

FIESER, Juliana married David Troxel.
FINNEGAN, Peter (1:87), son of Michael and Rosanna Finnegan, married Ap 12, 1832 Mary Gilbert, daughter of John and Elizabeth Gilbert; said Mary Gilbert had been married previously to ____ Bernhart.
Issue: Henry (1:148), born N 13, 1834; baptized F 23, 1835.
FIROR (VIERUHR), ____ (1:242) married Maria Barbara Wilhide, who later married Jacob Weller; said Maria Barbara died Jl 17, 1754.
Issue: John Henry (1:242).
FIROR, Elizabeth married David Eiker.
FIROR, Hannah Rebecca married Wilfred Six.
FIROR, Jacob Levi married Amanda Crabbs.
Issue: Frederick Lewis (2:121,227), born Je 9, 1856; baptized Je 16, 1856; died Jl 17, 1856; buried at Apple's Church Jl 18, 1856.
FIROR, John son of Leonhard and Elisabeth Fierur (Firor) married (1) Magdalena Werfels.
Issue: William (1:112), born Ja 31, 1820; baptized F 13, 1820.
FIROR, John son of Leonhard Firur (Firor) and Elizabeth, married (2) on Ag 21, 1834 Juliana Stauffer (1:217; 2:147), daughter of John Christian and Barbara (Weller) Stauffer; born Ap 21, 1815; baptized My 28, 1815.
Issue: Calvin Leander (1:148), born F 23, 1835; baptized Mr 11, 1835.
FIROR, Levi.
Issue: Margaret A. Elizabeth (2:220), born N 20, 1851; died Je 20, 1850; buried at Apple's Church Je 21, 1850. [dates as transcribed]
FIROR (FÜHRUHR), Leonard married Elizabeth Pauss.
Issue: Maria Magdalena married Christian Harbaugh.
FIROR, Magdalena married Wilfred Six.
FIROR, Peter married Mary _____.
Issue: Howard Orlandes (2:133), born N 30, 1874; baptized Jl 27, 1875.
FIROR, Sophia married James Krieger.
FIRST, Jacob married Margaret Schmidt.
Issue: Magdalena (1:210), born O 10, 1809, baptized S 9, 1810.
FISHER, Cornelius or Frederick (2:163) married O 10, 1877 Mollie Florence Colliflower (2:54), both of Graceham; she was the daughter of Michael Joseph and Harriet Elizabeth (Shuff) Colliflower, and was born My 14, 1859 and baptized Je 29, 1859.
Issue: Nora Edith (2:71,254), born O 27, 1878; baptized F 2, 1879; died F 8, 1879; buried at Graceham F 9, 1879.
Alverda May (2:72), born D 4, 1879; baptized Ap 18, 1880.
FISHER, Magdalena, born Mr 30, 1817; died My 15, 1864; buried My 17, 1864 at Stone Church in Mechanicstown. (2:240).
FISHER, Nathanael (2:150) married in Ag, 1846 Magdalena Hoover.
FLATT, William M. married Mary Ann Allendar.
Issue: Augustus Francis (1:145), born D 18, 1832; baptized Mr 24, 1833.
FLAUTT, Ann married William Herman.
FLAUTT, Jacob married Emilia Wolf.
Issue: Mary Ann (1:84) married Jeremiah Brown.
FLEAGLE, Henry.
Issue: Virgie Florence (2;136), born Jl 28, 1880; baptized Ag 31, 1880.
FLEMING, Samuel married Hannah Coons.
Issue: Jemima Ann (2;112), born F 2, 1845; baptized Mr 27, 1845.
FLEY, Michael had by Margaret Kruschong, widow, an illegitimate daughter, Maria Magdalena (1:204), who was born Mr 10, 1807 and was baptized My 7, 1807.
FLICK, George married Mary Kuhn.
Issue: Mary Magdalena (1:136), born Jl 31, 1827; baptized Ap 16, 1828.
FLOREY, Wilfred L. (2:153) married Ja 19, 1854 Sarah Ann Leidy.
FOGLE or VOGEL, ____.
Issue: Henry (2:113), born N --, 1836; baptized N 16, 1845.
Samuel (2;113), born S 31 [sic], 1839; baptized N 16, 1845.

27

Solomon (2:113), born N --, 1840; baptized N 16, 1845.
Susannah (2:113), born Je 26, 1843; baptized N 16, 1845.
Sarah Elizabeth (2:113), born Je 26, 1843; baptized N 16, 1845.
FOGLE or VOGLE, John T. or F. (2:155), married O 15, 1857 Susan Elizabeth
    Colliflower (2:27), daughter of John and Matilda (Wilheid) Colliflower;
    born N 23, 1834; baptized Mr 11, 1835.
Issue: John Milton (2:59), born Ag 27, 1863; baptized D 25, 1863.
    Mary Catharine Susan Elizabeth (2:129), born My 27, 1866; baptized
        O 21, 1866.
    Emma Effie Matilda (2:129), born Jl 17, 1868; baptized S 13, 1868.
    Harvey Lewis Washington (2:68), born Jl 18, 1875; baptized O 24,
        1875.
FOGLE, Margaret Rebecca married (1) _____ Eichelberger and (2) Joseph H. W.
    Fick.
FOGLE, William N. (2:159), married Ap 16, 1867 Mary Margaret Barton.
FORDNEY, Caspar of Mechanicstown married Barbara Meister.
Issue: William David (1:140), born O 15, 1830; baptized N 28, 1830.
FOREMAN, George Washington (2:253), born Mr 27, 1808; died Ag 20, 1877 at
    Mechanicstown and buried in the cemetery there Ag 22, 1877. He married
    Phoebe Ann Wilhide (1:218; 2:289) daughter of Conrad and Elizabeth (Süss)
    Wilhide; born Ag 15, 1815; baptized O 8, 1815.
Issue: Mary Adaline (2:26,209), born My 22, 1834; baptized Jl 20, 1834;
        died D 29, 1835; buried D 31, 1835.
    Charles Valentine (2:28), born O 10, 1835; baptized Ja 17, 1836.
    Edwin (2:31), born S 10, 1837; baptized N 19, 1837.
    Albert (2:37), born F 12, 1840; baptized Ap 19, 1840.
    Harriet Amelia (2:41), born O 27, 1842; baptized Ja 29, 1843.
    Martha Ellen (2:112,218), born N 29, 1844; baptized Mr 29, 1845;
        died Jl 29, 1847; buried Jl 30, 1847.
    Henry Clay (2:115), born Ja 10, 1847.
    Mary Martha (2:46), born O 8, 1850; baptized Ap 10, 1851.
    Julia Catharine (2:48), born D 12, 1853; baptized Mr 28, 1854.
FOREMAN, Valentine (2:224); born S 4, 1774; died Mr 26, 1854; buried at
    Mechincstown Mr 28, 1854.
FORNEY, William.
Issue: Anna Ros. Cath. (2:237), born My 31, 1862; died Mr 11, 1863; buried
    at Mechanicstown Mr 12.
FÖRST, Elizabeth married Godfrey Höllwart.
FOX, George married Ann Elizabeth.
Issue: Elizabeth (1:86) married William Brown.
FOX, John P. (2:150) married Ap, 1847 Charlotte Eigenbrod.
FRANK, Peter (2:235), born Je 1, 1832; died F 25, 1862; buried Ap 13, 1862
    at the Frederick County Almshouse.
FREDERIC, Jacob married Mary Ann Derr.
Issue: Daniel Stauffer (1:137), born F 26, 1828; baptized S 25, 1828.
FREEZE, Julia married Josiah Wilhide.
FRENSCH, Peter married Christian Holzmann.
Issue: Anna Rebecca (1:203), born Ag 25, 1806; baptized F 12, 1807.
    Samuel (1:206), born F 20, 1808; baptized Ag 21, 1808.
    John (1:210), born Mr 18, 1810; baptized Jl 8, 1810.
    William (1:216), born Ja 11, 1813; baptized Ja 18, 1815.
    Maria (1:219), born Ag 7, 1815; baptized N 10, 1816.
FRESHMAN, George (2:160) married Je 28, 1868 Ellen Catharine Wilhide.
FREY, Abraham (1:127,170b), eldest son of Daniel Frey; born S 3, 1765;
    baptized D 12, 1789; married F 12, 1788 Susanna Günther (1:92), second
    surviving daughter of Peter Günther; Probationer S 26, 1790.
FREY, (John) Daniel, born O 15, 1742; baptized D 25, 1785; died My 3, 1807;
    buried My 5, 1807.
Issue: Abraham (1:127,170b), born S 3, 1765; married Susanna Günther.

FREY, (John) Daniel (1:173,262), born O 15, 1742; baptized D 25, 1785; died
    My 3, 1807; buried in the churchyard My 5, 1807; married (Maria) Catharina
    _____ (1:108,173), born O 18, 1741; baptized D 25, 1785; Communicant Je
    9, 1787.
Issue: John Daniel (1:173b), born My 2, 1769; baptized Jl 24, 1791.
    Maria Barbara (1:166b), baptized O 14, 1787; married Christian
        Frederick Günther.
    Anna Elizabeth, baptized O 11, 1789; married John George Gump.
    Christian (1:234), born Ap 5, 1776; died Je 24, 1784; buried in the
        churchyard Je 26, 1784.
    Catharina (1:234), born Ap 28, 1779; died Je 23, 1784; buried Je
        24, 1784 in the churchyard.
FREY, Jacob married Elizabeth Kamp daughter of John and Anna Elizabeth Kamp.
Issue: John Elias (1:174b), born Ag 31, 1791 at 1 p.m.; baptized S 9,
    1791.
FREY, Magdalena married Christian (or Christoph) Paus.
FRIES, _____ (1:89) married Sarah Six, daughter of Philip and Isabella Six;
    born Ap 18, 1816; she later became the wife of Edward O. [or P.] Norris.
FRÖHLICH, Barbara married John Shuff.
FRÖHLICH, Christian, Junior, married Susanna Haberstick (Sarah 1:214,221,265
    or Selle 1:211).
Issue: Elizabeth (1:211), born Je 24, 1811; baptized Je 24, 1811.
    John (1:214), born Mr 16, 1813; baptized My 2, 1813.
    Henry (1:218), born Jl 22, 1815; baptized Ap 28, 1816.
    Christian (1:221,265), born S 11, 1817; baptized Mr 1, 1818; died
        Ag 12, 1818; buried Ag 13, 1818. The cause of the child's death:
        diarrhoea.
    Thomas (1:111), born Ag 11, 1819; baptized O 3, 1819; married Mary
        Ann Rodenheiser.
FRÖHLICH, Daniel (1:85) son of Henry and Margaret Fröhlich; married D 17,
    1829 Elizabeth Hertzog, daughter of Peter and Catharine Hertzog.
FRÖHLICH (FRAILEY) David (2:253), died N 9, 1877 at Union Bridge; buried N
    10, 1877 at Creagerstown, aged 72 plus.
FRÖHLICH, Frederick, farmer, married Ellen McHenry.
Issue: Eliza (1:196), born Ap 28, 1803; baptized Je 26, 1803.
    Matilda (1:196), born Ap 28, 1803; baptized Je 26, 1803.
    Henry (1:200), born Ja 26, 1805; baptized Je 9, 1805.
    Martha (1:207), born Ag 1, 1807; baptized S 18, 1808.
FRÖHLICH, Henry (2:197); Came to this country with the Hessian troops in the
    Revolution; died Mr 25, 1830 due to weakness of age, at the age of 74-1-
    11; buried Mr 27, 1830. He was the father of 14 children.
FRÖHLICH, Henry married Maria _____.
Issue: Elizabeth, born O 23, 1786; died Je 21, 1818; married John Smith.
FRÖHLICH, Henry, farmer, married Margaret Wilhide (not a member) (1:82); she
    died S 15, 1822; buried S 17, 1822.
Issue: John (1:187), born Ja 25, 1799; baptized Mr 24, 1799.
    Solomo[n] (1:193), born Ja 20, 1802; baptized Ja 24, 1802; married
        Eliza Walker.
    William (1:208), born My 16, 1809; baptized My 28, 1809; married
        Catharina Williard.
    Margaret (1:131) married John Born.
    Daniel married Elizabeth Hertzog.
FRÖHLICH (FRAILEY), James H. (2:160), married Mr 10, 1870 Sarah E. Weller.
Issue: Harry Walker (2:66), born 1872; baptized My 26, 1872.
FRÖHLICH (FRALEY), John married Elizabeth Stauffer.
Issue: Mary Frances (2:127), born Je 18, 1854; baptized Mr 10, 1864.
    Emma Jane (2:127), born My 23, 1857; baptized Mr 10, 1864.
    Alice Ellen (2:127,254), born Mr 14, 1860; baptized F 25, 1864;
        died Je 28, 1879; buried at Mechanicstown Je 29, 1879.

29

Anna Bell (2:127), born Ja 19, 1862; baptized Mr 10, 1864.
FRÖHLICH (FRAILEY), John married Elizabeth _____.
Issue: Ellen Rebecca (2:239), born Ap 16, 1860; died F 26, 1864; buried at
Creagerstown F 27, 1864.
FRÖHLICH, John Henry (also spelled FRALEY) (2:151), married Ja 2, 1851 Mary
Ann Stauffer.
Issue: Laura Virginia (2:47); baptized My 30, 1852.
Sarah Elizabeth (2:50), born Jl 21, 1853; baptized Jl 11, 1856.
William Henry (2:50), born F 13, 1855; baptized Jl 11, 1856.
Charles Baker (2:60), born O 12, 1863; baptized O 10, 1864.
Harriet Lillian (2:61), born O 16, 1865; baptized Mr 28, 1867.
FRÖHLICH (FRAILEY), Solomon (1:85,193), born Ja 20, 1802, the son of Henry
and Mary Frailey (Fröhlich); he was baptized Ja 24, 1802 and married D 30,
1828 Eliza Walker daughter of John and Elizabeth Walker.
Issue: Margaret Elizabeth (1:139), born D 23, 1829; baptized Ja 31, 1830.
FRÖHLICH (FRALEY), Thomas (1:90,111), born Ag 11, 1819; baptized O 3, 1819;
married Je 8, 1840 Mary Ann Rodenheiser.
FRÖHLICH, William (2:209), born Mr 25, 1831; died Ja 28, 1836; buried Ja 30,
1836.
FRÖHLICH, William (2:198; 1:208) of the Catoctin; born My 16, 1809, the son
of Henry and Margaret (Wilhide) Fröhlich; he was baptized My 28, 1809;
married Ja 1, 1829 Catharina Williard; he died Ag 28, 1830 of ardent fever
and was buried Ag 29, 1830.
Issue: _____ (son)
FRÖHLICH, William had by Eliza Elisabeth Lammerson, an illegitimate daugh-
ter, Sarah (1:99), born F 2, 1840; baptized Ja 8, 1840 [sic].
FULLER, Catharine married Thomas Weare.
FURGESON, Josephine (2:224), born Ap 16, 1853; died Mr 17, 1854; buried at
Mechanicstown Mr 19, 1854.

GALL, Eva married Nicholas Engel.
GALL, William married Elizabeth Schreiber.
Issue: Louis Edward (1:110), born Mr 3, 1844; baptized Ap 10, 1844.
GAMMEL, James married _____ Bekkenbach.
Issue: James (1:192), baptized D 27, 1801.
GARRET, Christian had, by Catharine Graber, an illegitimate daughter Mary
Ann (1:143), born F 22, 1830; baptized My 6, 1832.
GARRETT (GERRETH), John married Catharine Colliflower.
Issue: Anna Maria (1:205), born S 11, 1807; baptized Mr 1, 1808.
GARRETT (GERRETH), Joseph married Elizabeth Colliflower.
Issue: Bernard (1:203), born N 14, 1806; baptized Ja 5, 1807.
Alice Susanna (1:207), born Jl 22, 1808; baptized S 24, 1808.
Joseph (1:210), born My 17, 1810; baptized Jl 15, 1810.
GARRISON, Elizabeth married Richard Lillie.
GARVER, Mary Ann married Fr. William Weddle.
GAUGH, Anna Milinda married Charles Dorsey.
GAUGH, Eva married John Shoop.
GAUGH, Laura married (1) _____ McKinney (?); and (2) Amadeus Wilhide.
GEISBERT, Deborah married Elias (C.) Weller.
GERNAND, Edward married Louisa Bassford.
Issue: Murvin Edward Jacob (2:63), born Jl 3, 1868.
GERNAND, Emanuel (1:205; 2:145) of Westminster, Maryland, son of John Adam
and Anna Catharine (Weller) Gernand; born Ap 9, 1808; baptized Ap 24,
1808; married N 5, 1829 Rebecca Süss (1:204; 2:286), daughter of Gottfried
and Anna Maria (Krämer) Süss; born Ap 5, 1807; baptized Ap 26, 1807;
Communicant Ag 13, 1823.
Issue: Charlotte Rebecca (2:17), born S 15, 1830; baptized O 8, 1830.
Edwin Kraemer (2:33), born N 13, 1838; baptized Ap 21, 1838.

GERNAND, Eugene Jacob (2:20,157,253,294) son of John Jacob and Sybilla (Wilhide) Gernand; born S 16, 1831; baptized O 9, 1831; married O 10, 1861 Harriet C. Stull; killed on the Baltimore & Potomac Railroad by the night express O 2, 1877; buried O 6, 1877 Graceham Cemetery.
Issue: Milton Eugene (2:58), born Jl 14, 1862; baptized S 10, 1862.
   Edwin Howard (2:59), born D 18, 1863; baptized My 1, 1864.
   Alice May (2:61), born Ag 23, 1866; baptized D 2, 1866.
   Charles Sumner (2:63), born Ja 1, 1868; baptized Ag 2, 1868.
   Cora Ella (2:64), born Ja 14, 1870; baptized Jl 17, 1870.
   Frank Wilson (2:67), born My 1, 1872; baptized N 28, 1872.
GERNAND, John, joiner (1:81,132,179) of Mechanicstown, son of John Adam and Anna Catharina (Weller) Gernand; born near Graceham Mr 31, 1795; died of consumption Mr 17, 1822; buried Mr 19, 1822; married Ja 11, 1818 Rosina Gump who was born in Frederick County and who was the daughter of _____ and Maria Gump.
Issue: Anna Maria Cecilia (1:112), born N 16, 1819; baptized N 28, 1819.
GERNAND, John Adam, tanner (1:108,128; 2:192), born Jl 15, 1755 in Frederick County; died N 14, 1825; buried N 16, 1825; readmitted to communion N 20, 1790; both his parents died before he married; he married My 19, 1789 Anna Catharine Weller (1:79,92,108,161) who was born Ap 27, 1768 near Graceham, the daughter of John Jacob and Anna Margaretha (Harbaugh) Weller, and she was baptized My 1, 1768; she died of consumption O 29, 1820 and was buried O 31, 1820. She was a Probationer O 11, 1789 and a Communicant N 20, 1790.
Issue: Thomas (1:170b), born My 4, 1790 at 11 a.m.; baptized My 16, 1790; married Maria _____.
   Anna Johanna (1:174b,240), born D 27, 1791 at 6 p.m.; baptized D 27, 1791; died of convulsions Ja 12, 1792; buried in the churchyard Ja 13, 1792.
   William (1:175b), born N 26, 1792 at 7 a.m.; baptized D 2, 1792; married Anna Elizabeth Johnson; died O 2, 1825.
   John (1:81,179), born Mr 31, 1795 at 6 a.m. near Graceham; baptized Ap 5, 1795; married Rosina Gump; died of consumption Mr 17, 1822; buried Mr 19, 1822.
   John Jacob (1:183), born My 26, 1797 at 3:30 a.m.; baptized My 28, 1797; married (1) Elizabeth Williar, (2) Anna Theodora Becker and (3) Sybilla Wilhide.
   Joseph (1:80, 188), born near Graceham N 15, 1799; baptized N 17, 1799; died of consumption Ap 10, 1821; buried Ap 11, 1821.
   Anna Margaret (1:193), born Ap 29, 1802; baptized My 9, 1802.
   Anna Rosina (1:197), born F 26, 1804; baptized Mr 11, 1804; married Martin Rauser.
   Elias (2:192; 1:202), born F 17, 1806; baptized Mr 2, 1806; died N 7, 1826; buried N 9, 1826.
   Emanuel (1:205), born Ap 9, 1808; baptized Ap 24, 1808; married Rebecca Süss.
   Louis Weller (1:212,263), born N 19, 1811; baptized D 1, 1811; died of convulsions F 26, 1812; buried F 28, 1812.
   Jonathan (2:210; 1:215), born O 4, 1813; baptized O 10, 1813; died of consumption D 10, 1836; buried D 11, 1836.
GERNAND, John Jacob, weaver (1:132; 2:143,247) of Graceham, son of John Adam Gernand and Anna Catharina (Weller) Gernand; born in Frederick County My 26, 1797; baptized My 28, 1797; died N 26, 1871; buried at Graceham N 28, 1871; he married 3 times, (1) on Mr 25, 1819 Elizabeth Williar (1:81), daughter of Andrew and Margaret (Herbach) Williar; born O 14, 1787 at 4 p.m.; died of Puerperal fever Ap 11, 1822; buried Ap 13, 1822.
Issue: Mary Amanda (1:113), born Je 29, 1820; baptized Jl 30, 1820; married Frederick Hankey.
   Andrew Augustus (1:118), born Mr 10, 1822; baptized Ap 13, 1822.

GERNAND, John Jacob, weaver (2:143), born in Frederick County My 26, 1797;
he was the son of John Adam and Anna Catharina (Weller) Gernand; he married three times, (2) on Ja 19, 1823, Anna Theodora Becker (2:143,197)
daughter of John Frederick Becker, breeches-maker, and his wife Anna
Elizabeth (Schneider); said Anna Theodora was born Ja 8, 1803 in Salem,
North Carolina, and came here in May, 1819 with the Kluges; she died Ap 6,
1830 of abdominal sphacelation resulting from childbirth; buried Ap 8,
1830.
Issue: William Henry (2:3,293), born O 29, 1823; baptized N 16, 1823; a
    Communicant in 1843.
    Josephine Eliza (2:6), born Ag 12, 1825; baptized S 4, 1825; mar-
    ried Jacob Boblets.
    Salome Angelica (2:11), born O 15, 1827; baptized N 11, 1827; mar-
    ried Raymond Sylvester Seiss.
    Anna Theodora (2:16,207), born Mr 31, 1830; baptized Ap 8, 1830;
    died of sore throat O 19, 1834; buried O 21, 1834.
GERNAND, John Jacob (1:132; 2:143,145) son of John Adam and Anna Catharina
(Weller) Gernand; born My 26, 1797; Communicant Ag 13, 1819; he married
three times, (3) on O 10, 1830 Sybilla Wilhide (1:198; 2:286) daughter of
Frederick and Catharina (Peitzel) Wilhide; born My 31, 1804; baptized Jl
1, 1804; a Communicant O, 1820; died [D 2, 1886].
Issue: Eugene Jacob (2:20,294), born S 16, 1831; baptized O 9, 1831;
    married Harriet C. Stull; died O 2, 1877.
    Mary Emeline (2:23), born F 10, 1833; baptized Mr 17, 1833; married
    Bernard Colliflower.
    Leander Wilson (2:28), born Ja 28, 1836; baptized F 21, 1836.
    Sarah Ellen (2:34, 156), born Ag 7, 1839; baptized Ag 25, 1839;
    married Henry T. Bachman.
    Edward Theodore (2:39), born S 18, 1841; baptized O 17, 1841.
GERNAND, Joseph Alfred (2:5, 152) son of William and Anna Elizabeth (Johnson) Gernand; born N 27, 1824; baptized Ja 19, 1825; died [Je 11, 1909 and
buried at Apple's Church]; married N 23, 1852 Sarah Ann Elizabeth Walters
who died [F 2, 1854, aged 28-1-26, and is buried at Apple's Church].
GERNAND, Joseph Alfred son of William and Anna Elizabeth (Johnson) Gernand;
born N 27, 1824; baptized Ja 19, 1825; he married (2) Harriet S. _____,
who died [Ap 14, 1899, aged 73-3-23].
Issue: Eliza Jane (2:232), born D 15, 1856; died Mr 15, 1859; buried at
    Apple's Church Mr 16, 1859.
    Emma Kate (2:240), born D 27, 1863; died Mr 12, 1865; buried at
    Apple's Church Mr 13, 1865.
GERNAND, Mary married Henry Haspelhorn.
GERNAND, Thomas (1:170b) son of John Adam and Anna Catharina (Weller) Ger-
nand; born My 4, 1790; baptized My 16, 1790; married Maria _____.
Issue: William Dorson [Dawson?] (1:81,222), born N 29, 1813 at Philadel-
    phia; baptized Ja 12, 1819; came to live with his uncle William
    Gernand when he was 4); died Jl 24, 1822; buried Jl 25, 1822.
GERNAND, William, shoemaker (1:132, 175b; 2:192), of Graceham, son of Adam
and Anna Catharina (Weller) Gernand; born N 26, 1792 in Frederick County;
baptized D 2, 1792; died O 2, 1825; buried O 3, 1825; married Je 18, 1816
Anna Elizabeth Johnson (1:114,221); born in Frederick County; baptized
when an adult on My 11, 1818.
Issue: Anna Catharine (1:221,266), born Je 15, 1818; baptized Ag 24, 1818;
    died of convulsions Mr 14, 1819; buried Mr 16, 1819.
    Caroline Emilie (1:113), born Je 26, 1820; baptized Jl 28, 1820;
    married Ephraim Bobletts.
    Mary Melinda (2:2), born F 26, 1823; baptized Ap 13, 1823.
    Joseph Alfred (2:5), born N 27, 1824; baptized Ja 19, 1825; married
    (1) Sarah Ann Elizabeth Waters and (2) Harriet S. _____.

GERNAND, William Henry (2:152) son of John Jacob and Anna Theodora (Becker) Gernand; married Ag 7, 1851 Anna Maria Süss (2:224) daughter of John and Elizabeth (Schuler) Süss; born Ag 24, 1831; died at Westminster, Maryland Mr 12, 1854; buried at Graceham Mr 14, 1854.
Issue: Elizabeth Rebecca (2:224), born Mr 4, 1854; baptized Mr 11, 1854; died Je 28, 1854; buried Je 29, 1854.
GIBBONS, Elizabeth married _____ Hammer.
GIEBLER, John Peter married Elizabeth _____.
Issue: John (1:177), born Je 11, 1793; baptized Jl 20, 1793.
GIESE, Daniel married Elizabeth Bowus.
Issue: A. Catharine married Jacob H. Welty.
GIESE, Henry, widower, blacksmith and farmer, (1:128) married Rosina Glatt Ja 20, 1800 (1:260); she was born Ag 30, 1760 in Heidelberg Township, Berks County; she was the daughter of George Glatt, farmer, and Maria Elizabeth (Dock) Glatt; she was formerly the wife of John Romig (or Jacob Romig, 1:260); she died N 3, 1804; buried N 4, 1804.
Issue: William (1:191), baptized Ag 17, 1800.
      Joseph (1:194), born Ap 9, 1802; baptized Ag 1, 1802.
      Elias (1:196), born Je 21, 1803; baptized Ag 6, 1803.
      Solomon (1:199), born O 28, 1804; baptized O 31, 1804; died soon after baptism.
GIESE (GESEY), [John] married Elizabeth Hankey (2:234) daughter of Isaac and Susanna Magdalena (Apple) Hankey; she was born Ap 15, 1793; died S 17, 1861; buried Apple's Church S 19, 1861.
GIESE (GEASEY), Magdalene, born S 5, 1788; died Ag 27, 1856; buried Ag 28, at Apple's Church. (2:228).
GIESE (GEASY), Mary married John Welty.
GIESE (GEESEY), Mary Ann married George Brown.
GILBERT, _____ married Eve _____, a member of the Dutch Reformed Church; she was born Ag 10, 1787; died Mr 30, 1860 of Pleurisy, while on a visit to her children; she was buried at Graceham Ap 1, 1860.
Issue: Ephraim
      Joshua
GILBERT, Clement Evers (2:136), born Ja 9, 1880; baptized Jl 28, 1880.
GILBERT, Ephraim married Catharine S. V. Webb.
Issue: Mary Catharine (2:230), born Ja 31, 1849; died D 21, 1857; buried at Graceham D 23, 1857.
GILBERT, Ephraim W. (2:154) married Mr 6, 1856 Sophia Theresa Boller (2:26) daughter of John and Catharine (Reidenauer) Boller; born N 19, 1834; baptized Ja 1, 1835.
Issue: Sarah Missouri (2:51), born D 17, 1856; baptized Mr 1, 1857.
      Mark Calvin (2:54), born D 6, 1858; baptized Ja 9, 1859.
      Clara Bell (2:55), born Ja 30, 1861; baptized Mr 3, 1861.
GILBERT, Hannah married Joshua Hetterli.
GILBERT, John married Elizabeth _____.
Issue: John B. (1:87) married Catharine Grimes.
      Mary (1:87) married (1) _____ Bernhart and (2) Peter Finnegan.
GILBERT, John B. (1:87) son of John and Elizabeth Gilbert, married N 27, 1832 Catharine Grimes, daughter of Samuel and Catharine Grimes.
GILBERT, Joshua (2:52), born Ag 28, 1833; baptized Mr 28, 1858; married Sarah Caroline Boller (2:34) daughter of John R. and Catharine (Reidenauer) Boller; she was born N 25, 1839; baptized D 31, 1839.
Issue: John Henry (2:122), born S 20, 1857; baptized F 7, 1858.
      Benjamin Franklin (2:54), born S 6, 1859; baptized O 16, 1859.
      William Hagen (2:58), born Je 2, 1863; baptized O 4, 1863.
      Joseph Elvin (2:60), born S 8, 1865; baptized O 9, 1865.
      Charles Wesley (2:63, 255), born F 6, 1868; baptized Ag 30, 1868; died Ap 10, 1880; buried at Mechanicstown Ap 11, 1880.
      Harvey Milton (2:68), born Je 12, 1870; baptized N 21, 1875.

33

George Edward (2:248), died Je 24, 1875, aged 3 years; buried Je
    25, 1875 at Stone Church, Mechanicstown.
    Gertrude Elizabeth (2:68), born Je 4, 1875; baptized N 21, 1875.
    Marshal Luther (2:70), born Je 1, 1877; baptized S 2, 1877.
GILBERT, Julia E. married Harrison Reever.
GILBERT, Susan married Enos Cover.
GILBERT, Virginia married William Cover.
GINNIVAN, Reuben married Catharine Merkly.
    Issue: Alexander Washington (1:96), born D 26, 1838; baptized D 31, 1838.
GLAS, Susanna married Abraham Hahn.
GLATT, Elizabeth married John Woodring.
GLATT, George married in Heidelberg in Pennsylvania Maria Elizabeth Dock
    (1:260); she was born in Bissweilen, Alsace, Mr 24, 1720; she died O 4,
    1804 and was buried O 5, 1804; she later married Tobias Böckel.
    Issue: Rosina (1:260), born in Heidelberg Ag 30, 1760; died N 3, 1804;
        buried N 4, 1804; married (1) Jacob Romig and (2) Henry Giesy.
    6 others
GLOCK, Adam married Susan Herbner.
    Issue: William Henry (2:130), born Ag 31, 1868; baptized S 27, 1868.
GNÄDIG, Catharíne married John Wegele.
GOLDSBOROUGH, Dr. Leander W. married Sarah Duncan or Dunkin.
    Issue: William Duncan (1:141; 2:200), born F 17, 1831; baptized Ag 10,
        1831; died S 8, 1831; buried S 9, 1831.
        Charles Edward (1:149), born D 16, 1834; baptized My 13, 1835.
GORDON, Daniel married Susanna Brown.
    Issue: Elizabeth (1:214), born D 4, 1807; baptized Ja 21, 1813.
        Maria (1:214), born D 7, 1811; baptized Ja 21, 1813.
GORLZ, Moses married Margaret Wolf.
    Issue: Sarah Catharine (2:116), born F 10, 1849; baptized O 14, 1849.
GÖTZ, Maria Catharine married George Hörr.
GOUSHON, Abraham married Anna Matilda Staub.
    Issue: John Christian Luther (1:104), born Mr 23, 1842; baptized O 24,
        1842.
GRABER, Catharine, had an illegitimate child by Christian Garret.
GRAHAM, Maggie married William Nelson Wilhide.
GREE, Leonard married Susanna _____.
    Issue: Maria (1:211), born F 26, 1810; baptized Mr 10, 1811.
GREEN, John Thomas (2:161) married O 13, 1870 Elizabeth Jane Jamison.
GREEN, William married Betse Dens.
    Issue: William (1:209), born Je 22, 1804; baptized Ag 20, 1809.
        Christopher (1:209), born Ap 9, 1806; baptized Ag 20, 1809.
        James Madison (1:209), born Mr 15, 1809; baptized Ag 20, 1809.
GREEN, William (2:238), born F 27, 1805; died Ag 23, 1863; buried at Stone
    Church, Mechanicstown Ag 24, 1863.
    Issue: Daughter married _____ Wolfe, near John Weller's.
GREIDER, Eugene P. married Sarah F. _____.
    Issue: Emma Matilda (2:56), born Jl 20, 1861; baptized S 15, 1861.
        Howard Sangston (2:60; 241), born N 6, 1864; baptized Ja 15, 1865;
        died Je 24, 1865; buried at Graceham Je 25.
        Paul Michael (2:61), born S 3, 1866; baptized N 4, 1866.
GREISS, Daniel married Johanna Regina Spieker, daughter of _____ and Maria
    (Bühler) Spieker.
    Issue: Emanuel (1:213), born N 16, 1806; baptized N 22, 1806.
        Farona (1:205), born Ja 1, 1808; baptized Ja 17, 1808.
        Marian (1:210), born O 26, 1810; baptized Mr 24, 1810.
GRIMES, Augusta Ann married Robert Leander Wilhide.
GRIMES, Catharine married Dennis Hanley.
GRIMES, Frank S. (2:164) of Double Pipe Creek, married Emma F. Routzahn of
    Ladiesburg, N 27, 1879.

34

GRIMES, James married Rebecca _____.
Issue: Lydia Ann Elizabeth (1:141), born Je 29, 1831; baptized S 6, 1831.
GRIMES, Samuel married Catharine _____.
Issue: Catharine married John B. Gilbert.
GROFF, Elias son of ____ and Elizabeth Groff, married Amanda Biggs.
Issue: William Henry (1:139), born Ap 26, 1828; baptized S 27, 1829.
GROFF, Zebulon (1:87) son of Joseph and Magdalen Groff, married Mr 6, 1832
Deborah Switzer, daughter of Jonas and Anne Isabella Switzer.
GROSCH, Andrew.
Issue: Andrew (1:164), born F 15, 1773 at 1 a.m.
Frederick (1:165), born O 28, 1774; baptized N 5, 1774.
GROSCHONG, John married Anna Kotter (or Kortes, Cortis); she was formerly
the wife of Samuel Weker.
Issue: Anna (1:207), born Jl 1, 1808; baptized Mr 16, 1808.
Henry (1:211), born Ag 8, 1810; baptized Ap 23, 1811.
Hannah (1:217), born F 8, 1815; baptized Mr 7, 1815.
GROSHON, Ephraim (2:154) married D 20, 1855 Frances Ellen Weller (2:18)
daughter of John and Deborah (Krieger) Weller; she was born F 18, 1831;
baptized Mr 23, 1831.
Issue: Laura Catharine (2:51), born N 8, 1856; baptized Mr 1, 1857.
GROSS, David had by Sarah McWilliams an illegitimate son John (1:214), who
was born N 3, 1812; baptized D 2, 1812.
GRUBE, Anna Johanna married The Reverend John Martin Beck.
GUMP (or GUMPF), George (1:107), married Rosina Mack (1:107); both Communic-
ants O 8, 1858.
Issue: John (their fourth child) (1:260, 264), born Ap 10, 1739; died D
23, 1816; married (1) Elizabeth Juliana Weller and (2) Mally
Mikecky.
GUMP, Isaac (1:132, 180) son of John George and Anna Elizabeth (Frey) Gump;
born in Frederick County F 28, 1795; baptized My 31, 1795; married Je 2,
1816 Maria Löhr who was born in Frederick County.
Issue: Sophia (1:221), born Jl 16, 1817; baptized Ap 5, 1818.
GUMP, John (1:91, 107, 125, 264), the 3rd son and 4th child of George and
Rosina (Mack) Gump or Gumpf; he was born near Frederick, Maryland Ap 10,
1739; Probationer Mr 10, 1765; Communicant Mr 28, 1767; he died D 23,
1816; buried D 25, 1816; he was married twice, (1) to Elizabeth Juliana
Weller (1:91, 107, 246) daughter of Jacob and Maria Barbara (Wilhide)
Weller; she was born at Upper Monocacy Ap 16, 1744; Probationer Mr 10,
1765; Communicant Mr 28, 1767; she died D 26, 1795 and was buried D 28,
1795. John Gump and Elizabeth Juliana Weller were married F 2, 1762.
Issue: John George (1:160), born N 25, 1766 at 11 a.m.; baptized N 30,
1766; married Anna Elizabeth Frey.
John (1:161), born Jl 16, 1769 at 6:30 a.m.; baptized Jl 16, 1769;
married Anna Maria Williar.
Anna Elizabeth (1:163), born F 12, 1772 at 4:00 a.m.; baptized F
16, 1772.
John Jacob (1:165, 230), born S 5, 1774 at 6 p.m.; baptized S 18,
1774; died Ag 13, 1775; buried Ag 15, 1775 in the churchyard.
John Jacob (1:166), born O 8, 1776; baptized O 13, 1776; married
Christina Favorite.
Eva Rosina (1:156, 233), born My 3, 1779; baptized My 9, 1779; died
of consumption Ja 9, 1782; buried Ja 11, 1782.
Anna Rosina (1:169), born Jl 3, 1782; baptized Jl 7, 1782.
GUMP, John, farmer (1:161, 260) son of John and Elizabeth Juliana (Weller)
Gump; he was born Jl 16, 1769; baptized Jl 16, 1769; died Ag 30, 1804;
buried Ag 31, 1804; married Mr 1793 Anna Maria Williar who was born in
Frederick County, Maryland My 23, 1763, and who died of dropsy D 15, 1819;
buried D 16, 1819. (1:267).
Issue: Benjamin (1:176), born Mr 19, 1793 at 6 a.m.; baptized Ap 19, 1793.

Elizabeth (1:180, 247), born Mr 1, 1795; baptized My 25, 1795; died S 21, 1797 and buried S 22, 1797 in the churchyard.

Elias (1:184), born Je 9, 1797; baptized Jl 16, 1797.

William (1:187), born Ja 19, 1799; baptized My 19, 1799.

Jonathan (1:195), born N 15, 1802; baptized Ja 7, 1803.

Elizabeth (1:199), born Mr 5, 1805; baptized Ap 14, 1805.

GUMP, John (1:264), son of George and Rosina (Mack) Gump; he was born Ap 10, 1739; died D 23, 1816; buried D 25, 1816; married (2) Mally Mikechy.

GUMP, John George, farmer (1:92, 128, 160), eldest son of John and Elizabeth Juliana (Weller) Gump; he was born N 25, 1766 at 11 a.m.; baptized N 30, 1766; probationer O 11, 1789; married S 1, 1789 Anna Elizabeth Frey (1:169b), daughter of John Daniel and Maria Catharine Frey; she was baptized O 11, 1789.

Issue: John (1:171b), born Jl 29, 1790 at 2-3 a.m.; baptized Jl 29, 1790.

Anna Catharine (1:175b), born F 27, 1792 at 6 a.m.; baptized Mr 1, 1792; married Jacob Favorite.

Isaac (1:180), born F 28, 1795; baptized My 31, 1795; married Maria Löhr.

John Daniel (1:184), born S 5, 1797; baptized S 10, 1797.

Maria Barbara (1:190), born N 25, 1800; baptized N 30, 1800.

John George (1:198), born Mr -- (1803 or 1804?); baptized Ap 11, (1803 or 1804?)

John Jacob (1:201), born O 25, 1805; baptized N 3, 1805.

Simon Peter (1:205), born Mr 16, 1808; baptized Mr 15, 1808.

Anna Margaret (1:210), born Ap 22, 1810; baptized Je 11, 1810.

Anna Elizabeth Juliana (1:214), born O 8, 1812; baptized D 13, 1812.

Eva Rosina (1:218), born My 12, 1815; baptized Ag 20, 1815.

GUMP, John Jacob (1:166), born O 8, 1776; baptized O 13, 1776; married Christina Favorite.

Issue: Joseph (1:260, 199), born D 27, 1804; baptized Ja 1, 1805; died Ja 2, 1805; buried Ja 3, 1805.

Elias (1:201), born N 22, 1805; baptized Ja 5, 1806.

Andrew (1:204), born N 17, 1807; baptized Ja 17, 1808.

Israel (1:209), born N 1, 1809; baptized D 25, 1809.

Jeremiah (1:212), born D 18, 1811; baptized D 29, 1811.

Beatus (1:264), born D 7, 1813; died Ja 9, 1814 of convulsions; buried Ja 20, 1814.

John Jacob (1:216, 264), born Ja 9, 1815; baptized F 5, 1815; died Mr 7, 1816 of blue cough and convulsions; buried Mr 9, 1816.

Sarah Anna (1:219), born D 17, 1816; baptized Ja 19, 1817.

GUMP, Rosina, daughter of _____ and Maria, married John Gernand.

GUMP, Rosina married Henry Paul.

GÜNTHER, Christian Frederick (1:92, 127), son of Peter and Maria Günther of Hebron (he was their second child and first son); he was a Probationer O 14, 1787; he married S 28, 1786 Maria Barbara Frey (1:166b), the second child and first daughter of John Daniel and Maria Catharine Frey; she was baptized O 14, 1787.

Issue: Maria Catharina (1:175), born Jl 22, 1787 at 4-5 a.m.; baptized Jl 22, 1787.

John Christian (1:169b, 239), born Jl 13, 1789 at 1-2 a.m.; baptized Jl 19, 1789; died N 18, 1789 of chest sickness; buried in the churchyard N 20, 1789.

John Peter (1:171b), born N 11, 1790 at 11 a.m.; baptized N 14, 1790.

Maria Barbara (1:176), born Mr 8, 1793 at 4 a.m.; baptized Mr 10, 1793.

GUNTHER (GUNDER), John F. (2:153), married Ann M. Eyler D 8, 1853.

GÜNTHER, Susanna daughter of Peter, married Abraham Frey.

GURLEY, Mary married William Martin.
GURLEY, Thomas married Amanda Stoll.
Issue: Charlotte Louisa (1:150), born F 20, 1835; baptized Ap 3, 1836;
    married Charles A. Eyler.
    Mary Jane (1:152), born Ja 1, 1837; baptized Jl 23, 1837.
    Amanda (1:96); born Jl 7, 1838; baptized Mr 10, 1839.
    Lycurgus (1:102), born Jl 17, 1840; baptized D 11, 1842.
    Melinda Ann (1:106), born N 21, 1843; baptized Jl 7, 1844.
    Margaret Ellen (2:122), born O 25, 1855; baptized S 11, 1856.
GWINN, John married Jane _____.
Issue: William (1:167b), born S 9, 1788; baptized at Taneytown S 11, 1788.

HAAS, Frederick, Lutheran pastor, married Elizabeth _____.
Issue: Frederick Jacob (1:221), born N 22, 1817; baptized F 2, 1818.
HAAS, Maria married John Protzman.
HABER, Anna Elizabeth married (1) _____ Schmidt and (2) Peter Brunner.
HABER, George married Catharina Schneider.
Issue: Catharina married Michael Williard.
HABERSTICK, Susanna or Sarah married Christian Fröhlich.
HAHN, Abraham (1:89) married My 7, 1837 Ann Catharine Hann.
HAHN, Abraham married Susanna Glas(en).
Issue: Peter (1:204), born Je 5, 1807; baptized Jl 12, 1807.
HAHN, America Virginia (2:222), died My 13, 1853 aged 2-7-5; buried at
    Creagerstown My 14, 1853.
HAHN, Anna Maria (2:226), born Ag 30, 1846; died O 22, 1855; buried at
    Creagerstown O 24, 1855.
HAHN, Cassandra Matilda married Henry Boller.
HAHN, Francis D. married Catharine Elsrode.
Issue: Calvin Amadeus (2:118), born O 10, 1851; baptized My 16, 1852.
    Louis Henry (2:120), born Je 13, 1854; baptized Jl 21, 1854.
HAHN, George married Maria Catharine _____.
Issue: John Jacob (1:164), born S 16, 1772 at 9 a.m.; baptized S 20, 1772.
HAHN, Jacob married Mary Magdalena Acker.
Issue: Mary Ann (1:136), born Mr 29, 1827; baptized Ja 5, 1828.
    Susan (1:85), married Lawrence Baltzell.
    Elizabeth married Philip Handley.
HAHN, John married Catharine Adlesberger.
Issue: James Melanchton (1:150), born Ap 19, 1836; baptized My 6, 1836.
HAHN, John married Mary Catharine Wedell, daughter of George and Mary Ann
    Wedell.
Issue: Mary Ann (1:142), born Mr 20, 1832; baptized Ap 4, 1832.
HAHN, John Adam married Maria Catharine.
Issue: John (1:165), born S 18, 1774 at noon; baptized S 25, 1774.
HAHN, Magdalena had an illegitimate son by Leonard Moser, Jr.
HAHN, Maria Elizabeth married John Lawrence Krieger.
HAHN, Sophia; born at Emmaus Ag 9, 1768, a twin; baptized at Emmaus Ag 14,
    1768; came to Manacosy from Emmaus with her parents in N 1771; died of the
    measles, which were prevalent, but which did not "come out" on her, F 24,
    1773; she was buried in the churchyard F 26, 1773.
HAILEY (or HALEY), Lawrence married Elizabeth Herbach.
Issue: John Francis (1:152), born Mr 5, 1836; baptized Jl 27, 1837.
    Thomas Milton (1:105), born Mr 5, 1839; baptized Ag 6, 1843.
    Ann Eliza (1:105; 2:161), born O 30, 1840; baptized Ag 6, 1843;
    married Harry G. Clifton.
    Ann Rebecca (1:105), born Jl 13, 1842; baptized Ag 6, 1843.
    Emma Jane Elizabeth (1:106), born Je 28, 1844; baptized Ag 4, 1844.
    Robert Annan (2:114), born N 7, 1845; baptized Ja 4, 1846.
HALEY, Ann Eliza (Dunker) married O 5, 1871 Harry G. Clifton (Luth.).

HALL, William married Martha Elizabeth Schreiber.
Issue: Ludwig (1:151), born Mr 14, 1836; baptized N 15, 1836.
HAMBURG, Catharine married Benjamin Kuhn.
HAMMER, _____ married Elizabeth Gibbons (1:147).
HAMMER, Jacob, distiller and brewer, (1:132), in the mountains near Emmitts-
    burg; son of Gottlieb and Agnes (Jetter) Hammer; he was born at Unter
    Türckheim, near Stuttgart, on My 26, 1798; he married Ag 19, 1819
    Priscilla Eyler (1:181; 2:292), daughter of Jonas and Anna Regina
    (Herbach) Eyler; she was born My 1, 1796 in the mountains; she was
    baptized Je 5, 1796; a Communicant O 8, 1817.
Issue: John Gottlieb (1:113), born Je 26, 1820; baptized Ag 13, 1820.
    Caty Anna (1:119), born Je 9, 1822; baptized S 16, 1822.
    Christian Samuel (2:4), born Je 17, 1824; baptized Je 22, 1824.
    Maria (2:8), born D 20, 1825; baptized Ag 27, 1826.
    Salome Angelica (2:12, 203), born Mr 3, 1828; baptized My 12, 1828;
        died of scarlet fever Ap 6, 1833; buried Ap 7, 1833.
    Jacob Jeremiah (1:140), born My 30, 1830; baptized S 12, 1830.
    Elizabeth Margaret (1:143), born F 27, 1832; baptized Ap 23, 1832.
HAMMETT, David Calvin (2:158) married F 22, 1863 Eleanora Krieger.
Issue: Charles Edward (2:61), born Ja 29, 1865; baptized My 29, 1866.
    James Howard (2:63), born Ag 19, 1869; baptized S 26, 1869.
HANCOCK (HANCOK), William married Elizabeth _____.
Issue: Solomon (1:218), born S 19, 1813; baptized O 15, 1815.
HANCOCK, William had by Mary Colliflower (sister of John Colliflower) an
    illegitimate son, Jeremiah (1:140) who was born Ag 11, 1829 and baptized D
    29, 1830.
HANCOCK, William married Anna Mary Colliflower (1:205; 2:248); she was born
    My 10, 1807 and baptized Mr 1, 1808; she died S 26, 1874 and was buried S
    27 on Dr. Henshaw's farm near Catoctin Furnace.
Issue: William (1:105), born Ag 28, 1842; baptized Ag 30, 1843.
    Susan Catharine (2:222), died Mr 17, 1853 aged 7-3-4; buried Mr 19,
        1853 at Mr. Brown's.
    Isabella (2:53), born F 15, 1844; baptized D 26, 1858.
HANDLEY, Dennis married Catharine Grimes (2:253); she died Ja 16, 1878, aged
    about 80 years, and is buried at Creagerstown.
Issue: Mary Elizabeth (1:97), born O 25, 1832; baptized Ag 4, 1839.
    John Stephen(1:146), born My 25, 1833; baptized F 20, 1834.
HANDLEY, Dennis married Elizabeth _____.
Issue: Philip married Elizabeth Hahn.
HANDLEY, Philip (1:87) son of Dennis and Elizabeth Handley; married Mr 14,
    1833 Elizabeth HAHN, daughter of Jacob and Magdalena (Acker) Hahn.
HANKEY, Frederick (2:148) married Mr 24, 1839 Mary Amanda Gernand (1:113),
    daughter of John Jacob and Elizabeth (Williar) Gernand; she was born Je
    29, 1820 and baptized Jl 30, 1820. According to their gravestone's at
    Apple's Church, he died Je 16, 1883, 72-4-13, and she died Ja 12, 1902.
Issue: Sarah Ellen (1:104), born Ja 1, 1843; baptized Je 4, 1843.
    Jacob Andrew (2:112), born F 13, 1845; baptized My 11, 1845.
    [Barbara Virginia, born Ap 9, 1854, died Ap 19, 1854 (according to
        gravestone at Apple's Church)].
HANKEY, Isaac [died Jl 19, 1840, aged 74-3-4, buried at Apple's Church],
    married Susanna Magdalena Apple (2:220); she was born Ja 22, 1773; she
    died Ja 5, 1851 and was buried Ja 7 [at Apple's Church.]
Issue: Isaac married Martha Lammerson.
    [Mary Ann died N 29, 1843; buried at Apple's Church].
    [Elizabeth, buried at Apple's Church] (2:234), born Ap 15, 1793;
        died S 17, 1861; married John Geasy.
HANKEY, Isaac (1:86), son of Isaac and Susanna Magdalena (Apple) Hankey;
    married Ag 21, 1831 Martha Lammerson (1:208), daughter of Richard and
    Barbara (Benser) Lammerson; she was born S 9, 1806 and baptized Je 25,

1809. [He died O 15, 1844, aged 45-6-0, and she died Ja 9, 1840; both are buried at Apple's Church.]
HANKEY, William D. (2:156) [born O 9, 1832; died Ja 27, 1894; buried at Fairfield Cemetery, Fairfield, Pennsylvania]; he married O 11, 1860 Ann Maria Wilhide (1:100), daughter of Jacob and Caroline (Weller) Wilhide; she was born Ja 5, 1841 and baptized F 14, 1841; [she died O 20, 1918 and is buried at Fairfield Cemetery, Fairfield, Pennsylvania].
Issue: Susanna Martha Caroline (2:56, 235), born Ag 19, 1861; baptized S 29, 1861; died My 4, 1862; buried My 6, 1862 at Graceham.
Elizabeth Emma Jane (2:253), born S 19, 1875; died N 5, 1876 near Gettysburg; buried at Apple's Church.
HÄNS, Maria Elizabeth married Lorenz Protzman.
HARBAUGH, Alexander, tanner, (1:133; 2:286), of Millerstown (Fairfield, Pennsylvania), son of Christian and Maria Elizabeth (Milliar) Harbaugh; he was born Je 13, 1793 in Frederick County; a Communicant Mr 30, 1820; he married Ap 4, 1820 Rosina Süss (1:190; 2:286), daughter of Godfrey Süss, tanner, and Anna Maria (Krämer); Rosina was born N 27, 1800 in Frederick County, and baptized N 30, 1800; she was a Communicant Mr 30, 1820.
Issue: Lewis Frederick (1:115; 2:293), born Ja 1, 1821; baptized Mr 14, 1821; a communicant Ap 21, 1838.
Maria Elizabeth (2:7), born Ja 3, 1824; baptized F 29, 1824.
William Siess (2:7, 202), born N 18, 1825; baptized F 26, 1826; died Ja 20, 1833 of scarlet fever; buried Ja 22.
Carolina (2:10, 194), born Ag 6, 1827; baptized S 3, 1827; died O 3, 1827 of whooping cough; buried O 5, 1827.
Martin Alexander (2:14, 202), born D 29, 1828; baptized Mr 27, 1829; died Ja 21, 1833 of scarlet fever; buried Ja 22, 1833.
Quintin (2:198), born Jl 9, 1830; baptized S 12, 1830 by a Reformed minister; died S 23, 1830; buried S 24, 1830.
Gustavus Adolphus (2:21, 294), born O 12, 1831; baptized F 2, 1832.
Felix Victor (2:24, 294), born Ag 9, 1833; baptized S 2, 1833.
Thomas Franklin (2:29), born D 30, 1835; baptized My 2, 1836.
Winfield (2:30), born F 18, 1837; baptized My 30, 1837.
Henrietta Louisa (2:33), born S 13, 1838; baptized Ap 7, 1838.
Amy Johanna (2:38, 241), born S 20, 1840; baptized N 1, 1840; died N 4, 1840; buried N 6, 1840.
Clementine Salome (2:40), born Ja 5, 1843; baptized Ja 22, 1843.
HARBAUGH, Catharine married William Smith.
HARBAUGH, Christian, Jr., weaver, (1:129; 2:225, 286), son of Christian and Maria Elizabeth (Williar) Harbaugh; he was born in Frederick County O 10, 1785; baptized O 26, 1785; Probationer N 25, 1804; Communicant O 8, 1808; died suddenly on Mr 22, 1855 and was buried Mr 23, 1855; he married N 25, 1806 Maria Magdalena Firor (2:231), daughter of Leonard and Elizabeth (Pauss) Firor; she was born N 21, 1785 in Frederick County; Communicant O 8, 1809; she died N 5, 1858 and was buried N 7, 1858.
Issue: Maria Matilda (1:207), born Ja 2, 1809; baptized Ja 14, 1809; married David Weller; she died in 1837.
Jethro (1:212, 263), born Je 25, 1811; baptized Jl 7, 1811; died Je 12, 1812 of convulsions; buried Je 14, 1812.
John William (1:215; 2:233, 293), born D 8, 1813; baptized D 21, 1813; confirmant Mr 31, 1833; communicant Ap 4, 1833; died O 22, 1860.
Catharina Theresa (1:219; 2:195), born Ap 18, 1816; baptized My 5, 1816; died of hectic fevor S 6, 1829; buried S 7, 1829.
Rebecca Elizabeth (1:222), born D 21, 1818; baptized F 7, 1819; married Isaac Weller.
Lavinia Augusta (1:117), born Jl 24, 1821; baptized O 27, 1821.
Maria Magdalena (2:3), born D 3, 1823; baptized D 26, 1823; married John Wilhide.

Sophia Charlotte (2:8), born Ap 25, 1826; baptized My 14, 1826.
Jeremiah Daniel (2:12, 293), born Ag 20, 1828; baptized O 8, 1828.
Levi Christian (2:18, 294), born F 19, 1831; baptized Mr 3, 1831.
HARBAUGH, Christian, farmer (1:92, 108; 2:209), born Ja 14, 1753;
Probationer Ap 16, 1786; Communicant Je 9, 1787; died of a stroke Mr 23,
1836; buried Mr 25, 1836; he married N 6, 1780 Maria Elizabeth Williar
(1:91, 108, 156; 2:190), daughter of Peter and Elizabeth Magdalena
(Schlim) Williar; she was born S 18, 1760 in Frederick County; she was a
Probationer Ap 16, 1786; a Communicant Je 9, 1787; she died S 28, 1824 and
was buried S 29, 1824.
Issue: Elizabeth (1:92, 261), Probationer Je 5, 1797; died unmarried on Ja
    9, 1805 aged 23-5-13, and was buried Ja 11, 1805.
    ----- (1st son)
    Christian (2nd son) (1:173), born O 10, 1785 at 11 p.m.; baptized
        O 26, 1785; died Mr 22, 1855; married Maria Magdalena Firor.
    John (1:166b), born J1 27, 1787 at 2-3 p.m.; baptized J1 30, 1787;
        married Anna Margaret Harbaugh.
    Elias (4th son & 5th child) (1:168b), born F 11, 1789 at 5-6 p.m.;
        baptized Mr 15, 1789; married Maria Weber.
    Henry (1:173b), born O 2, 1791 at 8 p.m.; baptized O 7, 1791;
        married (1) Maria Beierle and (2) Ann Hersh.
    Alexander (1:177), born Je 13, 1793 at 9 p.m.; baptized J1 14,
        1793; married Rosina Süss.
    Anna Maria (1:181), born O 24, 1795; baptized N 22, 1795; married
        Jacob Harbaugh.
    Rebecca (1:185), born F 12, 1798; baptized F 21, 1798; married
        Capt. John Eyler.
    Charlotte (1:189), born Je 21, 1800; baptized Je 30, 1800; married
        John Wilman.
    John Solomon (1:193), born F 5, 1802; baptized F 12, 1802.
    Sabina (1:201), born N 10, 1805; baptized N 28, 1805; married
        Frederick Beierle.
HARBAUGH, Cornelia Ann Elizabeth married Benjamin Franklin Boyer.
HARBAUGH, David (1:234), born Mr 5, 1756; died of an intense fever Ag 13,
1784; buried in the churchyard Ag 15, 1784; from his youth he was a quiet
and obedient to his parents.
HARBAUGH, David [died D 3, 1880, aged 72-6-21; buried at Foxville]; married
(1) Susan Brown [died O 20, 1860, aged 51-0-28; buried at Foxville].
Issue: Martin (1:142), born O 10, 1831; baptized Mr 4, 1832.
    Hamilton (1:103), born S 23, 1842; baptized Ja 22, 1843.
HARBAUGH, David (2:158), [died D 3, 1880, aged 72-6-21; buried at Fox-
ville]; married (2) on F 17, 1863 Mary Amanda (Catharine) Eyler (1:117),
daughter of (Captain) John and Rebecca (Harbaugh) Eyler; she was born Ag
29, 1821; baptized O 28, 1821; died [S 15, 1899].
HARBAUGH, Elias [died Ap 25, 1881, aged 78-6-21; buried at Jacob's Church in
Adams County]; married Elizabeth Eyler [died J1 16, 1895, aged 81-0-7;
buried at Jacob's Church in Adams County].
Issue: John Lewis (1:149), born N 25, 1835; baptized F 7, 1836.
HARBAUGH, Elias, wagon-maker (1:168b), in the mountains, son of Christian
and Maria Elizabeth (Williar) Harbaugh; he was born F 11, 1789; baptized
Mr 15, 1789; he married Maria Weber.
Issue: Frederick Alexander (1:115), born Ja 2, 1821; baptized F 10, 1821.
HARBAUGH, Elias married Rosina _____.
Issue: unbaptized son (1:82), born Ag 15, 1822 at Millerstown [Fairfield],
        Pennsylvania; died of convulsions Ag 24, 1822; buried Ag 25,
        1822.
HARBAUGH, Elias married Susanna Eyler (1:95).
HARBAUGH, Elizabeth married Charles Smith.
HARBAUGH, Elizabeth married Lawrence Hailey.

HARBAUGH, Elizabeth married Marcus Fetter.

HARBAUGH, Elizabeth married Peter McClain.

HARBAUGH, George (1:236-237), in the mountains, was born F 10, 1726 on the Kirschweiler Hof, near Kaiserslautern in the Palatinate; he married O 4, 1746 Catharine Williar (brought up Reformed) (1:239-240), sister of Peter Williard, with whom she came to Pennsylvania in the spring of 1744; she was born D 21, 1721 at Erlebach, near Kaiserslautern in the Palatinate; she died Ja 12, 1791 after an illness of three weeks was was buried in the churchyard. On F 13, George rode away from home on business, over the mountain into Pennsylvania. On his way back, about three miles from his house, it is supposed that he fell from his horse into a little Creek and was rendered helpless to save himself from drowning. His brother Ludwig, who passed by about a half hour later found him a corpse. George came to Pennsylvania with his parents in his 12th year and lived at Crice Creek in York County, whence he came here in 1754. They were here at the founding of this congregation O 8, 1758 and attended the first communion here. They were both members at York. He was Steward and Diener here until his corpulency made it necessary for him to resign. On F 11, 1787 he was at church, and that was the last time. His age was 61-0-13; he was buried F 19, 1787 in the churchyard. George and Catharine were the parents of 7 children, five of which survived them.

Issue: Anna Regina (1:155), born F 12, 1759; died [O 6, 1849]; married Jonas Eyler.

John George married (1) Elizabeth Binkele and (2) Maria Barbara _____.

John married (1) Maria Catharina Huber and (2) Elizabeth Boller.

Anna Maria, born F 26, 1754; died S 22, 1837; married Lawrence Krieger.

Anna Margaret, born Jl 21, 1749; died Ap 11, 1795; married John Jacob Weller.

Margaret, born O 11, 1761; died Ap 24, 1819; married Andrew Williar.

HARBAUGH, Henry (1:173b), son of Christian and Maria Elizabeth (Williar) Harbaugh; he was born O 2, 1791; he died [Ap 27, 1875 and is buried at Saint John's Reformed Church, Sabillasville]; he married (1) Maria Beierle [she was born Ja 12, 1810; died Mr 8, 1880; buried at St John's Reformed Church, Sabillasville].

Issue: George Washington (1:135), born Ag 22, 1827; baptized S 12, 1827.

Samuel Francis (1:140), born O 7, 1830; baptized N 14, 1830.

He married (2) Ann Hersh, and had the following issue:

Harriet Josephine (1:98), born Ap 16, 1840; baptized My 17, 1840.

Anne Louisa (2:112), born D 15, 1844; baptized F 9, 1845.

Henry Taylor (2:115), born O 10, 1846; baptized D 6, 1846.

HARBAUGH, Henry of Eyler's Valley; [he died F 21, 1871, aged 71-1-11 and is buried at Apple's Church]; he married Martha Ann Young (1:106), daughter of Philip and Nancy (Benner) Young; she was born O 10, 1817; baptized S 1, 1844; [she died Mr 12, 1888 and is buried at Apple's Church].

Issue: Sevilla (1:95), born Ap 15, 1838; baptized Je 30, 1838; [died Mr 2, 1919]; married Israel Boller.

Cecilia Ann Elisabeth (1:98), born Ag 11, 1839; baptized Mr 22, 1840.

Mary Isabella (1:102), born S 23, 1841; baptized Jl 10, 1842.

Catharine (1:103), born F 6, 1843; baptized My 19, 1843.

Nancy Maria (1:106), born Ag 9, 1844; baptized S 1, 1844.

Emma Jane Sophia (2:54), born Je 22, 1859; baptized S 24, 1859.

Martha Delila (2:114), born Ja 8, 1848; baptized Ap 11, 1848.

George Martin (2:115), born Ap 6, 1846; baptized Ap 17, 1846.

Diana Agnes (2:117), born S 11, 1849; baptized My 13, 1850.

John Henry Franklin (2:118), born Ja 18, 1851; baptized My 8, 1851.

William Hamilton (2:121), born N 1, 1854; baptized Ap 9, 1855.

Flora Mancella (2:124), born O 8, 1860; baptized Ja 29, 1861.

HARAUGH, Henry married Rebecca _____.

Issue: Catharine (1:116), born Mr 31, 1821; baptized Jl 1, 1821.

HARBAUGH, Jacob, junior (1:132), in the mountains 3 miles above Jacob Williar; son of John Herbach; said Jacob was born in Frederick County; he married Ap 13, 1819 (his first wife) Anna Maria Harbaugh (2:289), daughter of Christian Harbaugh, senior, and his wife Maria Elizabeth (Williar), in the mountains; said Anna Maria was born in Frederick County O 24, 1795; she was a Communicant Mr 19, 1818.

Issue: Jeremiah (1:113), born Mr 22, 1820; baptized Je 18, 1820.

Sabina Elizabeth (1:122), born O 20, 1825; baptized Ap 30, 1826.

Charles (1:138), born D 23, 1828; baptized Ap 26, 1829.

Mary Elisabeth (1:140), born Jl 13, 1830; baptized S 19, 1830.

Lydiann Margaret (1:95), born Ag 13, 1838; baptized S 23, 1838.

HARBAUGH, Jacob married Margaret _____. Reformed.

Issue: Susanna, born N 6, 1765; died F 26, 1802; married John Jacob Huber.

HARBAUGH, Jacob married Maria Elizabeth Harbaugh.

Issue: Charlotte Sevilla (1:143); born F 19, 1832; baptized My 27, 1832.

HARBAUGH, Jeremiah married Anne Witmer.

Issue: Mary Jane (2:48), born Jl 31, 1852; baptized Ag 1, 1853.

HARBAUGH, John (1:108) who resided in the mountains; later, Muskingum County, Ohio; he was the son of George and Catharine (Williar) Harbaugh; a Communicant N 13, 1785; he married (1) Maria Catharine Huber (of Mennonite extraction); (1:108,172); she was baptized when an adult on My 22, 1785; she was a Communicant N 13, 1785.

Issue: John (1:166), born Je 17, 1777; baptized Je 20, 1777; died Mr 23, 1824; married Elizabeth Koch.

Samuel (1:168), born Ag 11, 1779 in early morning; baptized Ag 24, 1779; married Anna Regina Krieger.

Catharine (1:169,236), born S 22, 1781; baptized S 24, 1781; she was accidentally shot through the heart with a flint by a 9 year old slave boy of her grandfather's and she died S 21, 1786; she was buried S 24, 1786.

David (1:171), born Ja 9, 1784; baptized Ap 23, 1784.

Benjamin (1:173), born Ja 25, 1786; baptized F 8, 1786.

Isaac (1:167b,237), born My 28, 1788; baptized Je 3, 1788; died of smallpox F 24, 1789.

Isaac Renatus (1:170b), born Mr 21, 1790 at 12-1 a.m.; baptized My 2, 1790.

Anna Elizabeth (1:177,245), born Ap 28, 1793 at 5 p.m.; baptized Je 5, 1793; she fell into the mill race which resulted in her death Je 26, 1795; buried in the churchyard Je 28, 1795.

Amos (1:181), born S 24, 1795 at 9 a.m.; baptized N 1, 1795.

HARBAUGH, John, widower (1:130), son of George and Catharine (Williar) Harbaugh; married (2) Ap 29, 1810 Elizabeth Boller who had previously been the wife of Philip Woodring.

HARBAUGH, John, tanner (1:132,166b), who resided in the mountains; son of Christian and Maria Elisabeth (Williar) Harbaugh; he was born in Frederick County Jl 27, 1787; baptized Jl 30, 1787; he married Ap 14, 1818 Anna Margaret Harbaugh who was born in Frederick County and who was the daughter of John Harbaugh, senior.

Issue: Juliana (1:222), born Ja 30, 1819; baptized Ap 13, 1819.

John Henry (1:112), born Mr 21, 1820; baptized My 14, 1820.

Alexius Jefferson (1:145), born Jl 5, 1833; baptized Jl 27, 1833.

HARBAUGH, John, joiner (1:129,166; 2:189), of Graceham; son of John and Maria Catharine (Huber) Harbaugh; he was born in Frederick County Je 17, 1777; baptized Je 20, 1777; he died Mr 23, 1824; buried Mr 25, 1824; he married at Graceham Mr 9, 1805 Elizabeth Koch (2:244,292), daughter of

George and Maria (Duckness) Koch; she was born in Lancaster, Pennsylvania
O 5, 1787; she was a Communicant at Graceham Ag 13, 1804; she died Ja 13,
1869 and was buried at Graceham Ja 15, 1869.
Issue: Vernillia (1:201), born Ja 12, 1806; baptized Ja 19, 1806.
Horatio (1:204), born Ap 30, 1807; baptized My 17, 1807.
Carolina (1:207), born S 18, 1808; baptized S 25, 1808.
Lavina (1:210), born Ja 17, 1810; baptized Ja 28, 1810; died My 10,
1863; married John Valentine.
Mary Ann (1:212), born O 12, 1811; baptized N 3, 1812.
Elizabeth (1:214), born Jl 8, 1813; baptized Jl 25, 1813.
Susanna (1:217), born F 14, 1815; baptized Mr 27, 1815.
Andreas Jackson (1:219), born O 22, 1816; baptized D 22, 1816.
Emilia Priscilla (1:111), born My 15, 1819; baptized Je 6, 1819.
Francis Marion (1:115), born Mr 1, 1821; baptized Ap 15, 1821.
Joseph Evans (2:1,189), born in Graceham F 28, 1823; baptized Ap 6,
1823; died of convulsions Ja 9, 1824; buried Ja 11, 1824.
HARBAUGH, John, blacksmith and farmer, married Susanna Huber.
Issue: Amalia (1:187); baptized Jl 21, 1799.
HARBAUGH, John George (1:91,126), eldest son of George and Catharine (Wil-
liar) Harbaugh; he was a Probationer N 14, 1784; he married N 27, 1770
Elizabeth Binkele (his first wife); (1:232), eldest daughter of Peter and
Margaret Binkele; she was born D 19, 1749; she died Ja 23, 1780; her body
was brought through the deep snow on a sled to the churchyard where burial
took place on Ja 25, 1780.
Issue: John George (1:163), born N 11, 1771 at 4 a.m.; baptized N 17,
1771.
John Jacob (1:164), born D 25, 1773 at 11 p.m.; baptized D 28,
1773.
Elizabeth (1:165), born in the morning O 19, 1775; baptized O 23,
1775.
John (1:167), born Mr 21, 1778; baptized Mr 25, 1778.
a daughter (1:232), born Ja 10, 1780; died same day and was buried
in the garden by the mother herself.
HARBAUGH, John George, son of George and Catharine (Williar) Harbaugh;
married secondly Maria Barbara _____ (1:92); she was a Probationer Ap
16, 1786.
Issue: Anna Maria (1:169), born Ap 7, 1782; baptized Jl 7, 1782.
Benjamin (1:170,233), born S 25, 1783; baptized S 29, 1783; died My
2, 1784; buried in the churchyard My 3.
Daniel (1:172), born Mr 22, 1785 at 10 a.m.; baptized Mr 29, 1785.
Maria Barbara (1:174,237), born Ja 5, 1787 at 4 a.m.; baptized Ja
8, 1787; died F 5, 1789 and buried in the churchyard. The cause
of death was smallpox.
Frederick (1:172b), born F 18, 1791; baptized Ap 3, 1791.
HARBAUGH, Joseph, farmer, in the mountains, married Susanna Kreiss, daughter
of Peter Kreiss.
Issue: Maria Magdalena (1:112), born O 23, 1819; baptized Mr 19, 1820.
Banjamin (1:117), born O 3, 1821; baptized N 13, 1821.
HARBAUGH, Juliana married John Stem.
HARBAUGH, Leonard C., of Harbaugh's Valley, married Mary Ann Miller.
Issue: Leonard Courteney (2:114,115), born F 9, 1846; baptized Je 21,
1846.
Lewis Calvin (2:116), born S 27, 1848; baptized N 5, 1849.
HARBAUGH, Levi married Minerva Ann Miller.
Issue: Theodore Washington (2:50), born Ap 21, 1855; baptized Je 10, 1855.
HARBAUGH, Lewis married Barbara Ann Hoffman.
Issue: Susan Elizabeth (2:49), born N 2, 1850; baptized Je 4, 1854.
Isaac Winfield (2:49), born O 20, 1851; baptized Je 4, 1854.

HARBAUGH, Milton married Laura Jane Eyler (2:37), daughter of Capt. John and
Rebeccca (Harbaugh) Eyler; she was born N 23, 1839 and baptized Mr 22,
1840.
Issue: Frank Irving (2:130), born Ag 16, 1869; baptized Ja 30, 1870.
HARBAUGH, Samuel (1:92), a Probationer D 11, 1786.
HARBAUGH, Samuel, blacksmith (1:129,168), son of John and Maria Catharina
(Huber) Harbaugh; he was born Ag 11, 1779 in Frederick County, Maryland;
baptized Ag 24, 1779; married N 22, 1803 Anna Regina Krieger (1:168),
daughter of Lawrence and Anna Maria (Harbaugh) Krieger; she was born Mr
12, 1781 in Frederick County; baptized Mr 18, 1781.
Issue: Joel (1:198), born S 27, 1804; baptized O 7, 1804.
HARBAUGH, Samuel married Eliza Ann Williar (1:220), daughter of Peter and
Elizabeth (Müller) Williar; said Eliza Ann was born D 25, 1816 and bap-
tized Ap 20, 1817.
Issue: Aramintha (1:152), born F 22, 1837; baptized Ap 1, 1837.
HARBAUGH, Savilla married Israel Boller.
HARBAUGH, Sophia married John Nagel.
HARBAUGH, Sophia Charlotte married George Hesser.
HARBAUGH, Susanna married John McClain.
HARBAUGH, Susanna married George Valentine.
HARBAUGH, Valentine of Harbaugh's Valley.
Issue: Sarah Emma Jane (2:240), born D 4, 1850; died S 7, 1864; buried at
Sabillasville S 8, 1864.
HARBAUGH, William, son of Yost Harbaugh, married Catharine Stemm.
Issue: Mary Jane (1:142), born S 3, 1831; baptized O 16, 1831.
Lucinda Adeline (1:145), born Ap 8, 1833; baptized Jl 27, 1833.
HARBAUGH, Yost married Ann Elizabeth Gump (1:140).
HARBAUGH, Yost married Elizabeth [Mong, according to reliable external
sources].
Issue: Mary Ann (1:85) married George Doffler.
HARDING, Elias, manager of the Furnace, married Helena Ellen _____.
Issue: Robert (1:190), born O 20, 1799; baptized N 10, 1800.
HARDING, George W. (2:164) of York County, Pennsylvania, married D 24, 1879
Ida S. Wilhide of Mechanicstown.
HARR, Everard or HERR, Eberhard, married Mary Magdalena Kauffman.
Issue: Ann Eliza (1:149), born O 18, 1834; baptized Je 28, 1835.
Rebecca Jane (1:150), born My 10, 1836; baptized Jl 20, 1836.
Mary Juliet (1:106), born Ag 29, 1840; baptized N 26, 1843.
Andrew James (1:106), born Ag 14, 1841; baptized N 26, 1843.
HARRISON (HERRESSEN), Henry married Petty _____.
Issue: Alexander (1:201), born Ap 20, 1805; baptized N 17, 1805.
HARRY, Isaac Renatus (2:208), born F 10, 1767; baptized My 15, 1786; died Mr
20, 1835; buried Mr 22, 1835; married in 1793 (firstly) Anna Cölln of
Lititz.
Issue: son, died young.
HARRY, Isaac Renatus (2:208), born in Philadelphia County F 10, 1767; bap-
tized at Lititz My 15, 1786; died Mr 20, 1835 of chest fever of three
month's duration; buried Mr 22, 1835; married, secondly, on O 12, 1795
Maria Barbara Feiser (1:261) who was born at York My 3, 1766; she died D
14, 1806 on the birth of her third daughter; she was buried D 16, 1806.
Issue: Anna Rosina (1:264,203), born N 28, 1806; baptized D 16, 1806; died
Mr 15, 1816 of convulsions; buried Mr 17, 1816.
Lydia (2:208) married Michael Mücke.
HARRY, Isaac Renatus (1:130), born F 10, 1767; baptized My 15, 1786; died Mr
20, 1835; buried Mr 22, 1835; married My 7, 1807 (thirdly) Margaret Eigen-
brod (1:167; 2:229,292), daughter of John Yost and Eva Maria (Schörer)
Eigenbrod; she was born Mr 24, 1779; she was baptized Mr 28, 1779; a
Communicant N 13, 1801; she died F 12, 1857 and was buried F 13, 1857.
Issue: Parmenio Renatus (1:211), born N 7, 1810; baptized N 25, 1810.

HARRY, Parmenio Renatus who was born N 7, 1810, son of Isaac Renatus and
Margaret (Eigenbrod) Harry, had by Antoinette Sybilla Smith, daughter of
John and Margaret (Born) Smith, an illegitimate son, Parmenio Renatus
(2:113) who was born Ag 1, 1846 and baptized Ag 3, 1846.
HARRY, Parmenio Renatus (1:211; 2:148), son of Isaac Renatus and Margaret
(Eigenbrod) Harry, was born N 7, 1810; baptized N 25, 1810; married O 10,
1841 Salome Süss (2:290) daughter of Godfrey and Anna Maria (Krämer) Süss,
who was born Je 17, 1810 at Graceham; she was a Communicant D 4, 1825; she
was formerly married to William Delaplane.
   Issue: Edwin Ebenezer (2:39,214), born Ap 10, 1842; baptized Jl 4, 1842;
          died Jl 4, 1842; buried Jl 6, 1842.
          Alice Venelia (2:41,215), born Jl 26, 1843; baptized Ag 27, 1843;
          died N 25, 1843; buried N 27, 1843.
HARRY, Parmenio married Elizabeth _____ (she survived him). She was born
Ap 17, 1825 at Graceham; died N 2, 1875 and she was buried N 4, 1875 at
Graceham.
   Issue: Clara Viola (2:53), born D 21, 1853; baptized N 14, 1858.
          Charles Albert (2:53), born Ja 2, 1855; baptized N 14, 1858.
          Parmenio Renatus (2:53), born S 15, 1857; baptized N 14, 1858.
HART, _____ married Susanna Stokes.
HART, William married Sarah Stewart.
   Issue: Elvira married Charles Worthington.
HARTMAN, Barbara married John Jacob Huber.
HARTMAN, Frederic married Elizabeth Margaret Miller.
   Issue: William (1:145), born Ap 27, 1833; baptized Je 2, 1833.
          Anna Catharine (1:147), born Jl 16, 1834; baptized Jl 27, 1834.
          Peter (1:149), born N 7, 1835; baptized D 13, 1835.
HASPELHORN, Elizabeth married John Pearl.
HASPELHORN, Henry (2:221) married Magdalena _____. He died Je 20, 1852,
aged 65-0-6, and was buried at Apple's Church Je 22, 1852.
   Issue: Elisabeth (1:145), born Ap 8, 1832; baptized F 9, 1833.
HASPELHORN (1:90) married Ja 11, 1842 Mary Gernand.
HAUVRE, Elizabeth married George Herman.
HAYS, Jane married Robert McCleave.
HEAD, Richard, on the way to Kentucky.
   Issue: Richard (1:259), born Ja, 1800 at Imenstown; died Ag 4, 1801;
          buried Ag 5, 1801 in the churchyard.
HECKEDORN, Jacob married Salome _____. (Lutherans).
   Issue: Christian (7th son), (1:175), born Ap 10, 1787 at 12-1 p.m.; bap-
          tized My 6, 1787.
          Rebecca, born D 26, 1788 towards noon; baptized N 28, 1789.
HECKMAN, George married Mary Koons.
   Issue: Jacob Mehring (1:148), born Je 17, 1834; baptized O 5, 1834.
HEDGES, Stephen, farmer, married Sally Butler.
   Issue: Mary (1:195), born Mr 7, 1802; baptized Mr 27, 1803.
          Rebecca (1:200), born D 19, 1803; baptized My 1, 1805.
HEFFNER, Elizabeth married Jacob Lochman.
HEFFNER, Henry married Harriet Ann Camplane.
   Issue: John Henry (1:110), born F 23, 1844; baptized O 27, 1844.
HEFFNER, John married Mary _____.
   Issue: Margaret Ann (2:115), born F 4, 1846; baptized Je 2, 1846.
HEFFNER, Michael of Mechanicstown married Lavinia _____.
   Issue: Charles Augustus (2:117,220), born Ap 26, 1850; baptized Jl 12,
          1850; died Ag 15, 1850; buried Ag 16, 1850 at Apple's Church.
HEFFNER, Peter married Charlotte Cole.
   Issue: Catharine married (1) _____ Renner, and (2) Daniel Cover.
HEFFNER, Susan married Cyrus Moser.
HEITSHEW, Charles F. married Mary E. Newman.
   Issue: Jesse Ellsworth (2:133), born Jl 19, 1875; baptized Jl 25, 1875.

HEKEDORN, Philippina married John Fever.
HELLER, Christina married Jonathan Shuff.
HENNING, Catharine married Benjamin Witmer.
HERBACH, See HARBAUGH
HERBERT, Benjamin Franklin (2:151) of near Hagerstown, married Ja 10, 1850
   Josephine Aurelia Wilhide (2:10,295), who was born Je 5, 1827 and baptized
   Jl 14, 1827; she was a Communicant O 9, 1842 and the daughter of Benjamin
   and Mary Barbara (Knouff) Wilhide.
   Issue: George Doyle (2:117), born Mr 6, 1850; baptized Ag 11, 1850.
      Frederic Dorsey (2:122), born Ag 5, 1856; baptized Mr 15, 1857.
      Emma Kate (2:125), born Ag 3, 1861; baptized Ap 6, 1862.
      William Henry (2:127), born Ap 20, 1864; baptized S 20, 1864.
      Adia (2:128), born F 15, 1866; baptized O 7, 1866.
HERBNER, Susan married Adam Glock.
HERMAN (HARMAN), Christian married _____ Heron.
   Issue: Joseph Albert (2:222), died Mr 20, 1853, aged 1-1-9; buried at
      Apple's Church Mr 21, 1853.
HERMAN, George married Elizabeth Hauvre.
   Issue: William Henry (1:152), born D 18, 1836; baptized S 10, 1837.
      Eliza (1:96), born O 15, 1838; baptized D 23, 1838.
HERMAN, George, Jr. (1:113) married Barbara Wilhide.
   Issue: Mary Anna (1:111), born Ag 3, 1819; baptized Ag 13, 1819.
HERMAN (HARMAN), Isaac married Mary _____.
   Issue: Emery Forest (2:72), born Mr 11, 1867; baptized Mr 11, 1880.
HERMAN, William, son of Christian and Maria Herman, married Ann Flautt.
   Issue: Mary Ann (1:139), born Je 23, 1829; baptized O 17, 1829.
HERON, _____ married Christian Harman.
HERTZOG, Peter married Catharina _____.
   Issue: Elizabeth (1:85) married Daniel Fröhlich.
HERZOG, Anna Catharine mother of Susanna Moser.
HESS, Delilah married Henry Leidy.
HESSER, George (1:85) married D 17, 1829 Amy Knauff (2:239), daughter of
   John and Catharine Knauff; she was born S 5, 1804; she died F 20, 1864 and
   buried at Graceham F 22, 1864.
   Issue: Hannah Catharine (1:141), born D 29, 1830; baptized F 21, 1831.
      Susan Rebecca (1:145), born Ja 28, 1833; baptized Mr 29, 1833.
      Emily Sophia (2:230), born Ag 7, 1835; a Lutheran confirmed D 31,
      1854; a Communicant Ja 1, 1855; died Ja 25, 1858; buried at
      Graceham Ja 26, 1858.
HESSER, George (2:159) married Mr 21, 1867 Sophia Charlotte Harbaugh.
HESSER, George Jacob (2:156) married at his step-father's house (Firney?) on
   D 30, 1860 Eliza Susan Newman.
   Issue: Allen Jacob (2:57), born O 20, 1861; baptized Je 8, 1862.
      Charles Milton (2:58,237), born My 3, 1863; baptized My 4, 1863;
      died My 3[sic], 1863; buried at Graceham My 5, 1863.
      George Newman (2:60,241), born S 15, 1864; baptized Mr 5, 1865;
      died Mr 20, 1865; buried at Graceham Mr 21, 1865.
HESSER, Lilly Ann married George Samuel Newcomer.
HESSER, Mary Isabella married John Tilghman Colliflower.
HESSERE, Susanna Rebecca married John Troxel.
HETTERLI, Joshua married Hannah Gilbert.
   Issue: Caroline (1:143), born Ja 27, 1831; baptized My 28, 1832.
HETTERLY, Jacob (2:160) married Je 10, 1869 Martha M. Eyler.
HETTERLY, Mary Ann Virginia (2:227), born Ja 27, 1855; died D 7, 1855;
   buried at Apple's Church D 9.
HEUMANN, Maria Wilhelmina married Joseph Perking.
HEWETT, Martha married William Burch.
HEWIT, Charles married Sophia Jane Wiles.
   Issue: Mary Ann (1:99), born N 12, 1839; baptized Je 8, 1840.

HEYNE, Henry married Elizabeth _____.
    Issue: Lucinda (1:87) married William Cover.
HILDEBEUTEL, Anthony married Maria Favorite.
    Issue: Sabina (1:218), born Ag 13, 1815; baptized S 9, 1815.
    Elizabeth (1:220), born Mr 11, 1817; baptized My 11, 1817.
HIRSCHEL, Peter married Anna Kunigunda Wilman, widow of _____ Miller.
    (1:151,152).
HÖFER, Rosina married Christian Henry Eigenbrod.
HOFFMAN, Barbara Ann married Lewis Harbaugh.
HOFFMAN, George, farmer (1:132), son of Michael and Catharine Hoffman; he
    married Je 27, 1819 Maria Magdalena Boller (2:195), daughter of Philip
    William and Catharine (Lanius) Boller who came here in 1804; said Maria
    Magdalena was born in Northampton County, Pennsylvania on F 22, 1795; she
    died of nerve fever S 12, 1828 and was buried S 14, 1828.
    Issue: 2 sons & 2 daughters.
HOFFMAN, John married Hanna Rosge.
    Issue: George Washington (1:111), born Jl 4, 1819; baptized Jl 17, 1819.
HOFFMAN, John Henry (2:150) married Mr 19, 1849 Jane E. Engler.
HOFFMAN, William Charles Henry (2:226), born Mr 8, 1855; died Jl 30, 1855;
    buried Jl 31, 1855 at Creagerstown.
HÖFLICH, Maria married John Rudifer.
HOLD, Jesse married Sophia _____.
    Issue: Emily (1:122), born S 5, 1825; baptized Ap 25, 1826.
HÖLLWART, Godfrey married Elizabeth Först.
    Issue: Caroline (1:98), born Ag 28, 1839; baptized D 26, 1839.
HOLTZ, Jacob, farmer, married Anna Barbara Morgenstern.
    Issue: Elizabeth, born Ap 30, 1795; married William Krieger.
HOLTZMAN, Juliana had an illegitimate child by William Ehrhart.
HOLTZMAN, Margaret married William Ehrhart.
HOLZMAN, Andrew of Kriegerstown married Barbara Schenkel (not Moravians).
    Issue: Anna Maria (1:175), born Ag 31, 1792 at 4 p.m.; baptized S 7, 1792;
        died S 8, 1792.
        Samuel (1:193), born S 2, 1801; baptized My 3, 1802.
HOLZMAN, Conrad married Eva _____.
    Issue: Catharina (1:185); baptized Ja 12, 1797.
HOLZMAN, Jacob, innkeeper, of Creagerstown.
    Issue: Thomas (1:196); baptized Jl 20, 1803.
HOLZMAN, Sem had by Peky Schenkel an illegitimate son Thomas (1:204), who
    was born My 1, 1807 and baptized Je 21, 1807.
HOLZMANN, Christina married Peter Frensch.
HOOVER, Augustus C. (2:242), born Ag 3, 1819; died D 6, 1865; buried at
    Mechanicstown D 8, 1865.
    Issue: David Byer (2:230), born N 8, 1857; died F 21, 1858; buried in the
        family burial ground F 23, 1858.
HOOVER, Christian married Elizabeth _____.
    Issue: Lavinia married Frederic Recher.
HOOVER, Christian married Magdalena _____.
    Issue: Magdalena (1:86) married Jacob Crise.
HOOVER, John (2:223), born D 8, 1777; died at Owings Creek F 9, 1854; buried
    at Ephraim Crouse's on F 12, 1854.
HOOVER, John M. C. (2:237), son of Daniel Hoover; said John M. C. was born
    My 1, 1837; died F 23, 1863 and buried at Creagerstown F 25, 1863.
HOOVER, John W. (1:89), married My 23, 1837 Elizabeth Black.
HOOVER, Magdalena married Nathanael Fisher.
HOOVER (HUBER), Maria Catharine married John HARBAUGH.
HÖRR, George married Maria Catharine Götz.
    Issue: Anna Catharine (1:141), born Jl 29, 1831; baptized S 18, 1831.

HOSLER, George (2:149) married Mr 8, 1842 Anna Juliana Christ (2:288); she
    was born Ja 16, 1818 and baptized My 11, 1818; she was the daughter of
    Jacob and Christina (Leinbach) Christ.
Issue: Minerva Ann (2:40), born N 27, 1842; baptized Ja 3, 1843.
    Sarah Ann Augusta (2:42), born Ap 15, 1844; baptized Je 2, 1844.
    Mary Jane (2:43), born Ap 22, 1846; baptized My 21, 1846.
    Aquila Winfield (2:45), born Je 29, 1849; baptized Ag 5, 1849.
HOUCKS, Mary Ann married William Deberry.
HOUGH, Mary Jane married Simon P. Rouzer.
HOWARD, John (2:150) married D, 1848 Sarah Pearl.
HUBBARD, David married Adeline Favorite.
Issue: Anna Maria (2:132), born Mr 11, 1863; baptized Mr 4, 1873.
    John Harvey (2:132), born F 3, 1865; baptized Mr 4, 1873.
    Barbara Alice (2:132), born N 30, 1866; baptized Mr 4, 1873.
    Addie Grace (2:134), born N 3, 1873; baptized Jl 27, 1875.
HUBER, Daniel, blacksmith (1:131; 2:196), in the valley, son of Jacob and
    Susanna (Harbaugh) Huber, in the mountains; said Daniel was born in
    Frederick County and was baptized My 3, 1792; he died of consumption F 2,
    1829 and was buried F 4, 1829; he married Ap 14, 1816 Mary Haberland who
    was also born in Frederick County.
Issue: Jacob (1:220), born Jl 23, 1817; baptized Ag 31, 1817.
    Susanna (1:112), born O 15, 1819; baptized N 1-, 1819.
    Mary Anna (1:117), born S 9, 1821; baptized O 28, 1821.
    Johannes (1:120), born Jl 2, 1823; baptized S 14, 1823.
HUBER, [John] Jacob, blacksmith, of Mennonite extraction (1:167b,266); born
    at Conococheague, Washington County, Maryland on Mr 2, 1762; he died Je
    8, 1788; died Je 14, 1819 and buried Je 15, 1819; he married (1) on Ja 20,
    1787 Susanna Harbaugh (1:92,108,259), daughter of Jacob and Margaret
    Harbaugh (Reformed); she was born in Maryland, in the mountains, on N 6,
    1765; she was a Probationer Je 8, 1788; a Communicant Ap 9, 1789; she died
    F 26, 1802 and was buried F 28, 1802.
Issue: Catharine (1:166b), born O 23, 1787 at 10 p.m.; baptized O 28,
    1787; married George Weller.
    Anna Margaret (1:171b), born S 12, 1790 at 12 at night; baptized S
    19, 1790.
    Daniel (1:175b), born My 3, 1792 at 5:30 a.m.; baptized My 13,
    1792; died F 2, 1829; married Mary Haberland.
    Regina (1:182), born Ag 6, 1796 at 4 a.m.; baptized Ag 14, 1796.
    Elizabeth (1:187,252,254), born Je 13, 1799; baptized Je 23, 1799;
    died N 7, 1799; buried N 9, 1799.
    Johana Sophia (1:190), born O 1, 1800; baptized O 12, 1800.
HUBER, John Jacob (1:266), born Mr 2, 1762; died Je 14, 1819; buried Je 15,
    1819; married (2) Barbara Hartman.
Issue: Solomon (1:201), born Je 20, 1805; baptized N 3, 1805.
HUEBENER, Samuel Renatus married Salome Tshudy.
Issue: Samuel Andrew (2:30), born Mr 3, 1837; baptized Mr 12, 1837.
    Johanna Salome (2:33), born Je 11, 1839; baptized Ja 20, 1839.
HUEFFEL, Charlotte Sophia married Samuel Reinke.
HUGHES, Hannah married William Armsperger [Adelsperger or Ellensperger?]
HUMERICH, John married Elizabeth STOLL.
Issue: Amanda Sevilla (1:148), born F 19, 1834; baptized O 21, 1834.
HUMERICH, John H. (2:164) of near Graceham; born [D 9, 1856]; married Mr 10,
    1880 Caroline Augusta Engel, daughter of Nicholas and Anna Eve (Gall)
    Engel; she was born O 21, 1858 and baptized Ja 6, 1859. John H. died [Ag
    16, 1930] and his wife died [S 12, 1928].
HUMERICH (HUMMERICH), Joshua married Susan Koons.
Issue: John Abraham (1:149), born S 28, 1834; baptized O 9, 1835.

HUMES, _____ married Mary Perkins (1:261), daughter of Joseph and Maria Wilhelmina (Heyman) Perkins; she died Ap 23, 1805; she was buried Ap 24, 1805.
HUMES, Thomas (1:262), adopted child of Jacob Huber, to whom he was loyal, industrious and obedient; he died F 1, 1809 of a feverish chest disease at the age of 22-9-4, and was buried F 3, 1809.
HUMMER, Anna Marie married Henry Fahs.
HUMMER, Henry married Sally Renner (1:212); she was baptized (as an adult) on S 22, 1811.
Issue: John (1:212), born S 19, 1811; baptized S 22, 1811.
HUMMER, Maria married John Sebastian.
HUMMER, Mary Ann married Ezra Wilhide.
HUMMER, Susan married Ezra Wilhide.
HUMMER, Susanna married Edward Kier.

IRONS (EIRONS), John married Mary Elizabeth _____.
Issue: Sarah Sophia (2:58), born Ja 13, 1862; baptized D 25, 1862.
IRONS, John S. (2:163) married Ag 14, 1878 Mary C. Biggs.
IRONS, Michael, farmer, near the Catholic Seminary, (2:221), died D 25, 1851; buried D 26; he married Elizabeth Boller (2:221,286), who was born Ja 10, 1798 in Northampton County, Pennsylvania; she was a Communicant Ag 12, 1821; she died [S 28, 1851].
Issue: Sarah Anna (1:114), born O 14, 1820; baptized N 21, 1820.
Sophia Susanna (1:122), born F 25, 1826; baptized Mr 10, 1826.
Maria Louisa (2:20), born My 17, 1831; baptized Je 19, 1831; died [Ag 27, 1926].
Catharina Anna (2:26), born Ap 29, 1834; baptized Je 22, 1834.
John Schüler (2:33), born Ja 5, 1838; baptized F 5, 1838.
Amanda Caroline (2:41), born Ap 20, 1843; baptized Je 4, 1843.
IRONS (EIRON), Rebecca married William A. Wireman.
IRONS (EIRON), Sarah Ann married _____ Petticourt.
IRVIN, Hannah Maria married Thomas W. Banks.
IRWIN, David, single, joiner, (1:81); he was taken sick and died Ag 1, 1822, while helping to build the new church; he was buried Ag 2.

JACKSON, Maria married Emanuel Süss.
JAMISON, Elizabeth Jane married John Thomas Green.
JANS (JOHNS or JANSEN), Henry (1:130), son of Peter and Catharine (Angst) Jans; he was born in Maryland and was a farmer by occupation; he married N 5, 1811 Catharine Sophia Stauffer (1:212) daughter of John Christian and Barbara (Weller) Stauffer, who was born Mr 29, 1790 in Maryland, and was baptized O 8, 1811.
Issue: Matilda (1:213), born Ag 24, 1812; baptized O 4, 1812; married Jacob Martin.
Maria (1:217), born F 12, 1815; baptized Mr 19, 1815.
Ludwig (1:117), born Ag 23, 1821; baptized N 8, 1821.
Daniel (1:121), born N 1, 1824; baptized Ja 15, 1825.
JANS, Marian married Daniel Shattuck Loy.
JANS, Peter (1:92,108; 2:187), born Ja 23, 1746 at Skippack, Pennsylvania; he was a Probationer Ap 16, 1786; a Communicant D 1, 1787; he died Mr 16, 1823 and was buried Mr 18, 1823; he married Ap 25, 1769 Catharina Angst (1:92,108); she was a Probationer Ap 16, 1786 and a Communicant D 1, 1787; she died Mr 26, 1813.
Issue: (6 sons and 5 daughters)
Maria Magdalena (1:174), born N 8, 1786 at 5 a.m.; baptized N 19, 1786.
Maria Catharina (1:168b), born D 20, 1788 in the afternoon and was baptized Ja 4, 1789.
Elizabeth (1:203), born D 5, 1770; baptized D 26, 1806.

49

Henry (1:130), married Catharine Sophia Stauffer.
JANSEN, Elizabeth married Nicholas Staub.
JANSON, William of Baltimore, married Mary Firor.
Issue: Mary Virginia (2:122), born My 7, 1856; baptized Ag 29, 1857.
JENNER, Maria Elisabeth married Henry Boller.
JODUM, Daniel married Susan Butler.
Issue: John (1:204), born Je 1, 1803; baptized O 24, 1807.
    Zacharias (1:204), born S 26, 1806; baptized O 24, 1807, he being
    badly burned and was expected to die.
JOHNS, David.
Issue: Isaac (1:183), born Ag 5, 1795; baptized Je 30, 1797 and died a few
    hours later.
    Rebecca (1:183), born Ap 22, 1797; baptized Je 30, 1797.
JOHNSON, Joseph of Carroll's Manor married Mary _____.
Issue: Joshua (1:159), born Jl 2, 1764; baptized S 9, 1764.
JOHNSON, Semmy had by Sophia Kuns an illegitimate daughter Rebecca (1:219),
    who was born My 23, 1816 and was baptized Ag 20, 1816.
JORDAN, William, cooper, married Jane More.
Issue: Margareth (1:191), born O 28, 1800; baptized My 19, 1801.
    Beaty Anna Hazlit (1:191), born O 28, 1800; baptized My 19, 1801.
JUNG, Casper married Catharine Glatt (1:191).
JUNG, Daniel had a daughter 'Selly Schu' who had an illegitimate son by
    Christopher Reich.
JUNG, Heinrich married Maria Lederman (1:151).
JUSTUS, Jean (1:247-248); came here in 1782; was an apprentice nailsmith
    with Godfrey Süss; he was born in Je, 1777; he caused his master much
    inconvenience by controversy as to his correct age, but in his last
    moments seemed to desire a reconciliation; he died D 17, 1797 and was
    buried D 18, 1797.

KAMP, Adam (1:91,107,233), born D 16, 1714 at Wohnsheim in the Palatinate;
    he came to America in 1741; he was a Probationer Mr 6, 1764; a Communicant
    Ja 26, 1765; he came to know the Moravians in Lancaster, in Nyberg's time;
    conducted himself in a quiet and upright way with everyone; he died Mr 8,
    1784--towards noon [of that day] he rode to the mill; towards evening,
    when he was supposed to be riding home, a boy found him lying half dead in
    the road about a mile from home. The boy notified his son John, and when
    they came to help him, he was without reason or hearing. He was taken to
    his son's house on a sleigh but remained in the same condition until
    towards midnight when he passed away; he was buried Mr 11, 1784; he
    married twice and was the father of three children by his first marriage;
    he married, secondly, Maria Ottila (this was also her second marriage);
    (1:91,108,230); she was born Ja 16, 1709 at Oppenheim in the Palatinate;
    she came to America with her first husband by whom she had six children;
    she came to know the Moravians after her second marriage; she was taken
    into the congregation Je 26, 1774; first communed Ja 4, 1775; she died S
    18, 1775 and was buried in the churchyard S 20, 1775.
KAMP, Elizabeth married David Brown.
KAMP, John son of Adam Kamp (1:92); a Probationer Ja 1, 1781; married Anna
    Elizabeth (or Maria Elisabeth 1:174b), daughter of Elisabeth Protzman,
    widow; she was a Probationer Ja 1, 1781.
Issue: Margaret (1:166), born Mr 27, 1777 in the evening; baptized Ap 1,
    1777.
    John Gottlieb (1:168), born early on D 13, 1779; baptized D 17,
    1779.
    Barbara (1:171), born D 27, 1782; baptized D 28, 1783.
    Catharina (1:174), born Je 17, 1786 at 3-4 a.m.; baptized Je 18,
    1786.

Anna Charlotte (7th child, 5th daughter) (1:167b), born Ag 1, 1788 in the afternoon; baptized Ag 3, 1788.
Anna Maria (1:174b), born N 5, 1791 at 5-6 a.m.; baptized N 6, 1791.
Elizabeth married Jacob Frey.
KAST, George of Carroll's Manor married Catharine _____.
Issue: Maria Margaret (1:158), born S 29, 1763 at 10 a.m.; baptized Ap 8, 1764, the sponsors being Franz Kast and his wife Margaretha.
KAUFFMAN, _____ married Magdalena Eyler (2:20).
KAUFFMAN, George married Elsie _____.
Issue: Elsie Anna, born Jl 20, 1784; died F 23, 1878; married George Eyler.
KAUFFMAN, George, over the mountain, married Jane Eldridge.
Issue: Sarah Ann (1:121), born My 2, 1825; baptized N 10, 1825.
Alexander (1:135), born F 9, 1827; baptized Ag 30, 1827.
Lewis (1:137), born Je 29, 1828; baptized Ag 10, 1828.
Henry (1:139), born Ap 3, 1830; baptized S 1, 1830.
Ephraim Frederic (1:143), born Ag 10, 1831; baptized Ap 29, 1832.
Anne Eliza (1:145), born F 21, 1833; baptized Je 30, 1833.
Harriet (1:148), born Jl 22, 1834; baptized Ja 11, 1835.
Joseph (1:150), born S 21, 1835; baptized Ap 3, 1836.
Mary Juliet (1:99), born Ap 23, 1840; baptized N 1, 1840.
George Washington (1:102), born Ap 9, 1842; baptized S 4, 1842.
KAUFFMAN, Leonard married Polly _____.
Issue: Joshua (1:111), born Mr 31, 1819; baptized S 5, 1819.
KAUFFMAN, Mary Magdalena married Everard Harr.
KEAN, Mary Ellen married Jacob Krieger.
KEHL, George married Susanna Roscher.
Issue: Joshua (1:212), born Mr 23, 1811; baptized Ag 3, 1811.
KEIPER, Barbara married Jacob Woodring.
KEMMEL, John married Barbara Leidy.
Issue: Maria (1:207), born D 11, 1808; baptized Mr 2, 1808.
James (1:212), born Ap 15, 1811; baptized O 28, 1811.
KERTSCHER, Andrew (1:91,226), born Ag 4, 1701 at Berns, near Altenburg, Saxony; he was a Probationer Jl 10, 1763; a Communicant Ap 19, 1764; he died at 11 a.m. O 22, 1767 and buried in the churchyard O 23, 1767; he married Dorothea _____ (1:231) who was born Je 30, 1701 in the duchy of Saxony; she was a Probationer Ja 10, 1763 and a Communicant Ap 19, 1764; she and her husband came to know the Moravians at York; she was received in the congregation Jl 10, 1763 and first communed D 8, 1764; she died F 19, 1776 and was buried in the churchyard F 21, 1776.
KESSLER, Catharine married Levi Feezer.
KESSLER, Levi (1:86), son of Michael and Susan Kessler; he married Ag 18, 1831 Magdalena Smith daughter of Peter and Magdalena Smith.
KESSLER, Michael married Susan _____.
Issue: Hannah married Christian Riddlemoser.
KETTERING, Mary Elizabeth (2:46), of Sabillasville, born Mr 8, 1851 and was baptized My 2, 1851.
KEY, John (1:86), son of Andrew and Elizabeth Key; married F 27, 1831 Mary McLamee, daughter of Francis and Mary McLamee.
KID, Anna married Moses Smith.
KIEFFER, Ludwig married Margaret McDonnell.
Issue: Catharina married Jacob Long.
KIER, Edward married Susanna Hummer.
Issue: Jeremiah (1:211), born Ag 27, 1810; baptized F 21, 1811.
KINSEY, George (1:88) married F 21, 1837 Jane Shuff.
KINSEY, Sarah married Reuben Ecker.
KLINGSOHR, _____ married Elizabeth Mack.
KLOTZ, Catharine married John Eyler.

KLUGE, John Peter, Minister at Graceham, married at Lititz on O 3, 1800 Anna
Maria Ranck (1:78), daughter of Philip Ranck (farmer) and his wife Barbara
(Stauffer); said Anna Maria was born near York, Pennsylvania on S 13,
1772; she died F 12, 1820 and was buried F 15, 1820.
Issue: Charles Frederick, born Jl 21, 1801 at White River, Indiana.
    Henrietta, born S 1, 1803.
    John Henry, born D 31, 1805.
    Christian Ludwig, born Jl 14, 1808.
    Carolina Emilia, born F 27, 1811.
    Clementine Louisa, born Ag 12, 1813.
KLUGE, John Peter, minister, married Elizabeth Eyerly.
Issue: Selma Angelica (2:1,89), born D 13, 1822; baptized D 23, 1822; died
    of tooth trouble D 9, 1823; buried D 12, 1823.
KNAUFF, Eve married William Reidenauer.
KNAUFF, Henry married Mary Ann Wile.
Issue: Mary Barbara, born My 18, 1798; married Benjamin Wilhide.
KNAUFF, John married Catharine _____.
Issue: Amy (2:239), born S 5, 1804; died F 20, 1864; buried F 22, 1864;
    married George Hesser.
    Mary (1:83), married Jeremiah Martin.
    Catharine married Benjamin Ogle.
KNAUFF, John married Catharine Biggs.
Issue: Ellen Rebecca (1:220), born Mr 11, 1817; baptized My 21, 1817.
    Sarah Ann Elisabeth (1:138), born O 28, 1828; baptized Ap 4, 1829.
KNAUFF, John (2:152) married Ap 29, 1852 Susan M. Biggs.
Issue: Laura Virginia (2:119), born F 16, 1853; baptized My 15, 1853.
KOCH, Adam married Elizabeth _____.
Issue: Mary (1:197), born S 10, 1803; baptized O 9, 1803.
KOCH, Catharine (2:245); died F 8, 1869, aged 84 years 2 months and 30 days;
buried at Graceham F 9, 1869.
KOCH, George (1:108), near the Monocacy; he married Je 2, 1778 Maria
Duckness (1:92,108,263) who was born in Philadelphia on Ap 23, 1758; she
was a Probationer Mr 30, 1794; both were readmitted to communion D 26,
1797; she died of cancer O 3, 1810 and was buried O 4, 1810.
Issue: Sarah (1:169b; 2:237), born O 7, 1789 at 7-8 a.m.; baptized O 18,
    1789; died My 28, 1863; buried My 29, 1863.
    Maria (1:177), born Ap 17, 1793 at noon; baptized Ap 30, 1793.
    Susanna (1:180), born My 2, 1795; baptized Je 14, 1795; married
    Joseph Cover.
    Rosina (1:185), born Ag 20, 1798; baptized O 7, 1798.
    Son (1:240), born Je 14, 1791; died Je 27, 1791 of facial convul-
    sions and was buried in the churchyard Je 28, 1791.
    Henry married Eleanora Hummer.
    5 others.
KOCH, Henry, son of George and Maria (Duckness) Koch, married Eleonora
Hummer.
Issue: Obadiah Duckness (1:201), born Ja 18, 1806; baptized Ja 30, 1806.
    Luellen [Llewellyn] (1:204), born My 7, 1807; baptized Je 15, 1807.
    Eliza (1:206), born Je 20, 1808; baptized Jl 11, 1808.
    Sophia Adelina (1:209), born Ag 7, 1809; baptized S 24, 1809.
    Jeremias (1:211), born My 25, 1811; baptized S 8, 1811.
KOEHN, Anna Margaret married Jacob Weller.
KÖHLER, Elizabeth married Jacob Fahs.
KOLB, Mrs. Mary Magdalena (2:248), born Jl 17, 1806; died O 5, 1874; buried
O 6, 1874 at the Lutheran and Reformed Church at Creagerstown.
KOONTZ, Ann married Samuel Jacob Wilhide.
KOONTZ, William married Anne Mehring.
Issue: Elias Washington (1:148), born Ag 8, 1834; baptized Ja 10, 1835.
KOTTER (CURTIS?), Anna married (1) Samuel Weker and (2) John Groschong.

52

KRALL, Anna married John Jacob Weller.
KRALL, Elizabeth married George Bush.
KRALL, Isaac (Renatus, added at baptism); (1:108,175); born Jl 18, 1754;
baptized Je 3, 1787; Communicant My 10, 1788; married Elizabeth _____
(1:92,108), daughter of Mrs. Busch; said Elizabeth was a Probationer O 14,
1787 and a Communicant My 10, 1788.
Issue: son
      daughter
      Maria (2nd daughter) (1:175,238); born My 12, 1787 at 7-8 p.m.;
        baptized Je 3, 1787; died of smallpox My 1, 1789 and was buried
        in the churchyard My 3, 1789.
      John George (2nd son) (1:168b,238); born Ap 26, 1789 at 2 p.m.;
        baptized My 3, 1789; died of facial convulsions My 6, 1789 and
        was buried in the churchyard My 8, 1789.
      Catharine (1:172b); born D 25, 1790 at 7 p.m.; baptized F 6, 1791.
KRALL, Mary Magdalen married Henry Stauffer.
KRÄMER, Michael married Elizabeth _____.
Issue: Elizabeth; born Ja 22, 1778; died Ja 15, 1851; married Ludwig
        Protzman.
      Anna Maria; born O 31, 1769; died Jl 30, 1856; married Godfrey
        Süss.
KRANZ, John Dietrich had by Christina Leimbach an illegitimate son, John
Dietrich (1:204), who was born Mr 9, 1807 and baptized Jl 12, 1807.
KRANZ, Johann Philip married Anna Catharine Miller.
Issue: Catharine Barbara (1:94), born S 15, 1837; baptized Ja 21, 1838.
      Edward Philip (1:97), born F 28, 1839; baptized My 19, 1839.
      Susanna Frederica (1:102), born Jl 26, 1841; baptized D 11, 1842.
KRAUSE, Elizabeth married William Theodore Miller.
KREIDLER, John, saddler, of Kriegerstown, married Catharine Schäfer.
Issue: Henry (1:193), born D 14, 1801; baptized My 3, 1802.
KREISS, Susanna, daughter of Peter, married Joseph Harbaugh.
KREMSER, Elizabeth married The Reverend Samuel Uttly.
KRIEGER (CREAGER, CREEGER, etc.), Abraham (1:209), son of Henry and Sophia
(Protzman) Krieger; he was born Jl 25, 1809 and baptized Ag 27, 1809; he
married Sarah Zentmeyer.
Issue: Francis Washington (2:205), born Je 25, 1832; died O 11, 1833 of
        brain inflammation; buried O 12, 1833.
      Josephine Elizabeth (1:101), born O 4, 1841; baptized Ja 27, 1842.
KRIEGER, Anna Elizabeth married Jacob Weller.
KRIEGER (CREEGAR), Augustus.
Issue: James Albert (2:220), born O 20, 1848; died F 10, 1851; buried F
        11, 1851.
      Emily Frances (2:235), born D 7, 1850; died Je 9, 1862; buried at
        Mechanicstown Je 11, 1862.
      Anna Elizabeth (2:236), born D 1, 1855; died Je 24, 1862; buried at
        Mechanicstown Je 25, 1852.
KRIEGER (KRIGER), Daniel (1:130; 2:194), son of Lawrence and Anna Maria
(Harbaugh) Krieger; he was born in Frederick County, Maryland on N 5,
1788; he died Ag 13, 1827 of consumption and was buried Ag 14, 1827; he
married O 14, 1810 Maria Barbara Eyler (1:168b), daughter of Jonas and
Anna Regina (Harbaugh) Eyler; she was born in Maryland Ja 17, 1789 and was
baptized F 15, 1789; "Welche in unerlaubten Umgang geraten."
Issue: Ezra (2:205;1:211), born My 13, 1811; baptized My 23, 1811; died S
        14, 1833 unmarried, of consumption; buried S 16.
      Parmenio (1:213; 2:195), born Ag 27, 1812; baptized S 13, 1812;
        died of consumption S 29, 1829; buried S 30, 1829.
      Anna Catharina (1:216), born My 3, 1814; baptized My 22, 1814; died
        of consumption, unmarried, D 8, 1833; buried D 9, 1833.

KRIEGER, George Washington, born Ja 23, 1818 and baptized Ap 5, 1818; married Rebecca Late.
Issue: William E. married Laura L. Ecker.
KRIEGER, Henry, miller, (1:130,171; 2:223,289), 3 miles from Lewistown, son of Lawrence and Anna Maria (Harbaugh) Krieger; he was born N 7, 1784; baptized N 7, 1784; a Communicant Ag 13, 1808; he died F 2, 1854 and was buried F 4, 1854; he married Mr 14, 1809 Sophia Protzman (1:174b; 2:206), daughter of Ludwig and Elizabeth (Rauser) Protzman; said Sophia was born Ja 25, 1792; she was baptized F 19, 1792; died in childbed Jl 4, 1834 and was buried Jl 6, 1834.
Issue: Abraham (1:209), born Jl 25, 1809; baptized Ag 27, 1809; married Sarah Zentmeyer.
    Elizabeth (1:212), born S 8, 1811; baptized S 29, 1811; married John Jacob Milliar.
    Anna Maria (1:215; 2:195), born O 24, 1813; baptized N 21, 1813; died Jl 22, 1829; buried Jl 23, 1829; she was deaf and dumb from birth.
    Rachel (1:218), born Jl 15, 1815; baptized Ag 20, 1815.
    Solomon (1:220), born Mr 13, 1817; baptized Ap 13, 1817; deaf and dumb.
    Lewis (1:222), born Ja 17, 1819; baptized F 18, 1819.
    Augusta Charlotte (1:114), born O 31, 1820; baptized D 3, 1820.
    Anna Rebecca (1:119), born S 6, 1822; baptized O 22, 1822.
    Angelina (2:5), born Ja 1, 1825; baptized F 20, 1825.
    Martin Henry (2:8), born O 5, 1826; baptized D 3, 1826.
    Jerome Francis (2:12,210), born S 25, 1828; baptized N 16, 1828; died S 5, 1837; buried S 7, 1837.
    Henrietta Sophia (2:17), born Ap 25, 1830; baptized My 30, 1830.
    Edward Theophilus (2:21), born My 3, 1832; baptized My 13, 1832.
    Simon (2:25,206), born My 21, 1834; baptized Je 3, 1834; died Jl 3 or 4, 1834.
KRIEGER, Henry married Sophia Dotterow.
Issue: Eliza Ann (2:32), born Ap 25, 1838; baptized Ag 12, 1838.
    John Wesley (2:34), born Ag 8, 1839; baptized Ja 24, 1840.
KRIEGER, Jacob married Mary Ellen Kean (2:250); she was born in Baltimore Ap 2, 1852; she died in St. Louis, Missouri F 2, 1876 and was buried at Mechanicstown Mr 9, 1876.
Issue: Mary Ellen (2:250), born in Baltimore Ja 18, 1876; died Jl 4, 1876; buried at Mechanicstown Jl 5, 1876.
KRIEGER, Jacob Frederick (2:44,164) of Mechanicstown, son of James and Elizabeth (Weller) Krieger; he was born F 17, 1848 and was baptized Ap 9, 1848; he married N 25, 1880 Mary C. Clem, also of Mechanicstown.
KRIEGER, James (or Jacobus) (2:148,287), son of John Jacob and Maria Catharina (Busch) Krieger; he was born Je 14, 1817; baptized Jl 20, 1818; a Communicant Ap 12, 1838; he married Ap 22, 1838 Elizabeth Weller (1:111; 2:229,287), daughter of Frederick and Sarah (Stauffer) Weller; she was born Mr 19, 1819; baptized My 2, 1819; a Communicant Ap 12, 1835; she died Ap 13, 1857 and was buried Ap 14, 1857.
Issue: Martha Matilda (2:34,211), born Ap 29, 1839; baptized My 20, 1839; died Ag 3, 1839; buried Ag 4, 1839.
    Sevilla Catharine (2:37), born Ag 10, 1840; baptized S 6, 1840; married Wesley Delaplane.
    Eleonora Adelaide (2:41), born F 16, 1843; baptized Mr 26, 1843.
    Juliana (2:42,218), born Jl 28, 1845; baptized Ag 24, 1845; died N 4, 1847; buried N 6, 1847.
    Jacob Frederick (2:44), born F 17, 1848; baptized Ap 9, 1848; married Mary C. Clem.
    Edward Robert (2:45,229), born Mr 11, 1849; baptized My 13, 1849; died S 12, 1856; buried S 13, 1856.

Anna Elizabeth (2:48), born My 11, 1853; baptized Jl 10, 1853; married Mahlon Witmer.

Amadeus James (2:50,228), born Ag 14, 1855; baptized O 28, 1855; died Ag 15, 1856; buried Ag 16, 1856.

James Hagen (2:57,238), born Mr 14, 1862; baptized My 25, 1862; died S 24, 1863; buried at Graceham S 25, 1863.

KRIEGER, James (2:155) married Ap 21, 1859 Sophia Firor.

Issue: John Wesley (2:59), born N 30, 1863; baptized F 2-, 1864.

Martin Luther (2:61), born My 5, 1866; baptized Jl 8, 1866.

[James H.] died [S 24, 1863, aged 1-6-10].

KRIEGER, John, Junior, innkeeper and merchant (2:194), son of Lawrence and Anna Maria (Harbaugh) Krieger; he was born Ag 6, 1777; he was married on Je 8, 1802 to Eva Eyler; he had been excommunicated, but was reinstated when he sent a letter asking forgiveness of the congregation; he died Mr 22, 1828 and was buried Mr 23, 1828.

Issue: Ezra (1:198,261), born Ag 16, 1804; baptized Ag 19, 1804; died Mr 11, 1805; buried Mr 12, 1805.

Theresa (1:200), born Ag 17, 1805; baptized O 6, 1805.

Eleonora (1:203), born Ja 10, 1807; baptized F 22, 1807.

Timothy (1:206; 2:193), born My 24, 1808; baptized My 26, 1808; died D 13, 1826 and buried D 15, 1826.

Uriah (1:210), born O 18, 1810; baptized O 28, 1810.

Frederick Louis (1:214,264), born Ja 18, 1813; baptized Ja 22, 1813; died Ja 28, 1813 of continual convulsions; buried Ja 31, 1813.

Sarah Anna (1:219,266), born Ag 19, 1816; baptized S 22, 1816; died N 27, 1818 of dropsical head; buried N 29, 1818.

Anna Margaret (1:221), born D 7, 1817; baptized Ap 12, 1818.

Maria Louisa (1:112), born Mr 21, 1820; baptized Ap 30, 1820.

Josephine Eliza (1:116), born Ap 30, 1821; baptized Jl 8, 1821.

Martha Matilda (2:2), born F 26, 1823; baptized Ap 27, 1823.

Sabina, born Mr 30, 1803; married Martin Schultz.

KRIEGER (CREEGAR), John Edward (2:224), born Mr 11, 1854; died Ap 22, 1854; buried at Mechanicstown Ap 23, 1854.

KRIEGER, John Henry (1:225), born [My 17, 1749]; died at 5-6 a.m. My 25, 1764 after 3 days illness, of small-pox; and was buried My 27, 1764.

KRIEGER, John Jacob (1:129,167; 2:218,286,291), son of Lawrence and Anna Maria (Harbaugh) Krieger; he was born My or Ag 24, 1779 in Frederick County; he was baptized My 25, 1801; he was a Communicant O 8, 1803; he died S 16, 1849 and was buried S 18, 1849; he married Mr 31, 1803 Maria Catharine Bush (1:191; 2:217), daughter of John and Anna Elizabeth (Stauffer) Bush; she was born Mr 26, 1784 and was baptized My 25, 1801; she was a Communicant D 4, 1803; she died Je 10, 1847 and was buried Je 12.

Issue: Ephraim (1:78,197), born D 23, 1803 in Frederick County; baptized Ja 22, 1804; died Jl 31, 1820 of dysentery; buried Ag 1, 1820.

Manasse (1:202), born My 27, 1806; baptized Je 1, 1806; married Margaret Reitenauer.

Deborah (1:205), born D 29, 1807; baptized Ja 24, 1808; married John Weller.

Levi (1:211), born D 25, 1810; baptized Ja 14, 1811; married Mary Ann Weller.

Seba (son); (1:214), born D 28, 1812; baptized Ja 22, 1813.

Amos (1:218,264), born N 20, 1815; baptized N 21, 1815; died N 21, 1815 and buried N 23; born too soon.

Jacobus (or James) (1:220), born Je 14, 1817; baptized Jl 20, 1818; married Elizabeth Weller.

John William (2:4,293), born Jl 20, 1824; baptized Ag 8, 1824; a Communicant in 1841; died in Mexico in the Mexican War.

KRIEGER, John Lawrence (1:91,107,234), born Mr 15, 1715 at Bettelhausen in Wittgenstein; he married in 1741 or 1742 Maria Elizabeth Hahn (1:91,107,251-252) who was originally Reformed; she was born N 23, 1715 at Alertshausen in Wittgenstein; they came to America together in 1737 or 1738. They went to live 7 miles beyond York, on the Codorus, where their first two children were born, and thence came here in 1747. They became Probationers when this church was organized, O 8, 1758, and Communicants My 3, 1761. He came to know the Moravians through Lischy. He died Ag 28, 1784 of consumption resulting from a leg injury; he was buried Ag 29, 1784 in the churchyard; she died Jl 23, 1798 and was buried Jl 25, 1798; her father died when she was 4, and she was a servant for 13 years. She came to Pennsylvania in 1737 and served in Germantown for 3 years. Her health had been good, but in late years her faculties (particularly sight) were impaired and she could not attend services for a year and a day before she died; she remembered many hymns, however, and refreshed herself with them. (The words of a hymn dictated by her are given.) She was only confined to her bed for a fortnight.
Issue: John Jacob (1:156,225), born My 10, 1761 at 8 a.m.; baptized My 11, 1761; died My 16, 1761 and is buried on his father's farm.
John Lawrence; born My 26, 1754; died N 12, 1820; married Anna Maria Harbaugh.
Maria Barbara; born My 10, 1747; died Je 15, 1820; married John Weller.
Magdalena; married John Jacob Weller; she died D 28, 1765.
Anna Elizabeth; married _____ Ricksecker.
Anna Margaret, a Chordienerin at Lititz.
KRIEGER, Joseph (1:177), son of Lawrence and Anna Maria (Harbaugh) Krieger; he was born My 27, 1793 and baptized Je 2, 1793; he married Susanna Otto.
Issue: Octavius Augustus (1:111), born Jl 26, 1819; baptized Ag 30, 1819; married Maranda Zeller.
KRIEGER, Lawrence (1:79,91,108,126), son of John Lawrence and Maria Elizabeth (Hahn) Krieger; he was born My 26, 1754 in Frederick County; he was a Probationer N 13, 1782 and a Communicant Ja 22, 1785; he died N 12, 1820 and was buried at Graceham N 13, 1820; he married Ag 30, 1774 Anna Maria Harbaugh (1:91,108; 2:210), 3rd daughter of George and Catharine (Milliar) Harbaugh; she was born F 26, 1754; she was a Probationer N 13, 1782 and a Communicant Ja 22, 1785; she died of a stroke S 22, 1837 and was buried at Graceham S 23, 1837.
Issue: Anna Elizabeth (1:165), born N 13, 1775 in the morning; baptized N 19, 1775; married Conrad Wilhide.
John (1:166), born Ag 6, 1777; baptized Ag 10, 1777; died Mr 22, 1828; married Eva Eyler.
John Jacob (1:167), born My 24, 1779; baptized My 30, 1779; died S 16, 1849; married Maria Catharine Busch.
Regina (1:168), born Mr 12, 1781; baptized Mr 18, 1781; married Samuel Harbaugh.
Rosina (1:170), born F 13, 1783; baptized F 16, 1783; married Elias Weller.
Henry (1:171), born N 7, 1784 at 12 o'clock in the morning; baptized N 7, 1784; died F 2, 1854; married Sophia Protzman.
Maria Margaret (1:175), born My 16, 1787 at 7-8 p.m.; baptized My 20, 1787; married Elias Weller.
Daniel (1:167b), born N 5, 1788; baptized 25th Sunday after Trinity; died Ag 13, 1827; married Maria Barbara Eyler.
(Samuel (1:172b), born Mr 22, 1791 at 5-6 p.m.; baptized Mr 27, (1791; married Elizabeth Favorite.
twins (Joseph (1:172b), born Mr 22, 1791; baptized Mr 27, 1791; died Ag (4, 1792; buried Ag 6, 1792 in the churchyard.

Joseph (1:177), born My 27, 1793 at 2 p.m.; baptized Je 2, 1793;
married Susanna Otto.
William (1:181), born My 9, 1796 at 2 a.m.; baptized My 16, 1796;
died S 2, 1850; married Elizabeth Holtz.
KRIEGER, Levi (1:211; 2:147,219,287), son of John Jacob and Maria Catharina
(Bush) Krieger; he was born D 25, 1810 and baptized Ja 14, 1811; he was a
Communicant Ap 12, 1835; he died Ap 19, 1850 and was buried at Graceham Ap
20, 1850; he married S 8, 1835 Mary Ann Weller (1:218; 2:224,287), daugh-
ter of Frederick and Sarah (Stauffer) Weller; she was born Ap 9, 1816 and
was baptized Ap 10, 1816; she was a Communicant Ap 4, 1833; she died My
17, 1854 and was buried at Graceham My 19, 1854.
Issue: Ephraim (1:150; 2:210), born Ap 22, 1836; baptized Ap 22, 1836;
died Ap 23, 1836; buried Ap 24, 1836.
John Tilghman Augustus (2:31), born D 19, 1837; baptized Ja 24,
1838.
Sarah Matilda (2:37), born Ja 25, 1840; baptized Ap 5, 1840.
Joseph Hamilton (2:39), born F 20, 1842; baptized Ap 3, 1842.
Charles Leander (2:41), born Ag 17, 1843; baptized N 5, 1843.
Josephine Theresa (2:43), born O 15, 1845; baptized Ja 11, 1846.
Martha Sophia (2:44), born O 9, 1848; baptized D 24, 1848.
KRIEGER, Manasse (1:202), son of John Jacob and Maria Catharine (Bush)
Krieger; he was born My 27, 1806 and was baptized Je 1, 1806; he married
Margaret Reidenauer.
Issue: Ephraim Augustus (1:152), born Ag 3, 1837; baptized Ag 27, 1837.
KRIEGER, Margaret had an illegitimate son by Joseph (Ogle?).
KRIEGER, Octavius Augustus (1:90,111), son of Joseph and Susanna (Otto)
Krieger; he married Ag 8, 1842 Maranda Zeller.
KRIEGER, Peky had an illegitimate son by Daniel Rauser.
KRIEGER, Samuel, shoemaker (1:131,177b), of Graceham, son of Lawrence and
Anna Maria (Harbaugh) Krieger; he was born in Frederick County on Mr 22,
1791 and was baptized Mr 27, 1791; he married D 7, 1815 Elizabeth Favorite
(2:193) who was born in Frederick County in 1793; she was a Member here My
11, 1818; she died Ap 16, 1827 of an ardent gall fever, and was buried Ap
18, 1827.
Issue: Eliza (1:219,265), born S 15, 1816; baptized N 3, 1816; died of
convulsions Ja 16, 1817 and was buried Ja 17.
George Washington (1:221), born Ja 23, 1818; baptized Ap 5, 1818,
married Rebecca Late.
Jeremiah Augustus (1:80,116), born Mr 27, 1821; baptized Ap 7,
1821; died of convulsions Ap 8, 1821; buried Ap 9.
Mary Ann (1:119), born Ag 13, 1822; baptized S 22, 1822; married
George Washington Late; she died [D 12, 1898] and was buried at
Graceham.
Sarah Anna (2:4), born D 23, 1823; baptized Je 6, 1824.
Elizabeth (2:9), born O 26, 1826; baptized Ap 18, 1827.
KRIEGER, Sarah married Charles Augustus Reidenour.
KRIEGER, William, joiner (1:133; 2:220) of Mechanicstown, son of Lawrence
and Anna Maria (Harbaugh) Krieger; he was born in Graceham on My 9, 1796;
he died S 2, 1850 and was buried S 4, 1850; he married S 2, 1819 Elizabeth
Holtz, daughter of Jacob Holtz, farmer, and Anna Barbara (Morgenstern);
said Elizabeth was born Ap 30, 1795.
Issue: Mary Ann Matilda (1:80,115), born S 18, 1820 in Frederick County,
Maryland; baptized D 31, 1820; died S 21, 1821; buried S 23,
1821.
Theodore Francis (2:3), born Ag 22, 1823; baptized D 21, 1823.
Eleonora Elizabeth (1:121; 2:203), born Jl 29, 1825; baptized D 11,
1825; died Mr 24, 1833 of inflammation of the brain; buried Mr
24, 1833.

William Lawrence (2:12), born S 18, 1827; baptized D 25, 1827; died
My 10, 1866; married Elizabeth Margaret Rouzer.
Catharina Matilda (2:15,197), born Je 15, 1829; baptized Ag 13,
1829; died Je 20, 1830 of cholera morbus and teething; buried Je
22, 1830.
Daniel Manasse (2:18,198), born O 30, 1830; baptized O 31, 1830;
died N 4, 1830; buried N 6, 1830.
Nicholas Jacob (2:18,198), born O 30, 1830; baptized O 31, 1830;
died N 5, 1830; buried N 6, 1830.
son, stillborn (2:205) O 31, 1833; buried N 1, 1833.
Robert Nelson (2:27,210), born Je 29, 1835; baptized Jl 5, 1835;
died Mr 25, 1836; buried Mr 26, 1836.
Anna Minerva (2:30,217), born Jl 8, 1836; baptized S 7, 1836; died
Je 27, 1845; buried Je 29, 1845.
stillborn (2:214) O 20, 1840; buried O 20, 1840.
KRIEGER, William E., Lutheran, (2:161), at the Ridge, son of George Washing-
ton and Rebecca (Late) Krieger; he married at the age of 25 years, on Ja
26, 1871, Laura L. Ecker, also a Lutheran, at the Ridge; she was aged 22
when married; she was the daughter of Reuben and Sarah (Kinsey) Ecker.
KRIEGER, William Harvey (2:236), born Ja 6, 1845; died Je 17, 1862; buried
Je 17, 1862 at Mechanicstown.
KRIEGER, William Lawrence (2:152,242), son of William and Elizabeth (Holtz)
Krieger; he was born S 18, 1827; he died My 10, 1866 and was buried at
Apple's My 12, 1866; he married Ja 18, 1853 Elizabeth Margaret Rouzer.
Issue: Lilly Ann (2:121), born O 16, 1855; baptized Ap 8, 1856.
Thaddeus (2:123), born Ap 28, 1858; baptized S 9, 1858.
Harry (2:124), born Ag 20, 1860; baptized F 27, 1861; died [F 15,
1917]; married [Ida].
George (2:128,242), born O 26, 1864; baptized Jl 27, 1865; died Ag
15, 1865 and buried at Apple's Ag 17, 1865.
William Theodore (2:129), born N 26, 1866; baptized Ja 31, 1867.
KRUGS, Daniel married Susan Martin.
Issue: Rufus (1:101), born O 16, 1841; baptized Jl 10, 1842.
KREUSCHONG, Margaret, widow, had an illegitimate child by Michael Fley.
KUHN, Benjamin married Catharine Hamburg.
Issue: Daniel (1:220), born S 15, 1816; baptized Mr 23, 1817.
Lewis (1:222), born O 15, 1818; baptized Ja 31, 1819.
Catharine Anna (1:115), born D 22, 1820; baptized Ja 14, 1821.
KUHN, Cyrus C. (2:153) married O 11, 1853 Mary Jane Eyler (2:8,225), daugh-
ter of Frederick and Margaret (Williar) Eyler; said Mary Jane was born Ag
17, 1826 and was baptized O 1, 1826; she died Jl 30, 1854, aged 27-11-5,
and was buried Ag 1, 1854 at Mechanicstown.
Issue: Mary Jane (2:120), baptized Ag 1, 1854.
KUHN, Elizabeth married Leonard Smith.
KUHN, Gabriel, farmer, married Catharine Spies.
Issue: William (1:196), born F 1, 1803; baptized Jl 30, 1803.
KUHN, George married Elizabeth Protzman.
Issue: Henry Edward (1:94), born Je 4, 1837; baptized Mr 26, 1838.
Milton (1:96), born Jl 17, 1838; baptized Mr 1, 1839.
KUHN, George R. (2:152), married Ag 19, 1852 Mary Amanda Cover (1:144),
daughter of William and Elizabeth (Seiffert) Cover; she was born N 15,
1831 and was baptized S 2, 1832.
KUHN, Henry married Elizabeth _____.
Issue: Mary (1:87) married Ephraim Carmack.
KUHN, Joseph married Sarah Ovelman.
Issue: Margaret Ellen (1:140), born O 22, 1830; baptized D 20, 1830.
William Henry (1:145), born O 20, 1832; baptized Mr 24, 1833.
Leander Hamilton (1:100), born S 15, 1839; baptized Mr 17, 1841.
KUHN, Mary married George Flick.

KUHN, Philip.
Issue: Elizabeth Margaret (1:163), born Mr 1, 1772 at 6 a.m.; baptized Mr
16, 1772.
KUHN, Sarah married Joseph Favorite.
KUHNS, Ann married John Stoll.
KUHNS, Hannah married Samuel Fleming.
KUMS, Joseph married Masse Simes.
Issue: Joseph (1:209), born Ap 26, 1809; baptized Ag 20, 1809.
KUNS, Anna Margaret married Jacob Stauffer.
KUNS, David (KOONS) married Margaret Martin.
Issue: Emily Catharine (1:139), born F 10, 1830; baptized Mr 15, 1830.
KUNS, Elizabeth, daughter of George, married Laurence Ehrensperger.
KUNS (KOONS), Mary married George Heckman.
KUNS, Sophia had an illegitimate child by Semmy Johnson.
KUNS (KUNZ), Sophia married Jesse Shuff.
KUNS (KOONS), Susan married Joshua Humerich.
KUNS (COONZ), Susanna married Jacob Witmer.
KURTZ, Elizabeth married Frederick Bowers.

LAEMBKE, Christian William, merchant, (1:255-257), son of Franz Christ.
Lambky who was pastor at Nazareth and his wife Maria Catharina (Wier); he
was born Ap 18, 1763 at Nazareth, Pennsylvania; he finished his schooling
at Pädogogium at Nazareth, then began learning business at the store
there; member of the Big Boys Choir in his 12th year; member of the Single
Mens Choir Ag 29, 1782; a Probationer Ja 19, 1777; a Communicant F 27,
1779; he moved in 1785 to Store at Bethlehem, but soon returned to
Nazareth and served in the Pensions-Anstalt; he married in Lititz on Je
19, 1792 Anna Maria Demuth, daughter of Christopher and Anna Elizabeth
Demuth; after his marriage, in 1792, he moved to Graceham where he estab-
lished a store; he died My 8, 1800 and was buried in the churchyard My 11,
1800; at the end of 1799 he began to sustain severe abdominal pain which
proved to be gall colic; nevertheless he played the organ for the Christ-
mas celebrations. His death was especially regretted because of his
musical talent which he used for the benefit of the congregation.
Issue: Charlotte Willhelmina (1:177), born My 28, 1793 at 10 p.m.;
baptized Je 2, 1793.
Carolina Elisabeth (1:179), born Ja 24, 1795 at 4 p.m.; baptized F
1, 1795.
Mathildis Amalia (1:182), born D 16, 1796 at 6:30 a.m.; baptized D
25, 1796.
Augusta Eloisa (1:188), born Ag 25, 1799; baptized S 1, 1799.
LAMISON, Mary married Frederick B. Wiles.
LAMMERSON, Conrad (1:86) son of Conrad and Rosanna Lammerson married Ja 19,
1831 Cynthia Adams, daughter of James and Elizabeth Adams.
Issue: James Alfred (1:146), born My 28, 1832; baptized S 2, 1833.
LAMMERSON, Eliza Elizabeth had an illegitimate child by William Fröhlich.
LAMMERSON, Elizabeth married Ezra Williar.
LAMMERSON, Richard, potter at the furnace, married Barbara Benser.
Issue: Jacob (1:199), born Je --, 1804; baptized Ap 14, 1805.
Martha (1:208), born S 9, 1806; baptized Je 25, 1809; married Isaac
Hankey.
Richard (1:208), born Ja 9, 1808; baptized Je 25, 1809.
LAMMERSON, Richard married Sarah McWilliams.
Issue: Margaret Ellen (1:137), born Jl 6, 1828; baptized Ag 24, 1828.
LANDERS, _____, daughter of the storekeeper, died Mr 8, 1850 and was buried
Mr 9 at Apple's Church.
LANG, Christina married Christian Staub.
LANG, Magdalena married Francis Zoller.
LANIUS, Catharine married Philip William Boller.

LANIUS, Jacob married Maria _____.
  Issue: Anna (2:190), born D 23, 1794 at York; died S 16, 1824; buried S
    17, 1824; she was unmarried.
LATE, Catharine (2:225), born Je 28, 1819; died D 21, 1854; buried at
    Creagerstown D 22, 1854.
LATE, George Washington [born Je 14, 1819 and died D 5, 1903]; he married
    Mary Ann Krieger (1:119), daughter of Samuel and Elizabeth (Favorite)
    Krieger; she was born Ag 13, 1822; baptized S 22, 1822; [she died D 12,
    1898].
  Issue: John Luther (2:116), born F 25, 1850; baptized Mr 17, 1850; [he
      died My 15, 1892].
    William Edward (2:116), born F 25, 1850; baptized Mr 17, 1850;
      married Mannie Derr.
    Albert Theodore (2:48), baptized My 15, 1853.
    George Franklin (2:49), born N 13, 1853; baptized Ag 27, 1854.
    Clara America (2:51), born Ag 27, 1856; baptized Ja 25, 1857.
    Ida Ellen Virginia (2:54), born Je 20, 1859; baptized S 25, 1859.
    Harry Ellsworth (2:60), born N 27, 1864; baptized Ag 13, 1865;
      [died O 23, 1892].
LATE, Rebecca married George Washington Krieger.
LATE, Rebecca married Jacob Wilhide.
LATE, William Edward (2:116), son of George Washington and Mary Ann
    (Creegar) Late; he was born F 25, 1850 and was baptized Mr 17, 1850; he
    married Mannie Derr.
  Issue: Anna Mary (2:136), born Je 19, 1877; baptized Mr 24, 1878.
LAYTON, Henry had by Catharine Woodring an illegitimate daughter, Maria
    Magdalena (1:220) who was born Mr 23, 1817 and was baptized Ap 27, 1817.
LAYTON, Henry (1:132) married Ag 1, 1816 Helena (or Magdalena) Protzman
    (1:180), daughter of Ludwig and Maria Elizabeth (Rauser) Protzman; she was
    born Je 1, 1795 and was baptized Je 28, 1795.
LEFEVER, Esther married Abraham Smith.
LEFEVER, (LE-FAVOUR), John, farmer, married Catharine Mertz.
  Issue: Jacob (1:195), born F 1, 1803; baptized Mr 1, 1803.
    _____ (1:199), baptized D 19, 1804.
LEFEVER, Marie married Jacob Smith.
LEHMAN, Jacob married Catharine _____.
  Issue: Mary married John Stimmel.
LEHMAN, Susan married Solomon Wilhide.
LEIBER, (LIVERS), Anthony had by Catharine Barbara Süss an illegitimate son,
    Anthony (1:206; 2:237) who was born Jl 2, 1808 and was baptized Ag 8,
    1808; he [the son] died Ap 17, 1863 and was buried at Graceham Ap 19,
    1863. Said Catharine Barbara Süss (1:169; 2:230,292) was the daughter of
    John George and Maria Barbara (Eigenbrod) Süss; she was born N 29, 1781
    and baptized D 2, 1781; she was a Communicant D 4, 1802; she died Ap 2,
    1858 and was buried at Graceham Ap 3, 1858.
LEIBER (LIVERS), Anthony had by Maria Leinbach an illegitimate daughter,
    Jane (1:208) who was born O 19, 1806 and who was baptized Jl 19, 1809.
    Said Maria Leinbach was the daughter of Samuel and Maria (Ditnermesser)
    Leinbach.
LEIBER (LIVERS), Anthony had by Sarah McWilliams an illegitimate son
    Nathaniel (1:216) who was born D 17, 1813 and who was baptized Ap 17,
    1814.
LEIDY, Barbara married John Kemmel.
LEIDY, Henrietta married Cyrus Cover.
LEIDY, Henry married Delilah Hess.
  Issue: Samuel (1:207), born Ap 15, 1808; baptized N 23, 1808.
LEIDY, Jacob married Margaret Milhouse.
  Issue: Anna Rebecca (1:212), born Ag 4, 1811; baptized O 28, 1811.
    Margaret (1:214), born Ja 6, 1813; baptized Ja 27, 1813.

LEIDY (LIGHTY), Jacob married Sarah _____.
   Issue: Sarah Anna (1:122), baptized Ap 30, 1826.
LEIDY, Mary had an illegitimate daughter by Dr. Ligget.
LEIDY, Sarah Ann married Wilfred L. Florey.
LEIDY, William (1:90) married My 18, 1843 Lydia Ann Brown.
LEINBACH, Benjamin married Elizabeth _____.
   Issue: Catharine married William Falder.
LEINBACH, Catharina (2:18), adult, single; baptized O 8, 1830.
LEINBACH, Christian (1:127,241), son of Frederick and Elizabeth Leinbach; he
   was born at Skippack on F 13, 1739; he died Jl 13, 1792 after a short but
   painful illness and was buried in the churchyard; he married Ap 30, 1782
   Anna Rosina Paus (1:91,108), daughter of Christian and Magdalena (Frey)
   Paus; she was a Probationer O 17, 1784 and a Communicant Je 2, 1792.
   Issue: Elizabeth (1:170), born S 5, 1783; baptized S 7, 1783.
      Susanna (1:172), born My 29, 1785; baptized Je 5, 1785.
      Christina (1:174), born F 24, 1787 at 4-5 p.m.; baptized Mr 4,
         1787; married Jacob Christ.
      (Juliana (1:168b), born Je 19, 1789 at 4-5 a.m.; baptized Je 21,
         1789.
twins (Magdalena (1:168b,245), born Je 19, 1789 at 4-5 a.m.; baptized Je
         21, 1789; died Je 3, 1795 of smallpox; buried in the churchyard
         Je 4, 1795.
      Sarah (1:173b), born Ag 11, 1791 at 1 p.m.; baptized Ag 14, 1791;
         married Louis Matthews.
LEINBACH, Christina had an illegitimate son by John Dietrich Kranz.
LEINBACH, Friedrich (1:234), born Jl 15, 1703 in Hochstadt in Hanau; came to
   America in 1723; he married Je 2, 1737 Elizabeth _____ (1:233); she was
   born Je 2, 1717 and was baptized My 6, 1742 by the Reverend Mr. Jünger; he
   was a Probationer in 1742; she was admitted to Communion in 1742; theycame
   here from Oly in Ap, 1767; she died Je 5, 1783 after complaining of pain
   in the chest for a few days; she was buried in the churchyard Je 7, 1783;
   he died Jl 6, 1784 and was buried Jl 7, 1784. They were the parents of 17
   children, of whom 14 survived the mother and father; three of the surviv-
   ing children were Moravians:
      Christian, born F 13, 1739 at Skippack; died Jl 13, 1792; married
         Anna Rosina Paus.
      Jacob
      Johanna married Jacob Protzman.
LEINBACH, Jacob, son of Frederick and Elizabeth Leinbach.
   Issue: Elizabeth (1:163), born D 18(?), 1771 in the evening; baptized D
      29, 1771.
LEINBACH, Johanna Salome married Henry Frederick Schuman.
LEINBACH, Samuel married Maria Ditnermesser.
   Issue: Rebecca (1:208), born Je 20, 1809; baptized Jl 19, 1809.
      Samuel (1:217), born N 23, 1814; baptized F 22, 1815.
      Maria had an illegitimate daughter by Anthony Leiber.
LEINBACH, Sarah married Louis Matthews.
LENDY, John married Judith _____.
   Issue: Elizabeth (1:206), born Ap 22, 1808; baptized Jl 22, 1808.
LEONHART, Elizabeth married John Wohlfahrt.
LEWICK, John married Anna _____.
   Issue: Maria (1:221), born O 19, 1817; baptized Ja 18, 1818.
LEWIG, Maria married Samuel Eyler.
LICHTY, Catharine married Andrew Reidenour.
LICHTY, Sarah married David Manahan.
LIEBERKNIGHT, Lydia married Gerhard Beck.
LIENEFELDER, Nicholas, farmer, married Catharine Sauer.
   Issue: Emilie (1:193), born Ja 5, 1802; baptized F 27, 1802.

LIGGET, Dr. had by Mary Leidy an illegitimate daughter Juliana (1:95) who
was born Ag 2, 1837 and baptized S 18, 1838.
LILLIE, Richard married Elizabeth Garrison.
Issue: Maria (1:210), born Jl 2, 1809; baptized My 22, 1810.
LINGFELDER, Margaret married John Spengler.
LINGEFELDER, Nicholas married Elizabeth Cover.
Issue: Sarah (1:197), baptized D 11, 1803.
LITTLE, William (1:85), son of Peterand Elizabeth (Cover) Little; he married
My 4, 1830 Mary Ann Traxel (1:100 says Mary Ellen), daughter of Elias and
Sarah Traxel.
Issue: Maria Martha (1:96), born Ja 14, 1838; baptized F 1, 1839.
        Sarah Isabella (1:100), born Ja 30, 1840; baptized Ja 30, 1841.
        Martha Ellen (1:144), born Ja 14, 1831; baptized S 2, 1832.
LOCHMAN, Caspar married Juliana _____.
Issue: Jacob (1st son) (1:159), born Ja 24, 1765 at 11 p.m.; baptized Ja
        27, 1765.
LOCHMAN, Jacob; came to Maryland in 1752; married (1) Elizabeth Haffner.
Issue: Dorothea (1:244), born Jl 12, 1743 in Lancaster, Pennsylvania; died
        N 20, 1794; married Peter Brunner.
LOCHMAN, Jacob (1:226) married (2) in 1750 at Lancaster Maria Catharina
Dielforter who was originally Reformed; she was born Mr 15, 1715 at
Gernborn, duchy of Zweibrücken; she came to America in 1749; her first
husband was Engelhard Süssman q.v. They came to Maryland in 1752, and
joined the Moravians in 1757. She died Ja 13, 1788, having been helpless
from a stroke for two years, and was buried Ja 15, 1788; he died at 9 p.m.
F 13, 1764 in his 55th year, of pneumonia, and was buried F 15, 1764.
Issue: Jacob
        Magdalena
        Catharina
LOCHMAN, Jacob and Maria Catharine were Probationers Je 13, 1762 (1:91);
they were Communicants Ja 1, 1763 (1:107).
LOHR, Abraham (2:150) married Ag 10, 1848 Georgiana Stull.
Issue: William Albert (2:116), born Jl 11, 1849; baptized Jl 22, 1849.
        Anna McCaffry (2:242), born My 24, 1862; died Mr 29, 1866; buried
        Mr 30, 1866 at Apple's.
LOHR, Joseph N. (2:154) married Ag 17, 1856 Nancy A. M. Strawsbaugh.
LOHR, Mary married John Smith.
LONG, Daniel married Caroline Platt.
Issue: Francis Wellington (1:147), born Ag 30, 1833; baptized S 15, 1833.
LONG, Jacob (1:83), son of Daniel and Maria (Grimm) Long; he married D 28,
1827 Catharina Kieffer, daughter of Ludwig and Margaret (McDonnell)
Kieffer.
Issue: Jacob (1:142), born Je 2, 1831; baptized O 13, 1831.
LONG, John (1:86), son of Henry and Margaret Long, married S 20, 1831 Eliza-
beth Rau, daughter of John and Barbara Rau.
LONG, Nancy Ann married Peter Waldman.
LOT, Elizabeth married Henry Black.
LOY, Daniel Shattuck married Marian Jans (1:101 says Jansen).
Issue: Margaret Catharine (1:96), born Ap 16, 1836; baptized Ja 20, 1839.
        Mary Jane (1:96), born Ag 4, 1837; baptized Ja 20, 1839.
        William Henry (1:96), born N 28, 1838; baptized Ja 20, 1839.
        Calvin Wesley (1:101), born O 31, 1840; baptized Ag 22, 1841.
        Irving Washington (2:114), born S 8, 1846; baptized Ap 10, 1848.
        Zachariah Stewart (2:115), born Ap 15, 1848; baptized My 1, 1848.
LOY, Eve married John Schopp.
LOY, George married Louisa Sharrett.
Issue: Elizabeth Elweiry (1:222), born O 24, 1818; baptized Ap 1, 1819.
        Ezra Nathaniel (1:142), born D 3, 1830; baptized F 15, 1832.
        Catharine Margaret (1:144), born N 16, 1832; baptized F 6, 1833.

LOY, George married Lucy Shaddock.
Issue: Isaiah Frederic (1:137), born Mr 1, 1828; baptized Je 25, 1828.
LOY, George had by Susanna Sebastian an illegitimate son Frederick who was
    born Ap 15, 1809 and who was baptized O 22, 1809.
LOY, Mary (2:219), died My 24, 1850, aged about 88 years; she was buried My
    26, 1850.
LUCKENBACH, Elizabeth married Henry Eyler.
LUCKENBACH, John married Nancy Schenck.
Issue: David (1:221), born Ag 20, 1818; baptized O 11, 1818.
    Mary Anna (1:111), born D 14, 1818; baptized Jl 11, 1819.
    Johannes (1:117), born Jl 23, 1821; baptized S 9, 1821.
(The conflict in dates of birth of Mary Anna and David is not explained.)
LUCKENBACH, Margaret married Jacob Eyler.
LUGINSLAND, David married Catharine Weller (1:140).
LYNN, Ellen married John W. Martin.
LYNN, Isabella married George Ohler.
LYONS, William (2:223), son of Thomas and Maria Lyons; he was born S 15,
    1806 at Lancaster, Pennsylvania; he died F 8, 1854 and was buried F 10,
    1854; he married Elizabeth Reinly.
Issue: Margaret Emelina (1:147), born N 29, 1833; baptized My 18, 1834.
    Lewis (1:97), born Ag 27, 1835; baptized D 25, 1839.
    Priscilla (1:98), born Ja 8, 1838; baptized D 25, 1839.
    Francis (1:98; 2:226), born N 2, 1839; baptized D 25, 1839; died Ag
        16, 1855; buried Ag 18, 1855 at Graceham.
    Thomas (1:104), born Ap 26, 1841; baptized O 24, 1841.
    Elizabeth (2:41), born Ag 1, 1843; baptized S 10, 1843.
    Edward (2:112,222), born Ja 23, 1845; baptized Ap 13, 1845; died My
        5, 1853; buried My 6, 1853.
    Levi (2:113), born D 2, 1846; baptized F 14, 1847.

McCLAIN (McLANE), John married Susanna Harbaugh.
Issue: Hiram (1:141), born F 28, 1831; baptized My 1, 1831.
    Peter Elias (1:145), born D 2, 1832; baptized Mr 10, 1833.
    Simon (1:148), born S 23, 1834; baptized D 14, 1834.
    Joseph (1:151), born Je [26?], 1836; baptized Ag 21, 1836.
    John Franklin (1:96), born D 15, 1838; baptized F 10, 1839.
McCLAIN, Joseph married Susanna Eyler.
Issue: Susanna Elizabeth (1:95), born Jl 15, 1838; baptized Ag 26, 1838.
    Elias (1:98), born Mr 25, 1840; baptized My 17, 1840.
    Peter (1:101), born Ap 22, 1842; baptized Jl 10, 1842.
McCLAIN, Joseph married Susanna Goslen.
Issue: Mary (or Polly) married John Miller.
McCLAIN (McCLANE), Peter married Catharine Rau.
Issue: Julian[a] (1:104), born N 22, 1844; baptized My 14, 1843.
McCLAIN (McLANE), Peter married Elizabeth Harbaugh.
Issue: Catharine Anne (1:143), born Mr 23, 1832; baptized My 27, 1832.
    Isabella (1:146), born D 10, 1833; baptized F 8, 1834.
    Mary Jane (1:149), born O 13, 1835; baptized F 7, 1836.
McCLAIN, Peter married Nancy _____.
Issue: Harry Irwin (2:129), born Mr 2, 1867; baptized Jl 5, 1867.
    Elias Reuben (2:129), born D 1, 1865; baptized Jl 5, 1867.
McCLAIN (McCLANE), Susan married William Stem.
McCLEAVE, Robert of near Millerstown married Jane Hays.
Issue: Mary Ann (1:138), born O 7, 1828; baptized Je 21, 1829.
McDONALD, _____, in the Back Woods, married _____ Warning.
Issue: Susanna (1:267), born Mr --, 1795;) baptized by Schlegel
    Sarah (1:267), born My 20, 1797   ) on a trip to Cumberland
    Alexander (1:267), born My 4, 1799) and Bedford, Je 12, 1799.
McDONNELL, Margaret married Jacob Long.

McFEE, Elizabeth married Ignatius Brown.
McGINNESS (or McINNES), Mary Ann married Samauel Favorite.
McGUIGAN, James A. (2:158) of Mechanicstown married D 17, 1863 Maranda V.
Arthur, also of Mechanicstown.
McHENRY, Benjamin married Johanna _____.
Issue: Benjamin (1:174b), born Ja 29, 1791; baptized O 1, 1791.
McHENRY, Ellen married Frederick Frohlich.
McHENRY, Henry married Mary Otto (2:235); she was born S 14, 1791; she died
Mr 15, 1862 and was buried at Mechanicstown Mr 16, 1862.
Issue: Luke Tiernan Brien (1:141), born N 11, 1830; baptized Mr 27, 1831.
McKINEY, _____ married Laura Gaugh; she later married Amadeus Wilhide.
Issue: Nellie Myrtle (2:135), born F 20, 1872; baptized S 25, 1877.
McKINNEY, John married Hannah Moorhead.
Issue: John (1:122), born Jl --, 1825; baptized Ap 25, 1826.
McKISSIC (McKISY), William married Elizabeth _____.
Issue: Juliana (1:222), born Jl 30, 1818; baptized Ap 18, 1819.
William (1:120), born Ja 6, 1823; baptized Je 2, 1823.
McLAMEE, Francis married Mary _____.
Issue: Mary married John Key.
McLAMEE, Sarah married David Shealor.
McLANE, Elizabeth married James McMillan.
McMILLAN, James married Elizabeth McLane.
Issue: William Augustus (1:146), born Je 25, 1833; baptized O 20, 1833.
Joseph Washington (1:147), born Ag 3, 1834; baptized Ag 24, 1834.
McWILLIAMS, Sarah had an illegitimate son by Anthony Leiber.
McWILLIAMS, Sarah had an illegitimate son by David Gross.
McWILLIAMS, Sarah married Richard Lammerson.
MACK, Anna Rosina married John Frederick Schlegel.
MALONEY (MELONY), Jeremiah married Magdalena Moser, daughter of Leonard and
Elizabeth Moser.
Issue: Elizabeth (1:208), born Ap 24, 1809; baptized Je 7, 1809.
Sarah (1:211), born Ja 30, 1811; baptized Mr 31, 1811.
MANAHAN, Alfred married Jane _____.
Issue: George Willis Myers (2:128), born Ap 8, 1866; baptized Jl 1, 1866.
MANAHAN, David married Sarah Lichty.
Issue: Lewis (1:105), born My 23, 1841; baptized Ag 16, 1843.
Hiram (1:105), born S 14, 1842; baptized Ag 16, 1843.
Susan Elizabeth (1:106), born Ap 30, 1844; baptized Ag 4, 1844.
MANAHAN, James married Maria _____ (1:222 says Magdalena).
Issue: Henry (1:218), born Ag 1, 1815; baptized F 8, 1816.
David (1:220), born Mr 17, 1817; baptized Ag 31, 1817.
Barbara (1:222), born F 4, 1819; baptized Ap 18, 1819.
MANAHAN, Jonas married Sarah _____.
Issue: Margaret (1:218), born Je 1, 1815; baptized F 8, 1816.
Anna (1:221), born D 27, 1817; baptized Je 21, 1818.
MANAHAN, Rachel (or Regina) married John Williard.
MANAHAN, Samuel married Judith Eyler (2:32).
MARKER, Peter (2:154) married S 11, 1856 Rebecca Anna Eyler, daughter of
Frederic and Margaret (Williar) Eyler.
MARKS, Anna Maria married Jaocb Protzman.
MARTIN, Christian (1:130), son of David and Catharina Martin, married O 6,
1807 (or 1808) Maria Magdalena Willhide (2:197), daughter of John and
Maria Barbara (Weller) Willhide; she was born O 28, 1787 in Frederick
County; she died Mr 27, 1830 of a feminine illness, and was buried Mr 28,
1830.
Issue: Alice (1:206), born Mr 20, 1808; baptized My 1, 1808.
Jacob (1:209), born Ag 13, 1809; baptized S 10, 1809.
John (1:211), born Ag 27, 1810; baptized Mr 24, 1811.
David (1:217), born Ja 12, 1815; baptized Mr 12, 1815.

Maria (1:220), born My 2, 1817; baptized Je 15, 1817.
MARTIN, Daniel Ed (2:159) married Ag 30, 1866 Sarah M. Crouse.
MARTIN, David A. married Mary A. Baker.
Issue: Carrie Annie Mary (2:73), born Ag 2, 1880; baptized Ja 25, 1881.
MARTIN, Emanuel (1:86), son of David and Catherina (Ripley) Martin; he
    married F 15, 1831 Amy Doyle, daughter of Samuel Doyle.
Issue: Samuel (1:144), born S 16, 1831; baptized O 23, 1832.
MARTIN, Harriet married Martin Snyder.
MARTIN, Jacob (1:87), son of Christian and Maria Magdalena Martin, married F
    16, 1832 Matilda Jans, daughter of Henry and Catharine (Staufer) Jans.
MARTIN, Jeremiah (1:83), son of David and Catharina Martin, married O 25,
    1827 Mary Knauff, daughter of John and Catharina Knauff.
Issue: John David (1:138), born S 26, 1828; baptized Ap 4, 1829.
    Jacob William (1:141), born S 6, 1830; baptized F 21, 1831.
MARTIN, Jeremiah married Mary Jane _____.
Issue: William Milton (2:125), born N 7, 1859; baptized Mr 17, 1861.
    Minie Myrtle (2:128), born O 13, 1864; baptized F 11, 1865.
MARTIN, John W. (2:157) married F 3, 1863 Ellen Lynn.
MARTIN, Margaret married David Koons.
MARTIN, Margaret Ann Elizabeth married Jonathan Myers.
MARTIN, Mary married Sammy Ogle.
MARTIN, Sophia married John W. Deberry.
MARTIN, Susan married Daniel Krugs.
MARTIN, William married Mary Gurley.
Issue: Margaret Elizabeth (1:106), born Ag 16, 1843; baptized My 12, 1844.
MARTZ (MERTZ), Catharine married John Lefever.
MARTZ, Catharine married Peter Young.
MATTHEWS (MATTHES), _____ (1:134) married Polly Ehrhard, who later married
    Jonathan Shoff.
MATTHEWS, Elizabeth married (1) _____ Robinson and (2) Frederick Wilhide.
MATTHEWS, Jacob married Susan Beierle.
Issue: Mary Rosanna (1:142), born Je 26, 1831; baptized O 2, 1831.
MATTHEWS (MATTHÄUS), Louis (1:131), son of Philip Matthews; said Louis was
    born in Frederick County and married D 21, 1814 Sarah Leinbach who was
    born Ag 11, 1791 in Frederick County, the daughter of Christian and Anna
    Rosina (Paus) Leinbach; said Sarah was baptized Ag 14, 1791.
MEFFERT, John married Catharina Eyler (1:95,96).
MEFFERT, John (an illegitimate child) (1:131; 2:221,287,291), born F 9, 1790
    in Frederick County; he was a Communicant Ag 13, 1815; he died My 26,
    1852, aged about 62 years, and was buried My 27. He married My 4, 1812
    Catharine Eyler (2:218,287), daughter of Jonas and Regina Eyler; she was
    born Jl 4, 1791 in Frederick County; she was a Communicant Mr 26, 1812;
    she died S 20, 1847 and was buried S 22, 1847.
Issue: Anna Maria (1:214), born Mr 18, 1813; baptized Ap 3, 1813; married
    William Henry Boller.
    Amalia (1:217), born My 7, 1815; baptized Je 4, 1815; died of blood
    poisoning Ag 1, 1832; buried Ag 3, 1832.
    Theresia (2:200; 1:220), born Ap 10, 1817; baptized My 4, 1817;
    died Ap 7, 1832 of swelling of the knee; buried Ap 9, 1832.
    Rachel (1:222), born Mr 3, 1819; baptized Mr 21, 1819; she had
    illegitimate sons by Charles F. Boller and Israel Christ.
MEHRING, Anne married William Koontz.
MEISTER, Barbara married Casper Fordney.
MELCHER, Apollonia married Georg. Brunner.
MEREDITH, Simon married Mary Ann Schrieber.
Issue: Fenton Alonzo (1:151), born My 27, 1836; baptized Ag 31, 1836.
    Mary Florilla (1:100), born S 11, 1840; baptized N 3, 1840.
    Lydy Elisabeth (1:104), born F 21, 1843; baptized Je 5, 1843.
    Alpheus Havanton (2:115), born Ap 5, 1846; baptized Je 2, 1846.

Veniah Theophilus (2:116), born My 31, 1849; baptized Jl 22, 1849.
William Norris Shriver (2:120), born Mr 2, 1854; baptized My 21, 1854.
MERIK, Joseph married Susanna Sebastian.
Issue: Marianna (1:218), born Ap 18, 1815; baptized S 17, 1815.
MERKEN, Henry, farmer, married Elizabeth Margaret Kuhn.
Issue: Elizabeth Margaret (1:190), born S 29, 1800; baptized N 21, 1800.
MERKLY, Henry married Lydia Stauffer.
Issue: William Elias (1:94), born N 2, 1837; baptized D 18, 1837.
MERKLY, Catharine married Reuben Ginnivan.
METCALFE, G. Charles (2:231), born Ja 13, 1841; died Ap 14, 1858; buried Ap 15 at Lewistown.
METCALFE (MEDCALFE), Martha married Frederic Stauffer.
METZ, John Jacob, potter and farmer, married Philippina or Peppina Devis (1:200 says Phoebe); she was baptized Ag 13, 1804 when an adult (1:198).
Issue: Salome (1:200), baptized Ap 28, 1805.
John Jacob (1:203), born N 14, 1806; baptized Ja 5, 1807.
Benjamin (1:203), born N 14, 1806; baptized Ja 5, 1807.
Rebecca (1:208), born D 8, 1808; baptized Ap 3, 1809.
MILHOUSE, Margaret married Jacob Leidy.
MILLER, _____ married Anna Kunigunda Wilman (1:151,152).
MILLER, _____ married Sarah Grim (1:136).
MILLER, Ann Eliza (2:247), born Ag 17, 1811; died O 1, 1871; buried O 3, 1871 in Haugh's cemetery.
MILLER, Anna Maria married Richard Waggeman.
MILLER, Barbara married Samuel Rogers.
MILLER (MÜLLER), Catharine married Henry Ricksecker.
MILLER, Catharine married John Philip Kranz.
MILLER, Catharine married Lorentz Williard.
MILLER, Charles (2:245), member of the United Brethren Church; died F 16, 1869; aged 59 years 10 months and 8 days; buried at Otterbein Chapel F 18, 1869.
MILLER, Edward married Susan, née Miller.
Issue: John Henry (2:131), born My 17, 1870; baptized S 25, 1870.
MILLER, Elizabeth married James Davis.
MILLER (MÜLLER), Elizabeth married Peter Williar.
MILLER, Elizabeth married William Ward.
MILLER, Elizabeth Catharine married John George Rauch.
MILLER, Elizabeth Margaret married Fredericc Hartman.
MILLER, Eve Elizabeth married Jacob Adam.
MILLER, Frederick married Elizabeth [Wesner?].
Issue: John (1:106), born S 5, 1843; baptized N 26, 1843.
MILLER, Frederic had by Mary Ann Cover an illegitimate daughter Anna Lavinia (1:141) who was born Jl 5, 1831 and baptized S 6, 1831.
MILLER, George (2:158) married Ag 23, 1863 Sarah M. Wilhide.
MILLER, Henry married Margaretha Miller.
Issue: Peter Wilhelm (1:151), born Ag 13, 1836; baptized S 18, 1836.
MILLER, Jacob, near the Furnace, married Nancy _____.
Issue: Charles (2:45), born Je 5, 1848; baptized Mr 28, 1849.
MILLER, Jacob (1:84), son of John Peter and Sarah Miller, married D 25, 1828 Anne Roxbury, daughter of William Roxbury.
MILLER, Jacob married Rebecca _____.
Issue: Elizabeth Moorhead (1:121), born F 19, 1822; baptized O 29, 1824.
George Clevedian (1:121), born My 29, 1824; baptized O 29, 1824.
MILLER, Dr. James married Catharine _____.
Issue: Jessy Catharine (2:122), born F 24, 1856; baptized Ag 9, 1856.
Ida Eichelberger (2:122), born F 24, 1856; baptized Ag 9, 1856.
MILLER, John, farmer, in the mountains (1:133), son of Friedrich and Marian (Kuhn) Miller; he was born in Frederick County Mr 17, 1791; he married Ja

66

2, 1820 Mary or Polly McClain, daughter of Joseph and Susanna (Goslen) McClain, who was born in Frederick County F 27, 1801.
Issue: Mary Levinnia (1:112), born N 13, 1819; baptized Ja 2, 1820.
Hiram Ely (1:146), born Ag 29, 1832; baptized S 22, 1833.
Elizabeth Jane (1:149), born N 13, 1834; baptized F 7, 1836.
Thomas Jefferson (1:98), born S 10, 1837; baptized Ja 25, 1840.
Washington Monroe (1:98), born D 5, 1839; baptized Ja 25, 1840.
MILLER, John, son of John Peter Miller, married May Ann Busk.
Issue: Leah Ann Sarah (1:139), born Mr 18, 1829; baptized O 18, 1829.
MILLER, Levi O. (2:164) married Ja 15, 1880 Elizabeth J. Shingledecker.
MILLER, Magdalena married Daniel Eyster.
MILLER, Martha married Franklin Amadeus Colliflower.
MILLER, Mary Ann married Leonard C. Harbaugh.
MILLER, Minerva Ann married Levi Harbaugh.
MILLER (MÜLLER), Peter married Sarah _____.
Issue: Andreas (1:221), born My 27, 1818; baptized Jl 31, 1818.
MILLER (MÜLLER), Sarah married John Benhoff.
MILLER, Susan married John Henry Washington Wilhide.
MILLER, Susanna married John Beierle.
MILLER (MÜLLER), Susanna married Samuel Wilhide.
MILLER, William (2:155), of Frederick County, married N 4, 1856 Mary E. Bush.
MILLER, William Theodore married Elizabeth Krause.
Issue: William Clarence (2:133), born Ag 8, 1874; baptized O 6, 1874.
MOEHRING, George (married) had by Elizabeth Moyer (single), daughter of Jacob and Rachel Moyer, an illegitimate daughter Julian[a] (1:99) who was born My 29, 1840 and baptized Je 14, 1840.
MÖLLER, John Ludwig, potter (1:252-253), son of Joseph and ____ (Ziegler) Möller; he was born at Friedensthal in Pennsylvania My 23, 1752; he married at Littitz My 31, 1784 Gertrude Protzman; he died Mr 24, 1800 and was buried in the churchyard Mr 26, 1800.
Issue: Charles
       Elizabeth
       Louisa
       Catharina

John Ludwig Möller's parents placed him first in the 'Nurserey' at old Nazareth, then in the Anstalt at Bethlehem, whence in 1757 he was removed with the whole Anstalt to Nazareth Hall. Transferred 1761 to the Boy's Choir at Christiansbrunn. Thence he went with a colony of men and boys to Wachovia, arriving N 2 at Bethabara; the youngest in the company, the trip was very hard on him. Apprenticed to Br. Aust to learn the potter's trade, on his own request. In 1769 when they began to build Salem he went there with his master; a Probationer in his 18th year.

John Ludwig Möller (1:252-253)
"Meine 1. Eltern thaten mich erst in die damalige Nurserey nach alt Naz. u. darauf in die Anstalt nach Bethlm von wo ich im Jahr 1757 mit der ganzen Anstalt nach Naz: Hall versetzt wurde. Ich hatte hier von Innen u. Aussen oft selige Zeiten, verdarb ir aber solche dh. meinen Ungehorsam gegen den Hld u. meine Brüder; Ja ihre Worte: dass ein solches einmal zu Hause kommen wurde ist nachhero reichlich in die Erfüllung gegangen u. hat mir gar manche Thränen ausgepresst, bes: da ich ohne hinn immer mehr Lust zum Bösen als Guten empfand. Da ich 1761 schon nach Christiansbrun ins Knaben Chor versetzt wurde, bildete ich nur ein, nun recht viel Freyheit zu gniessen, allein ich empfand gerade das Gegentheil, denn ich hatte bey allem Schlecht seyn dennoch keine Ruhe im Herzen. Nach einige Zeit reiste ich in Gesellschaft eine Colonne Knaben u Brüder nach der Wachau u. kam den 2 ten. Nov. daselbst an in Bethabara, da ich der Jüngste in der

Gesellschaft war u. wir den Weg zu Fusse machten, so war die Reise für
mich höchst beschwerlich. Nach meiner eignen Wahl wurde ich zu Bruder.
Aust gethan das Töpferhandwerk zu erlernen, welches mich aber in der
Folge, da iches schwehr hatte sehr reuete. Mit meiner Bekehrung sah es
damals schlecht aus, ob ich wol oft dran dachte so blieb doch der Hang zur
Sünde u. Welt stärker in mir als mich dem Hld. zu ergeben. Ich lebte in
meinen eigenem Sinn dahin, fragte nicht Viel nach Gott u. Menschen; Ja
mein Herze wurde immer verstockter u. zwar so, dass ich nicht mehr Glauben
wolte u. konte, dass ein Gott sey. Da 1769 der Gem: Ort Salem zu bauen
angefangen wurde zog ich gleich fabs mit meinem Meister dahin. Verschied-
ene Versaml. u. wir auch besondre Unglücksfälle, bes: einen da ich lange
Zeit alles bewusst seyn Verloren hatte lies mir der Hld. zur zuen u
gründln. Anfassung für mein Herz dienen, so dass ich seine Treue Hand die
über mich elen den hielt, deutl. erkennen konnte Nichts desto weniger aber
schlug ich alle diese Heimsuchung in den Wind u. resolvirte sogar von der
Gem: zu gehen, welches ich auch wie wolunter grosser Angst des Herzens aus
Fichote, u. erst da ich dh eine hitzige Krankheit ganzherunter gebracht,
kam ich auf mein Bitten wieder Elend an Leib u. Seele in die Gem. zurück.
Ich ward vorher in meinem 18 Jahr in die Gem: aufgenommen, welches mich
ebenfalls in ein tiefes Nachdenken über meinen Zustand versetzte. Ich
wolte gern des Hlds Eigenthum seyn, aber doch auch der Sünde nicht absa-
gen, u. dieses men geschlagtes Leben endritte ich auch sollest meinem
Arbeite nicht, bis ich in einem Zustand der Verzweifel an ein Wasser, wo
es am tiefaten v. das Ufer am höchsten war, ging um mich zu ertränken,
wovon mich aber eine Stäotree Hand 3 mal zurükke heilt v. zwar das letzte
mal so deutl. als hörte ich eine Stimme, die zu mir spreche: was machst
der w. als wen mich Jemand fest hielte, v. daich mich nun doch allein
ssahe, warf ich mich hin zv Jesu Füssen u. hörte nicht auf zu Worgen bis
mir das Trost- Wort ins Herz schalte: Sey Getrost mein Sohn; deine Sünded
sind dir Vergeben, u. getrost noch Hause gehen u. mich meinem Arbeite
kindl. andritten konnte. 1780 d. 29t Aug genoss ich zum erstenmal Jesv
Leib u. Blut in Aben. Was ich da genossen kann ich nicht in worte brin-
gen. Jezo kannte ich erst meinen Hld dem ich so lange aus dem Weg gegangen u. der mich nun vor des Teufels Ketten erlöset hatte. 1782 in Aug.
reiste ich nach Pensylvanien, kam d. 15 ten in Bethlehem an u. zog darauf
nach Hope mich auf mein Handwerk einzurichten."

        In 1793 he came here to Graceham with his family and plied his
trade.   He was sick for several years, which inclined him toward the
Savior.   About 4 weeks before he died he developed an asthmatic condition.

MONDSHOUR (MONTSCHAUER), John married Sarah Smith; he died F 11, 1853, aged
76 years 2 months and 6 days; he is buried in Biggs's graveyard beyond
Monocacy, internment taking place F 12, 1853.
    Issue: Henry (1:113), born D 21, 1819; baptized Jl 2, 1820.
        Catharine married Jacob Favorite.
MONN, Anna Maria married Henry Demuth.
MOORHEAD, Hannah married John McKinney.
MORE, Jane married William Jordan.
MORE, John, farmer, married Sarah Dear.
    Issue: Nancy (1:194), born Ag 4, 1802; baptized O 3, 1802.
MOREHEAD, Mrs Hannah married John Rodeneiser.
MOREHEAD, Samuel married Mary Am. _____.
    Issue: William Israel (2:128), born Mr 12, 1866; baptized Jl 1, 1866.
MOREHEAD, William, shoemaker, married Hannah Wilhide.
    Issue: George Washington (1:116), born F 22, 1821; baptized My 25, 1821.
MORGENSTERN, Anna Barbara married Jacob Holtz.
MORGENSTERN, Catharine married Henry Wilhide.

MORGENSTERN, Philip, farmer, married Salome Morgenstern.
Issue: Susanna (1:192), born Je 15, 1801; baptized Ag 16, 1801.
MOSER, Anna Catharine (2:253), born Ap 11, 1847; died O 10, 1876 at Catoctin
Furnace; buried O 11, 1876.
MOSER, Catharine Lavina (2:231), born D 14, 1857; died Ap 17, 1858; buried
Ap 18, 1858 at Apple's Church.
MOSER, Cyrus, of Mechanicstown (2:149; 1:117), son of John and Hannah Ruth
(McWilliams) Moser; he was born D 22, 1821; he married D 23(?), 1845 Susan
Heffner.
Issue: Agnes Savanah (2:55), born Ag 2, 1860; baptized Ag 10, 1860.
Phoebe Ann (2:115), born My 10, 1846; baptized Je 2, 1846.
Ruth Ann Amelia (2:120,223), born Ja 14, 1854; baptized F 16, 1854;
died F 17, 1854; buried at Apple's Church F 18, 1854.
Charles Cyrus (2:126), born Ap 20, 1863; baptized Jl 31, 1863.
MOSER, John married Hannah Ruth McWilliams (1:217); she was baptized Je 26,
1815 (adult).
Issue: David (1:205), born F 4, 1808; baptized Ap 24, 1808.
John (1:209), born S 29, 1809; baptized N 12, 1809.
Amy (1:213), born Mr 25, 1812; baptized My 31, 1812.
William (1:216), born My 7, 1814; baptized D 26, 1814.
Thomas (1:220), born N 18, 1816; baptized Mr 16, 1817.
Cyrus (1:117), born D 22, 1821; baptized Ap 7, 1822; married Susan
Heffner.
Mary Ann (1:120), born Ja 24, 1824; baptized Ja 27, 1824.
MOSER, Leonard, farmer, married Elizabeth Schenkel or Schenkler (Lutherans).
Issue: Christian (4th son) (1:167b), born D 22, 1787; baptized D 27, 1787.
Margaret (1:185), born D 24, 1797; baptized Ja 21, 1798.
Sophia Theresa (1:195), born D 25, 1802; baptized D 30, 1802;
married Jonas Nathanael Eyler.
Elizabeth Christina (1:200), born S 7, 1805; baptized O 20, 1805;
married David Wilhide.
Elias (1:208), born F 24, 1809; baptized Ap 23, 1809.
Magdalena married Jeremiah Maloney.
MOSER, Leonard, farmer, baptized Mr 5, 1820; a Communicant Ag 12, 1821;
married Lydia Anna Wolfart (1:112; 2:287) who was aborn D 25, 1794 and
baptized Mr 5, 1820; a Communicant Mr 30, 1820.
Issue: Anna Margaret (1:213), born My 15, 1812; baptized Ag 2, 1812; had
an illegitimate son by William Brown.
Lyvina (1:216), born N 12, 1814; baptized D 26, 1814.
Henry (1:221), born O 20, 1817; baptized Mr 15, 1818.
Daniel (1:112), born Mr 31, 1820; baptized My 21, 1820.
Frederick Arnold (2:1,187), born D 31, 1822; baptized Ja 2, 1823;
died Ja 4, 1823; buried Ja 5, 1823.
Angelina (2:6), born Jl 14, 1825; baptized S 4, 1825.
Sarah Elizabeth (2:15), born Je 17, 1829; baptized Ag 23, 1829.
Leonard Ephraim (2:23), born My 7, 1833; baptized Ag 18, 1833.
MOSER, Leonard, junior, had by Magdalena Hahn an illegitimate son Leonard
(1:208) who was aborn Ap 12, 1809 and baptized Je 8, 1809.
MOSER, Leonhard married Sara _____.
Issue: John Michael (1:155), born Ag 1, 1759 at 2:30 a.m.; baptized Ag 5,
1759.
Samuel (1:156), born Ap 11, 1761; baptized Ap 12, 1761.
Francis (1:157), born Mr 15, 1763 at 9 a.m.; baptized Mr 17, 1763.
Christian (1:159), born Ja 5, 1765 at 11 p.m.; baptized Ja 6, 1765.
Anna Elizabeth (1:160), born Ja 30, 1767 at 8 a.m.; baptized F 1,
1767.
Henry (1:162), born S 12, 1769 in the afternoon; baptized S 17,
1769.

69

Joseph (1:163,230), born Jl 21, 1772 at 8 a.m.; baptized Jl 26, 1772; died Ap 17, 1773; buried in the churchyard Ap 18, 1773.
MOSER, Leonard; a Communicant O 8, 1758 (1:107).
MOSER, Maria Sarah, wife [of Leonard?]; she was a Probationer O 8, 1758 (1:91), and a Communicant Ja 11, 1761 (1:107).
MOSER, Magdalena (Mrs. Melony) had an illegitimate son by Jacob Wilhide.
MOSER, Michael.
Issue: John (1st son) (1:172), born Ag 16, 1784 at 1 a.m.; baptized Ap 27, 1785.
MOSER, Susanna (daughter of Anna Catharine Herzog) had an illegitimate son by Joseph Alfred Wilhide.
MOSER, W. H. (2:162), of Catoctin, married Mr 2, 1875 Mary Nolligen, also of Catoctin.
MOYER, Elizabeth (daughter of Jacob and Rachel) had an illegitimate daughter by George Moehring.
MÜCKE, Michael of Lititz (2:208) married Lydia Harry, daughter of Isaac Renatus and Maria Barbara (Feiser) Harry. Michael and Lydia (Harry) Mücke were the parents of three children.
MUMFORD, William married Susanna Dick.
Issue: Mary Ann Elizabeth (1:135), born F 20, 1827; baptized Jl 28, 1827; the sponsor was old Mrs. Elizabeth Dick.
MUMMA, Jacob R. of Hagerstown (2:149), married Ap 7, 1846 Catharine Ann Stull of Frederick County.
MUSGROVE, Stephen married Sarah Pfantz.
Issue: James Stephen (1:122), born D 13, 1825; baptized O 13, 1826.
MUTSCHLER, Sophia married John Henry Sowers.
MYERS (MEYER), _____ married Catharine Maus.
Issue: Catharine married George Zollinger.
MYERS, Elizabeth (2:223), born Je 10, 1773; died O 19, 1853; buried at Creagerstown O 20, 1853.
MYERS (MEYER), Elizabeth married Daniel Raudenbusch.
MYERS (MEYERS), John married Maria Elizabeth _____.
Issue: Maria Elizabeth (1:121), born O 19, 1824; baptized N 2, 1824.
twins (Joseph (1:122), born Ap 30, 1826; baptized Ap 30, 1826.
(Delila (1:122), born Ap 30, 1826; baptized Ap 30, 1826.
MYERS, Jonathan (2;155) married D 2, 1858 Margaret Ann Elizabeth Martin.
MYERS (MEYERS), Jonathan married Margaret Souther.
Issue: Margaret (1:267), born D 10, 1798; baptized Je 12, 1799 by Schlegel on a trip to Cumberland and Bedford.
MYERS, Joseph Martin (2:235), born F 21, 1861; died Ap 26, 1862; buried Ap 27, 1862 at Mechanicstown.
MYERS (MEIER), Maria married Adam Eyler.

NAFE, Henry married Lizzie _____.
Issue: Samuel Thomas (2:134), born Ag 1, 1870, baptized O 24, 1875.
NAGEL, John (2:240), born D 25, 1802; married Sophia Harbaugh; he died Ap 17, 1864 and was buried Ap 18, 1864 in Harbaugh Valley.
Issue: Thomas Jefferson (1:100), born N 4, 1840; baptized Ja 24, 1841.
William Henry (1:104), born Mr 13, 1843; baptized Je 11, 1843.
NALE (or NAIL), Theodore L. married Amanda O. Boller.
Issue: William Theodore (2:68), born O 22, 1874; baptized Je 8, 1875.
Odie Edith (2:70), born Jl 22, 1876; baptized S 2, 1877.
Lulu Edna (2:73), born Ag 1, 1880; baptized Ja 18, 1881.
NELSON, Rosa L. married John J. Davis.
NEWCOMER, George Samuel (2:159) married, by a Reformed minister, on N 7, 1867 Lilly Ann Hesser of Graceham.
Issue: Carrie Emma (2:63), born O 1, 1868; baptized My 21, 1869.
Howard Clayton (2:66), born -- -- ----; baptized (1872?).
NEWCOMER, Mary Jane married George Reuben Witmer.

NEWCOMER, Tobias of Graceham (2:163) married Ja 17, 1878 Sarah Troxel of
     near Emmittsburg.
NEWMAN, Eliza Susan married George Jacob Hesser.
NEWMAN, Mary E. married Charles F. Heitshew.
NIPPLE, John married Frances Welty.
     Issue: John Elias (2:134), born S 16, 1873; baptized Ja 20, 1876.
          Charles Francis (2:134), born My 28, 1875; baptized Ja 20, 1876.
NITSCHMAN, Susanna married Philip William Boller.
NOLLIGEN, Mary married W. H. Moser.
NORRIS, Edward O. [or P.], son of Edward and Rebecca Norris; he was born My
     27, 1815; he married Jl 5, 1838 Sarah Six (previously married to _____
     Fries); she was born Ap 18, 1816, the daughter of Philip and Isabella Six.
NULL, Elizabeth married John Williard.
NULL, Margaret Randolph married James Robinson.

OEHME, Catharine Elizabeth married John Smith.
OGLE, Benjamin (1:86), son of Ssamuel and Mary Ogle, married F 21, 1831
     Catharine Knauff, daughter of John and Catharine Knauff.
OGLE, Benjamin married Rebecca _____.
     Issue: Peter Stilly (1st son) (1:168), born O 18, 1779 in the evening;
          baptized D 3, 1779.
          Aron (1:168), born F 12, 1781; baptized F 23, 1781; died F 25,
          1781; buried in the churchyard F 26, 1781.
          Eli (1:170), born Jl 23, 1783; baptized Ag 3, 1783.
OGLE, Elizabeth married George Devilbiss.
OGLE, James.
     Issue: Mary (2nd daughter) (1:173), born F 18, 1786 at 4 p.m.; baptized F
          19, 1786; died F 19, 1786 at 3 p.m.
OGLE (OGEL), James, junior, farmer, married Elizabeth Ogel.
     Issue: James (1:188), born N 6, 1799; baptized N 11, 1799; died N 11,
          1799.
OGLE (OCLE), John, farmer, in the neighborhood, married Susanna Thomas.
     Issue: Catharine Matilda (1:113), born Ag 26, 1820; baptized S 23, 1820.
OGLE, Joseph married Elizabeth Valentine (Wallenthein).
     Issue: Maria (1:211), born N 15, 1810; baptized D 5, 1810.
          Margaret Sibilla (1:213), born My 21, 1812; baptized Je 11, 1812.
[OGLE? - (name blotted)], Joseph had by Margaret Krieger an illegitimate
     child Zephaniah (1:217) who was born D 19, 1814 and baptized Ap 23, 1815.
OGLE, Sammy, farmer, son of _____ and Maria _____. He married Mary
     Martin.
     Issue: (One of the grandmothers was Mary, née Biggs.)
          Mary (1:195), born N 15, 1802.
          Eme (1:202), born Ag 2, 1805; baptized Je 26, 1806.
OGLE, Thomas married Maria Beierle.
     Issue: Maria (1:205), born F 1, 1808; baptized Ap 7, 1808.
          Minerva Sibilla (1:211), born Ag 2, 1810; baptized D 9, 1810.
OHLER, Elisa married Benjamin Biggs, Esquire.
OHLER, George (2:153) married Ja 31, 1854 Isabella Lynn.
     Issue: Joshua Franklin (2:120), born D 7, 1853; baptized Ja 31, 1854.
ORR, Juliana married Joseph Wilson Biggs (M.D.).
OSLER, Anna married John Yingling.
OTT, Jacob married Susan Eyler.
     Issue: John Milton (2:245), died My 29, 1869, aged 11 years and 3 1/2
          months; buried at Otterbein Chapel My 31, 1869.
OTTO, Mary married Henry McHenry.
OTTO, Susanna married Joseph Krieger.
OVELMAN, Sarah married Joseph Kuhn.

71

PAGET, Richard married Mary Weller.
Issue: Robert Jacob (1:146), born Jl 26, 1833; baptized N 2, 1833.
PALMER, George.
Issue: Marietta (2:222), died My 21, 1853, aged 7-8-29; buried at Apple's Church My 22, 1853.
PARK(S), George (2:143,227), of Mechanicstown, born Jl 2, 1790 at Burnt Cabin, Pennsylvania; he was a Communicant Ag, 1849; he died Ap 17, 1856 and buried at Graceham Ap 18, 1856; he was a widower when he married Elizabeth Süss (2:218,287) on O 21, 1823; she was the daughter of Godfrey Süss, tanner and Anna Maria (Krämer); she was born My 8, 1793; she was a Communicant Mr 30, 1820; she died F 11, 1849 and was buried F 13, 1849.
Issue: Beata (2:191), stilborn D 15, 1824; buried same day.
      Hiram Alexander Shoke (2:9), born N 16, 1826; baptized Mr 10, 1827.
      Edward Jeremiah (2:13,293), born Ag 18, 1828 in Frederick County; baptized D 16, 1828.
      Jerome Hilary (2:16,224,293), born Ag 22, 1829; baptized D 10, 1829; died on the railroad Mr 7, 1854, aged 24-6-14; buried at Graceham Mr 9, 1854.
      son (2:198), stillborn O 27, 1830; buried same day.
      Wicliffe Hamilton (2:22,201), born S 28, 1832; baptized O 25, 1832; died O 29, 1832; buried O 30, 1832.
      Victor Amadeus (2:27,208), born Ja 22, 1835; baptized Ja 24, 1835; died Ja 25, 1835; buried Ja 26, 1835.
PARK, Hiram A. married Anna Maria Rheam.
Issue: Charles Augustus (2:120), born Jl 20, 1850; baptized Ag 16, 1854.
      Francis Edward (2:120), born Jl 15, 1854; baptized Ag 16, 1854.
      Orlean Melissa (2;123), born D 29, 1856; baptized O 12, 1858.
      James Ulysses (2:55), born N 13, 1858; baptized N 28, 1859.
PARRISH, Catharine Ellen married William Stoner.
PARRISH (PARISH), Elizabeth Jane married William E. Shriner.
PATTERSON, Elizabeth married George Zimmerman.
PATTERSON, Jane married (1) _____ Eckman and (2) Jacob Wise.
PATTERSON, John married Ann _____.
Issue: Jane married (1) _____ Eckman and (2) Jacob Wise.
PATTERSON, Lilli married Michael Zimmerman.
PAUL, Henry married Rosina Gump.
Issue: William Henry (2:14), born Ja 1, 1829; baptized Ap 12, 1829.
PAUS, Christian (or Christoph), (1:248-250), born O 5, 1710 in Bergord, Lower Hungary; his father died when he was one year old; he married at Bethlehem in 1745 Magdalena Frey (1:246-247), who was born Ap 22, 1710 at Falkner Swamp; she died Ja 11, 1797 and was buried in the churchyard Ja 13, 1797. They were the parents of five sons and four daughters; two sons and two daughters survived both.
Issue: John (1:240), born at Falkner Swamp F 27, 1761; died N 20, 1791 of colic pains; buried in the churchyard N 22, 1791.
      Anna Rosina married Christian Leinbach.

CHRISTOPH PAUS: Ich bin geboren d. 5t. Oct. 1710 zu Bergord in Nieder Ungarn. Mein Vater starb, als ich 1 Jahr alt war. In meinem 13ten Jahr brachte mich meine Mutter nach Oedenburg zu einer ledigen adelichen. Frauensperson für einen Aufwärter, wo ich es sehr gut im äussern hatte. Als ich 15 Jahr alt war, that mich meine Mutter zu einem Schuhmacher in die Lehre Nach 3 Jahren ging ich auf die Wanderschafft. In Dresden krigte ich das kalte ich das kalte Fieber. Nach dem ich mich erholt hatte, wollte ich die gerade Strasse nach Schlesien gehen; die gute Hand Gottes führte mich aber ins Gebirge nach Hirschberg. Als ich die Stadt vor mir saahe, musste ich weinen, ohne recht zu wissen, warum ? Ich krach unter eine Brüche u. weinte mich recht satt. Darauf kam ich in der Stadt zu einem Meister in Arbeit, dessen Sohn erweckt war. Ich handelte nach

meiner wilden Art, wie ich gewohnt war. Der Sohn meines Meisters sagte
mir: Du kommst nicht im Himmel! Ich dachte, das will ich bald ausfinden,
ging auf meine Schlafkammer, kniete nieder u. saagte: Lieber Gott! Mein
Geselle hat mir gesagt, ich sey nicht auf dem rechten Wege: offenbare mirs
doch. Ich wurde von Stund an unruhig über mich u. wollte mir selber
helfen, es wurde aber immer ärger. Wenn ich früh aufstund, nahm ich mir
vor mich zu bessern, u. wenn ich mich des Abends untersuchte, so ward es
nur noch schlimmer. Es hiesst bey mir: gib dich als einen armen Sünder
dem Heilende Jesu hin! Das verstand ich nicht recht; ich sagte: ich habe
ja nicht gestohlen oder todtgeschlagen. Ich fasste wieder neue Vorsätze
fromm zu werden aber immer vergebens. Ich wollte mich selber gut machen,
denn ich sahe wol, das ich ein böser Mensch sey, glaubte aber, als ein
solcher zu Gott nicht naher zu dürfen. Das währte so Sange, bis meine
Unruhe zu gross wurde u. ich mich als ein Sünder dem Herrn Jesu hingab.
Da krigte ich Gnade von Ihn; ich wurde losgemacht von der Sclaverey der
Sünde, u. konnte Ihn mit freudigem Herzen als meinen Heiland u. Versöhner
anbeten. O was hatte ich da für selige Zeiten! Ich erfuhr es: wo Verge-
bung der Sünden ist, da ist auch Leben u. Seligkeit. Die Liebe Gottes
wurde durch den Heil. Geist in mein Herz ausgegossen. In diesem Zustand
krigte ich einen Cameraden aus Sachsen, der gleiche Gnade erfahren hatte
u. wir hatten ein recht seliges Leben zusammen. Wir hörten dass besondere
Leute in Sachsen wohnten u. resolvirten, sie aufzusuchen. In Görlitz
nahmen wir Arbeit, u. als wir nach den besondren Leuten fragten, wiess man
uns nach Herrnhut, wo wir nun auch besuchten: wir würden brüderl. aufgenommen. Es war eben Sonntag. In der Predigt wurde mein Herz gleich mit
der gemeine verbunden. Nach einiger Zeit fand sich in Görlitz eine Socie-
taet von 13 erweckten Personen zusammen, die alle Sonnabendeine Versamm-
lung hatten. Der liebe heiland bekannte sich dazu u. wir waren wie Ein
Herz u. Eine Seele. Im jahr 1734 wurde denen Schwenkfeldern vom König
Ordre ertheilt, das Land zu räumen u. wir hatten unsere Versammlungen bey
einem Schwenkfelder, Names Wigener. Dieser zog fort u. unser Versammlungs
Ort ward da durch aufgehoben. Mir wurde es so mit Wigener nach Pennsyl-
vanien zu gehen. Wir wendeten uns deswegen an die Brüder nach Herrnhut,
die uns zu unserm Fortkommen behülflich waren. Wir reisten über Ebersdorf
nach Holland, gingen in Rotterdam zu Schiffe u. langten im Sept. 1734 in
Philadelphia an. In Schippack, wo sich mehrere aus Europa zusammen gefun-
den hatten, u. Br. Spangenberg bey uns war, hatten wir eine gemeinschaft-
liche Haushaltung u. ein Recht seeliges Leben.

Afterwards he was a Probationer, later a Communicant, at Bethlehem. They
stayed for a time at Bethlehem and Gnadenhütten, served in the Oeconomie,
but lost heart, left the Church and went to live in Falkner's Swamp for 20
years. Afterwards in various places and finally here where they joined
our church.

He enjoyed tolerably good health until about five years ago, but spent the
winters mostly in bed, as he could no longer stand the cold. He was
paralyzed in July, 1796 and bedridden ever since and had to be waited on
like a child. His demeanor was quiet, however, and he loved to recall the
past, often expressing with tears his regret that he had been a backsli-
der. After his wife's death he was taken to the home of his daughter,
Sister Leinbach, in Graceham. She [his wife] felt the effects of age for
a long time, but continued to care for her bedridden husband until May,
1796 when she began to have gouty attacks all over the body and she was
confined to her bed.

PAUS, Henry (2:211), born N 1, 1745 at Falkner Swanp; he served in the
Revolution; he was a Communicant Ap 15, 1824; he died D 31, 1839 and was
buried Ja 1, 1840.

PAUS, Susanna Verona (1:243), born Ja 16, 1768 at Falkner Swamp; she died My 13, 1794 and was buried My 14, 1794.

PEARL, John (2:151) married S 1, 1850 Elizabeth Haspelhorn.

PEARL, Sarah married John Howard.

PEIZEL, Henry (died 1786) married Juliana Wottring (1:260), daughter of John Daniel and Anna Maria (Rebmann) Wottring; she was born Ag 24, 1746 in York County, Pennsylvania; she had been previously married to Philip Weller; she died S 10, 1803 and was buried S 11, 1803.
Issue: John Henry (1:170), born My 13, 1783; baptized My 24, 1783.
        another child.

PEIZEL, Henry.
Issue: Louise (1:227); died S 5, 1769, aged 12; buried in the churchyard S 6, 1769.
        Catharina (1:227), died S 16, 1769, aged 16; buried in the churchyard S 18, 1769.

PERKING, Joseph (1:261), son of John and Anna (Doton) Perking; he was born in England in Ja, 1738; came to America about 1776; lived at Harper's Ferry; he married twice - first to _____ _____ and second to Maria Wilhelmina Heumann; he died D 1, 1806 and was buried D 4, 1806.
Issue: Mary; died Ap 23, 1805; married to _____ Humes.
        two other children.

PERKINS, Mary Ann married Samuel Schaeffer.

PERRY, Hannah C. married John Black.

PERRY, Louisa V. married Adam Railing.

PETERSEN, Ezra married Maria Pommer.
Issue: Israel (1:215), born My 13, 1812; baptized Ag 17, 1813.

PETTICOURT, _____, who resided in a Catholic community near the Seminary, married Sarah Ann Eiron (2:290); she was born O 14, 1820; she was a Communicant O 8, 1839.

PETTY (or BETTY), _____ married Margaret Sieseman (1:194).

PETTY, Mary married Michael Waldman.

PETTY, Polly married Michael Walkman.

PETTY, Thomas married Margaret, daughter of Mrs. Lochmann.
Issue: Magdalena (1:160), born Ag ?, 1766; baptized Ag 3, 1766.

PFANTZ, Sarah married Stephen Musgrove.

PITTENFER, John had by Maria Staufer an illegitimate son John (1:221) who was born F 11, 1818 and baptized F 22, 1818.

PITTENGER, William married Louisa _____.
Issue: Lewis Duncan (2:202), born Ag 5, 1828; baptized Ag 14, 1828 by a Methodist minister; died Ja 27, 1833 of scarlet fever and was buried Ja 28, 1833.

PLATT, Caroline married Daniel Long.

PLATT, Peggy Ann married William Joseph Weller.

PLATT, Sarah had an illegitimate daughter by Daniel Rouzer.

POMMER, Maria married Ezra Petersen.

POORMAN, Josiah baptized about 1847 (2:114).

POORMAN (PURMANN), Nelle married Frederick Rose.

PREISS, Georg married Sophia Eigenbrod (1:205).

PROTZMAN, _____ (female) married _____ Rap.

PROTZMAN, Daniel, farmer (1:259), son of Lorenz Protzman and Maria Elisabeth (Häns); he was born in York County N 16, 1749; he died Ag 8, 1802 and was buried Ag 9, 1802; he married (1) in Lancaster on N 26, 1780 Gertrude Baumgärtner (1:238), who was born in Lancaster County Je 22, 1752; in 1763 she and her parents went to live at Lititz; in her 21st year she spent some time in the Single Sisters House at Bethlehem, then returned home. She joined the church here, then went into service in Lancaster; she came here after her marriage; she died Ap 27, 1789 of childbed fever and was buried in the churchyard Ap 30, 1789.

74

Issue: Maria Barbara (1:168), born S 16, 1781 in the evening; baptized S
23, 1781; married Jacob Wünsch.
John (1:170), born Je 16, 1783; baptized Je 22, 1783.
John Henry (1:171,235), born F 4, 1785 at 5-6 p.m.; baptized F 13,
1785; died F 13, 1786 of injuries caused by a hard fall on the
head; buried in the churchyard F 14, 1786.
Elizabeth (1:167b), born D 25, 1787; baptized D 30, 1787.
John Daniel (1:168b), born Ap 19, 1789 at 8 p.m.; baptized Ap 26,
1789.
PROTZMAN, Daniel, son of Lorenz and Maria Elizabeth (Häns) Protzman, married
(2) Maria Spieker, née Bühler (1:259); this was also her second marriage.
No issue.
PROTZMAN, Daniel married Maria Bühler (1:189).
PROTZMAN (PROZMAN), Dan and Gertraut; Probationers My 25, 1785 (1:91);
Communicants Je 17, 1786 (1:108).
PROTZMAN, Elizabeth; a Communicant Jl 29, 1759.
PROTZMAN, Elizabeth married George Kuhn.
PROTZMAN, Gertrude married John Ludwig Möller.
PROTZMAN, Jacob (1:126), son of Lorenz and Maria Elizabeth (Häns) Protzman,
married My 10, 1768 Johanna Leinbach, daughter of Frederick and Elizabeth
Leinbach.
Issue: Elizabeth (1:162), born N 27, 1769 at 9 a.m.; baptized D 3, 1769.
John Jacob (1:163), born Jl 2, 1771 at 8 a.m.; baptized Jl 7, 1771.
Anna Rosina (1:164), born D 3, 1772 at 11 a.m.; baptized D 5, 1772;
married John Rächer.
John Frederick (1:165), born O 18, 1774 at 4 a.m.; baptized O 20,
1774.
Catharine (1:166), born Jl 31, 1776; baptized Ag 4, 1776.
Anna Maria (1:167), born O 17, 1778; baptized O 20, 1778.
Johanna (1:168), born early on Mr 14, 1780; baptized Mr 17, 1780
Anna Margaret (1:169,233), born Mr 14, 1782; baptized Je 20, 1782;
died My 19, 1784; buried in the churchyard My 20, 1784.
(John Christian (1:172), born Jl 28, 1785; baptized Jl 31, 1785.
twins   (Maria Barbara (1:172), born Jl 28, 1785; baptized Jl 31, 1785.
Daniel (1:166b,237), born Ag 8, 1787 at 1-2 p.m.; baptized Ag 8,
1787; died D 25, 1787 of convulsions; buried D 27, 1787.
John (1:171b,239), born Je 24, 1790 at 1-2 p.m.; baptized Je 24,
1790; died Je 28, 1790; buried in the churchyard Je 29, 1790.
PROTZMAN, Jacob, farmer, son of Jacob and Johanna (Leinbach) Protzman,
married Anna Maria Marks.
Issue: Jacob (1:189), born D 13, 1795; baptized Ap 24, 1800.
Elizabeth (1:189), born S 9, 1797; baptized Ap 24, 1800.
Samuel (1:189), born Jl 25, 1799; baptized Ap 24, 1800.
Sara (1:192), born Ag 1, 1801; baptized S 1, 1801.
(The father-in-law, with whom the family lived, objected strenuously to
baptizing the children, so it was long withheld.)
PROTZMAN, Jacob & Hannah; Probationers Je 25, 1786 (1:92); Communicants O
25, 1788 (1:108).
PROTZMAN, John married Maria Haas.
Issue: Catharine (1:182), born Ag 14, 1796; baptized S 25, 1796.
Sarah (1:189), baptized Je 29, 1800.
PROTZMAN, John, widower, (1:263); died Mr 12, 1811, aged 64 years and a few
days; buried Mr 13, 1811 in the churchyard.
PROTZMAN, John Ludwig (1:231), born Mr 26, 1718 at Wittgenborn, county of
Wächtersbach, in the Wetterau; married in 1746 to Anna Maria _____;
came to America in 1750 and lived for a time at York; he was taken into
the church at York Mr 5, 1752 and first communed My 4, 1753; he died Ap 5,
1778 after suffering 9 months with jaundice; buried Ap 7, 1778 in the
churchyard.

Issue: John Henry (1:158), born Je 1, 1764 between 11 & 12 p.m.;
    baptized Je 3, 1764.
PROTZMAN, Joseph, joiner, married Maria Elizabeth Brown.
Issue: David Alexander (2:2), born Ag 4, 1823; baptized Ag 10, 1823.
    Edward Eugenius (2:7), born S 19, 1825; baptized O 9, 1825.
PROTZMAN (PROZMAN), Lorenz (1:107), a Communicant O 8, 1758.
PROTZMAN, Lorenz (1:226), born Jl, 1721 at Witgenborn, county of Waechters-
bach; he married Maria Elizabeth Häns (who came to America in 1738); she
wasborn in D, 1726 at Cassel [read Cussel] in Zweibrücken; they lived in
marriage 17 years; he died D 9, 1767 at 10 p.m. and was buried D 11, 1767
in the churchyard; she died My 2, 1806 and was buried My 4, 1806 (1:261);
she lived to see 75 grandchildren and 41 great-grandchildren.
Issue: Jacob (1:126) married Johanna Leinbach.
    Daniel (1:259) married (1) Gertraut Baumgartner and (2) Maria
    Bühler.
    Anna Margaret (2:215), born Ja 11, 1754; died Mr 3, 1844; married
    John Williard.
PROTZMAN, Lorenz, son of Ludwig and Anna Protzman (1:166), married Elizabeth
    _____.
Issue: Francis Jacob (1:155), born Jl 23, 1760 at 10 p.m.; baptized Jl 27,
    1760.
    John Ludwig (1:159), born Mr 12, 1765 at 10 a.m.; baptized Mr 17,
    1765.
    Anna Maria (1:166), born Je 2, 1777; baptized Je 9, 1777.
PROTZMAN, Ludwig (1:130), son of _____ and Elizabeth; he was born in Maryland; he married My 12, 1811 Elizabeth Krämer (2:220,292); she was his
second wife; she was born in Lancaster, Pennsylvania Ja 22, 1778; she was
the daughter of Michael and Elizabeth Krämer, and she also married twice,
the name of her other husband being _____ Schuler. She died Ja 15, 1851
and was buried Ja 17, 1851.
Issue: Edmund (1:213), born Ag 23, 1812; baptized Ag 30, 1812.
    William (1:217), born Mr 9, 1815; baptized Mr 24, 1815.
    Elias Benjamin (1:220), born S 10, 1817; baptized O 5, 1817.
PROTZMAN, Ludwig, shoemaker, married in 1787 Maria Elizabeth Rauser (1:178,
187,263), daughter of Martin and Sarah Rauser; she was born F 22, 1772;
baptized O 8, 1794; she was of Dunker extraction; she died Ag 29, 1809 of
ardent nerve fever; she was buried Ag 30, 1809.
Issue: Rebecca (1:169b), born O 26, 1789 at 5-6 p.m.; baptized N 1, 1789;
    died N 7, 1852; married (1) Andrew Williar and (2) Frederick
    Favorite.
    Sophia (1:174b), born Ja 25, 1792 at 5 a.m.; baptized F 19, 1792;
    died Jl 4, 1834; married Henry Krieger.
    Salome (1:178,243), born Ap 5, 1794 at 10 p.m.; baptized Ap 13,
    1794; died of blue cough and was buried Ag 16, 1794 in the
    churchyard.
    Helena (1:180), born Je 1, 1795 at 6 a.m.; baptized Je 28, 1795,
    married Henry Layton.
    Benjamin (1:185,252), born Ja 27, 1798 at 6:15 a.m.; baptized F 4,
    1798; died Ap 16, 1799; buried Ap 18, 1799.
    Joseph (1:189), born My 15, 1800; baptized My 25, 1800.
    Henrietta (1:195), born O 25, 1802; baptized N 7, 1802.
    Abigail (1:204), born Ap 2, 1807; baptized Ap 19, 1807; married
    Elijah Süss.
    Franz Urias (1:208,263), born My 21, 1809; baptized My 28, 1809;
    died O 5, 1809; buried O 7, 1809.
PROTZMAN, Ludwig (1:92), a Probationer O 11, 1789.
PROTZMAN, Ludwig & Elizabeth (1:108), Communicants O 8, 1796.

PROTZMAN, Margaretha had by John [name blotted], in the mountains, an illegitimate son John Jacob (1:217) who was born Mr 10, 1815 and baptized Ap 23, 1815.
PROTZMAN, Maria had an illegitimate son by Jacob Wilhide.
PROTZMAN (PROZMAN), Maria Elizabeth, wife of Lorenz, was a Probationer O 8, 1758.
PROTZMAN (PROZMANN), Peky, daughter of Ludwig and Maria Elizabeth (Rauser) Protzman, had an illegitimate stillborn child S 14, 1811 (1:263). This child was buried in the churchyard S 15, 1811.
PRYOR, Catherine M. married John H. Wilhide.

RÄCHER (RECHER), Fredric (1:88), son of John and Rosanna Recher (Rächer), married S 16, 1834 Lavinia Hoover, daughter of Christian and Elizabeth Hoover.
RÄCHER, John, farmer, married Anna Rosina Protzman, daughter of Jacob and Johanna (Leinbach) Protzman; she was born D 3, 1772 and baptized D 5, 1772.
Issue: Frederick (1:192), born Je 23, 1801; baptized S 1, 1801.
RÄCHER, Peter married Elizabeth Protzman (Prozmann) (1:192).
RAILING, Adam (2:157) married Mr 20, 1862 Louise V. Perry, at the house of her grandfather Perry.
RAMSBURG, Stephen G. (2:156) married Mr 2, 1860 Barbara Ann Rebecca Weller.
RAMSBURG, Thomas C. married Julian Vogel.
Issue: Lilly May (2:132), born D 19, 1871; baptized D 21, 1873.
RANCK, Philip married Barbara Stauffer.
Issue: Anna Maria (1:78), born S 13, 1772; died F 12, 1820; married John Peter Kluge.
RANDALL (or REYNOLDS), Elizabeth Anna married Joseph B. (or C.) Schulz.
RAP, _____ married _____ Protzman. He died before O 7, 1819 when a daughter was baptized.
Issue: Katherine Anne (1:111), born Mr 16, 1819; baptized O 7, 1819.
RAU, Catharine married Peter McClain.
RAU, John married Barbara _____.
Issue: Elizabeth married John Long.
RAUCH, John George married Elizabeth Catharine Miller.
Issue: John George (1:149), born Jl 13, 1835; baptized Ag 23, 1835.
RAUDENBUSCH, Daniel married Elizabeth Meyer.
Issue: Susanna (1:215), born N 18, 1812; baptized S 5, 1813.
RAUSCH, George married Catharine Blumenstein.
Issue: Philip (1:142), born N 21, 1831; baptized Mr 4, 1832.
RAUSER, Abraham married Margaret Berger (1:209).
RAUSER, Daniel had by Peky Krieger an illegitimate son Joel (1:211) who was born Mr 6, 1811 and baptized My 23, 1811 at Lorenz Krieger's house.
RAUSER (ROUZER), Daniel had by Sarah Platt (daughter of Mary), an illegitimate daughter Mary Jane (1:144), who was born Je 11, 1826 and baptized D 23, 1832.
RAUSER (ROUZER), Eliza married Joshua Smith.
RAUSER (ROUZER), Elizabeth Margaret married William Lawrence Krieger.
RAUSER, Martin married Sarah _____.
Issue: Maria Elizabeth, born F 22, 1772; married Ludwig Protzman.
RAUSER, Martin, tanner, of Mechanicstown, married Rosina Gernand, daughter of John Adam and Anna Catharine (Weller) Gernand; she was born F 26, 1804.
Issue: William (2:10), born Ap 30, 1827; baptized Jl 10, 1827.
Sophia Catharine (1:139), born S 26, 1829; baptized O 25, 1829.
Martin (1:144), born Je 8, 1832; baptized Jl 23, 1832.
Elizabeth Margaret (1:147), born Ap 2, 1834; baptized Ap 27, 1834.
RAUSER (ROUZER), Simon P. (2:155) married F 17, 1859 Mary Jane Hough.
REECHER(?), Sophia married Daniel Fick.

REED, Jacob (1:87), son of James and Mary Reed, married N 13, 1832 Catharine Smeltz, daughter of John and Elizabeth (Rodeneiser) Smeltz.

REEVER, Harrison married Julia E. Gilbert (2:256); she was born N 12, 1849; she died D 16, 1880 and was buried D 18, 1880 at Taneytown.
Issue: Elizabeth Emma (2:70), born Ap 27, 1872; baptized Mr 25, 1878.
Alice Loretta (2:70), born S 19, 1874; baptized Mr 25, 1878.
Harrison Edward (2:70), born Ja 19, 1875; baptized Mr 25, 1878.
Gertrude Grace (2:70), born F 19, 1878; baptized Mr 25, 1878.

REHKOPF, Maria Lydia Anna (2:3,244), born N 3, 1799; baptized O 8, 1823; died N 11, 1868 and was buried N 12, 1868 at Graceham. She never married.

REICH, Christopher had by Selly Schu (daughter of Daniel Jung) an illegitimate son Christopher (1:207) who was born S 8, 1805 and was baptized O 19, 1808.

REIDENAUER, Adam married _____ Miller.
Issue: Mary married Nathaniel Rice.

REIDENAUER (REIDENOUR), Andrew married Catharine Lichty; she died Ja 23, 1853, aged 26-11-22; buried Ja 24, 1853 in the mountains above Harbaugh's Valley.

REIDENAUER (REIDENOUR), Andrew (2:153), married F 1, 1855 Mary Ann Wilhide.

REIDENAUER (REIDENOUR), Charles Augustus (2:150,226,293), born Ag 28, 1824; married Mr 26, 1848 Sarah Creeger; he died Ap 20, 1855 and was buried at Graceham Ap 21, 1855.
Issue: Alfred Augustus (2:116), born Ag 11, 1849; baptized O 14, 1849.
Washington Alexander (2:118,222), born Ap 23, 1852; baptized Jl 25, 1852; died Ap 11, 1853 and was buried Ap 13, 1853.
Comenius Frederick (2:49,226), born F 12, 1854; baptized Ag 20, 1854; died Ap 2, 1855; buried Ap 3, 1855.

REIDENAUER, Elizabeth married Benjamin Dubel.

REIDENAUER (REIDNAUER), George, of Hagerstown, married Ann Rebecca Weller.
Issue: Joseph Augustus (2:121), born D 8, 1855; baptized Ag 10, 1856.

REIDENAUER (REITNAUER), Jacob married Barbara Wiljahr.
Issue: Andrew (1:119), born My 29, 1822; baptized Jl 21, 1822.

REIDENAUER (REIDENOUR), Jacob (2:151), widower, married Mr 13, 1851 Catharine Eyler.

REIDENAUER (REITNAUER), Jacob, joiner (2:191), was born in Frederick County in 1799; he died Ag 1, 1825 and was buried Ag 2, 1825; he married (1) in 1801 Maria Schmitt (1:264) who was born My 15, 1779; she died D 3, 1815 of consumption and was buried D 5, 1815; they were married 14 years; Mrs. Barbara Schoff was mother of one of the parents.
Issue: Catharine (2:221,286), born Je 19, 1803; died S 23, 1851; married John R. Boller.
John (1:200), [baptized 1805?].
Adam (1:203,263), born F 12, 1807; baptized Mr 22, 1807; died Mr 6, 1812 of convulsions; buried Mr 8, 1812.
Henry (1:207), born N 15, 1808; baptized N 27, 1808.
Elizabeth (1:78,211) born in Mechanicstown, Maryland D 15, 1810; baptized Ja 26, 1811; died My 10, 1820; buried My 11, 1820.
Sophia (1:215), born Je 12, 1813; baptized Ag 1, 1813.

REIDENAUER (REITNAUER), Jacob, joiner, (1:132; 2:191) of Mechanicstown, was born in 1779; he died Ag 1, 1825 and was buried Ag 2, 1825; he married (2) Je 6, 1816 Gertrude Willjar (2:209), daughter of Andrew and Margaret (Harbaugh) Willjar; she was born N 10, 1784; she later became the wife of Philip William Boller; she died Je 11, 1835 of consumption and was buried Je 13, 1835.
Issue: Jacob (1:220), born Mr 20, 1817; baptized Mr 21, 1817.
William (1:222), born D 2, 1818; baptized Ja 24, 1819.
George (1:114), born O 7, 1820; baptized N 21, 1820.
Charles Augustus (2:5), born Ag 28, 1824; baptized O 5, 1824; married Sarah Creeger.

78

another son.

REIDENAUER (REIDNAUER), Jacob married Gertraut Willjahr (1:112).

REIDNAUER, Jacob married Mary Lichty (1:105 says Mary Ann).

Issue: William Henry (1:101), born Mr 17, 1841; baptized My 16, 1841.

Sarah Elizabeth (1:105), born My 21, 1842; baptized Ag 15, 1843.

REIDENAUER (REITENAUER), Margaret married Manasse Krieger.

REIDENAUER (REIDENOUR), Washington A. (2:163), married D 30, 1875 Amanda C. Ambrose of Smithfield.

Issue: Mary Anna (2:135), born My 10, 1876; baptized Jl 1, 1877.

REIDENAUER, William (1:90; 2:289), born D 2, 1818; a Communicant Whitsunday, 1841; married Ap 12, 1840 Eve Knauff.

Issue: Edward Theodore (2:38), born F 18, 1841; baptized Mr 1, 1841.

Cyrus Jothomus (1:105; 2:41), born Mr 10, 1843; baptized Jl 23, 1843.

John Adam (2:43), born Jl 17, 1846; baptized Ja 24, 1847.

Susan Catharine (2:45), born F 22, 1849; baptized My 27, 1849.

REIFSCHNEIDER, Levi S. (1:89), born D 5, 1811; married Je 24, 1838 Sevilla Sefton, daughter of Charles and Mary Sefton, who was born N 15, 1815.

REINHARD, Charles married Susan _____.

Issue: George William (2:125), born Jl 21, 1860; baptized Mr 24, 1862.

Mary Catharine (2:125), born F 1, 1862; baptized Mr 24, 1862.

REINHOLD, Ann married Jacob Williar.

REINKE, Amadeus A. married Ellen E. Rice.

Issue: Beata (2:219), died Jl 4, 1850.

Sarah Elizabeth (2:47), born Mr 27, 1852; baptized Ap 18, 1852.

William Henry (2:47), born Mr 23, 1853; baptized My 15, 1853.

REINKE, Samuel married Charlotte Sophia Hueffel.

Issue: daughter (stillborn) (2:194) Jl 28, 1828; buried Jl 29, 1828.

Emma Theodora (2:16,197), born S 3, 1829; baptized S 20, 1829; died Jl 8, 1830 of whooping cough and teething; buried Jl 10, 1830.

Raphael Rudolph (2:19,208), born Ap 29, 1831; baptized My 12, 1831; died Mr 5, 1835 of measles; buried Mr 7.

Clemens Leander (2:25), born Ap 28, 1834; baptized My 8, 1834.

REINLY, Elizabeth married William Lyons.

RENNER, _____ (1:89), married Catharine Heffner, daughter of Peter and Charlotte (Cole) Heffner; he died before Je 2, 1839 when she remarried, her second husband being Daniel Cover.

RENNER, Sally married Henry Hummer.

REYNOLDS (or RANDALL), Elizabeth Anna married Joseph B. (or C.) Schulz.

RHEAM, Anna Maria married Hiram A. Park.

RICE, Ellen E. married Amadeus A. Reinke.

RICE, Nathaniel (1:83), son of Philip and Anna Maria (Dehuff) Rice, married Mr 7, 1828 Mary Reitenauer, daughter of Adam Reitenauer and _____, late Miller.

RICE, Sarah L. married Edward Rondthaler.

RICKSECKER, _____ married Anna Elizabeth Krieger.

RICKSECKER, Benjamin married Charlotte F. Eberman.

Issue: Clara Elizabeth (2:52), born Ag 29, 1857; baptized S 20, 1857.

RICKSECKER, Henry married Catharine Miller (1:115).

RICKSECKER, Henry, schoolmaster, married Catharine Mueller.

Issue: Elizabeth (2:207), born Ja 22, 1798; died Ag 9, 1834; married Charles Williard.

Lea (1:205), born F 12, 1808; baptized Mr 12, 1808.

Grienberry (1:210) born O 15, 1810; baptized O 28, 1810.

Carl Heinrich or Henry Charles (1:79,111), born Ap 7, 1819 at Graceham; baptized My 20, 1819; died Ag 19, 1820 of diarrhea; buried Ag 20, 1820.

RIDDLEMOSER, Christian (1:87), married O 11, 1832 Hannah Kessler, daughter of Michael and Susan Kessler.

79

RIDGLEY, Richard, pourer at the Furnace, married Harriet Spears.
Issue: William (1:118), born Ja 22, 1822; baptized Ap 18, 1822.
RIFESNIDER, Matilda (daughter of John and Catharina) married Joseph Weller.
RINN (or RENN), Bernard married Margaret Strefer.
Issue: Elizabeth (1:204), born Je 25, 1807; baptized Ag 1, 1808.
Bernard (1:209), born Ag 25, 1809; baptized D 22, 1809.
RITTER, Catharine married Philip Williard.
RITTER, Tobias married Juliana Willjar, daughter of Peter and Maria or
Magdalena Elizabeth (Schlim) Willjar; she was born Je 2, 1763 and baptized
Je 5, 1763.
Issue: Maria Elizabeth (1:175), born Mr 4, 1787 at 5-6 a.m.; baptized Mr
22, 1787.
ROBESON, Daniel (2:208), born Ap 11, 1803; confirmed O 8, 1830; died N 22,
1834 of consumption; buried N 23, 1834; he married about 1826 Eliza or
(Elizabeth) Willjar (2:292), daughter of John and Sarah (McClain) Williar
[sic]; she was born N 17, 1809; she was a Communicant O 8, 1830.
Issue: Anna Margaret (1:135), born Ag 6, 1827; baptized O 7, 1827, the
sponsors being Lorenz and Catharina Willjar; died Mr 8, 1830 of
worms; buried Mr 10, 1830.
Sarah Ann (1:138) born D 15, 1828; baptized Ap 26, 1829.
Edwin Philander (2:20), born Ja1, 1831; baptized My 29, 1831.
Mary Jane (2:23), born Ap 1, 1833; baptized Ap 7, 1833.
ROBINSON (or ROBESON), Hezekiah (2:147), son of Alexander and Elizabeth
Robeson or Robinson; he married D 25, 1833 Mary Ann (or Anna Maria)
Williar (1:216; 2:211), daughter of Lorenz and Catharine (Miller) Williar
(after marriage she became a Methodist); she was born S 23, 1813 and
baptized Je 19, 1814; she was confirmed O 8, 1830; she died S 3, 1839 and
was buried S 4, 1839 in the Moravian Cemetery.
Issue: George Augustus (1:97), born Ag 28, 1839; baptized S 2, 1839.
Joseph Franklin (1:97), born Ag 28, 1839; baptized S 2, 1839.
ROBINSON, James married Margaret Randolph Null.
Issue: Daniel (1:97), born Ag 11, 1836; baptized S 2, 1839.
James Wilson (1:97), born D 21, 1838; baptized S 2, 1839.
RODENEISER (RODNEIS), Catharine married Jacob Schiller.
RODENEISER (ROTHNEISER), Catharine married Samuel Saylor.
RODENEISER, Elizabeth married John Smeltz.
RODENEISER (RODNEISS), Henry married Maria Carsen.
Issue: Maria (1:218), born Jl 26, 1814; baptized O 31, 1815.
ROD[E]NEIS[ER], John married Anna Maria Willheid, daughter of Frederick
Willheid.
Issue: John (1:206), born Ap 3, 1808; baptized My 8, 1808.
RODENEISER, John (widower), of Catoctin Furnace, married D 27, 1827 Mrs.
Hannah Morehead (widow), (1:83).
Issue: Mary (1:137), born Ag 19, 1828; baptized Ag 26, 1828.
Anne Rebecca (1:137), born Ag 19, 1828; baptized Ag 26, 1828.
RODENHEISER, Mary Ann married Thomas Fraley.
RÖDER, Catharine (or Mary), married Michael Williard.
RODGERS, Samuel S. married Josephine Matilda Clem.
Issue: George William Nelson (2:122), born D 29, 1856; baptized F 18,
1857.
ROESLER, John Charles, doctor, of Graceham, married Eva Catharine Wolf.
Issue: Amalia (1:265), died F 19, 1818 of convulsion at the age of 5
months; buried F 20, 1818.
Aurelia (1:222), born Ja 20, 1819; baptized F 4, 1819.
Carl August Justinus (1:79,112), born Ap 13, 1820 at Graceham;
baptized Je 11, 1820; died O 24, 1820; buried O 25, 1820.
ROGERS, Samuel married Barbara Miller.
Issue: Daniel (1:136), born S 16, 1825; baptized Ja 6, 1828.
Sarah Ann (1:136), born My 13, 1827; baptized Ja 6, 1828.

RÖHKOP, John Frederick married Susanna Schäfer.
Issue: Susanna (1:203), born S 1, 1786; baptized N 27, 1806; died N 28, 1806.
RÖHMANN (or RÖMER), Anna Barbara married Andrew Williar.
ROMIG, John (or Jacob? 1:260), farmer and miller, of Heidelberg Township, Berks County (1:128), died at York, Pennsylvania; he married Rosina Gladt (1:260), daughter of Georg and Maria Elisabeth (Dock) Gladt; she was born Ag 30, 1760 in Heidelberg Township, Berks County; she died N 3, 1804 and was buried N 4. They were the parents of 6 children. She later married Heinrich Giese.
RONDTHALER, Ambrose (2:289), born Je 8, 1813; a Communicant Ap 16, 1829; he married Ap 20, 1837 at Nazareth Matilda Caroline Busse who was born at Nazareth Ag 23, 1815.
Issue: stillborn (2:214) S 16, 1840; buried same day.
Mary Augusta (2:39,214), born Je 15, 1842; baptized Jl 5, 1842; died Jl 29, 1842; aged 45 days; buried Jl 30, 1842.
James Albert (2:42), born S 27, 1844; baptized O 13, 1844.
RONDTHALER, Comenius (2:150,290), of Funkstown, born O 6, 1819; married D 27, 1847 Catharine Theresia Weller (2:290), daughter of Frederick and Sarah (Stauffer) Weller; she was born S 17, 1825; she was a Communicant in 1841.
Issue: Frederick Emanuel (2:44), born (1848?).
Bertha Cornelia (2:117), born Ag 23, 1850; baptized O 13, 1850.
RONDTHALER, Edward married Sarah L. Rice.
Issue: Joseph (2:217), born N 6, 1844; died Jl 20, 1845; buried Jl 21, 1845.
Mary (2:44), born Jl 27, 1846.
Owen (2:44), born My 21, 1848; baptized Je 11, 1848.
RONDTHALER, Jane W. married Jesse Blickensderfer.
ROSCHER, Susanna married George Kehl.
ROSENSTEEL, James T. (2:160) married Ja 7, 1868 Annie L. Whitmore.
ROSGE, Hanna married John Hoffman.
RÖSLER, Julia Catharine Elizabeth married Arnold Richard Fahs.
ROSS, Frederick married Nelle Purmann.
Issue: Sophia (1:210), born S 18, 1809; baptized S 9, 1810.
ROTHROCK, Jacob had by Margaret Cleman an illegitimate daughter Anna Maria (1:155), who was born Je 24, 1759 and baptized O 8, 17--.
ROUTZAHN, Emma F. married Frank S. Grimes.
ROWE, Emma Jane (2:227), born Ap 17, 1854; died Je 20, 1856; buried Je 21, 1856 at Apple's Church.
ROXBURY, William.
Issue: Anne married Jacob Miller.
RUDIFER, John married Maria Höflich.
Issue: Maria (1:267), born Ap 21, 1799; baptized Je 12, 1799 by Schlegel on a trip to Cumberland and Bedford.
RUDOLPHI, Lydia Ann married Daniel Schaeffer.
RYAN, _____ married Isabel (Smeltzer ?).
Issue: Mary Elizabeth Frances (2:133), born Ag 3, 1873; baptized S 10, 1874.

SAUER, Catharine married Nicholas Lienefelder.
SAYLOR, Samuel, pourer at the Catoctin Furnace, married Catharine Rothneiser, daughter of Martha.
Issue: David (1:121), born Mr 29, 1825; baptized My 1, 1825.
Henry (1:135), born S 29, 1826; baptized N 12, 1826.
John (1:137), born Ag 8, 1828; baptized S 14, 1828.
Martha (1:139), born My 21, 1830; baptized Jl 4, 1830.
Mary (1:142), born F 1, 1832; baptized Mr 7, 1832.
SCHAEFFER (SCHÄFER), Catharine married John Kreidler.

SCHAEFFER, Daniel married Lydia Ann Rudolphi (2:215); she was born N 11 or
16, 1809; she died S 19, 1842 and was buried S 21, 1842.
Issue: Araminta Elisabeth (2:24), born Jl 26, 1833; baptized D 1, 1833.
Henrietta Angelica (2:28), born Mr 5, 1835; baptized Ag 16, 1835.
Washington Lafayette (2:31), born N 10, 1837; baptized Je 3, 1838.
Frances Maranda (2:40,216), born O 2, 1841; baptized Ag 21, 1842;
died My 16, 1845; buried My 17, 1845.
SCHAEFFER (SCHAEFERR), Henrietta Angelica (2:28), daughter of Daniel and
Lydia Ann (Rudolphi) Schaeffer, born Mr 5, 1835 and baptized Ag 16, 1835,
had an illegitimate son George Lafayette McClellan (2:126) who was born My
19, 1863 and baptized D 9, 1863.
SCHAEFFER, John married Margaret _____.
Issue: Eleonora (1:121), born Je 23, 1824; baptized O 14, 1824.
SCHAEFFER (SHAEFFER), John Frederick married Mary Ann _____.
Issue: Samuel Elijah (2:220), born Ja 20, 1842; died Ag 27, 1850; buried
Ag 28, 1850 at Lewistown.
Josiah Livingston (2:220), born O 13, 1847; died Ag 27, 1850;
buried Ag 28, 1850 at Lewistown.
John Daniel (2:117), born S 23, 1849; baptized Ag 28, 1850.
SCHAEFFER, Samuel (1:89), married F 1, 1839 Mary Ann Perkins.
Issue: William Carlton (1:96), born Ja 26, 1839; baptized F 1, 1839.
Charles (1:99), born O 18, 1840; baptized O 19, 1840.
SCHAEFFER, Sarah married Edward Eaton.
SCHAEFFER (SHAEFFER), Susan married Henry Steece.
SCHAEFFER (SCHÄFER), Susanna married John Frederick Röhkop.
SCHAEFFER (SHAFER), William G. (2:154) married N 13, 1856 Harriet Elizabeth
Dorsey.
SCHAFFNER, John Caspar married Catharine Schreiack.
Issue: Maria Catharine Johnson, born D 7, 1798; baptized Je 12, 1799 by
Schlegel on a trip to Cumberland and Bedford. (1:267).
SCHNECK, Nancy married John Luckienbach.
SCHENKEL, Barbara married Andrew Holzman.
SCHENKEL, Elizabeth married Leonard Moser.
SCHENKEL, Lorenz married Maria Seiphert (1:199).
SCHENKEL, Perky had an illegitimate child by Sam Holzman.
SCHIELER, Jacob married Catharine _____.
Issue: Margaret (1:210), born F 20, 1810; baptized O 29, 1810.
SCHIELY, David married Susanna _____.
Issue: Harriet (1:120), born O 20, 1822; baptized O 1, 1823.
SCHILLER, Jacob married Catharine Rodneis.
Issue: Maria (1:207), born My 29, 1808; baptized S 18, 1808.
SCHILS, Berez married Susanna Dindemang.
Issue: William (1:215), born Ag 15, 1806; baptized Ag 21, 1813.
Joseph (1:215), born Je 15, 1808; baptized Ag 21, 1813.
Elizabeth (1:215), born O 15, 1809; baptized Ag 21, 1813.
Jane (1:215), born D 12, 1811; baptized Ag 21, 1813.
Catharine (1:215), born D 16, 1812; baptized Ag 21, 1813.
SCHLEGEL, Joh. Friedr. married A. Ros. Mack (1:188).
SCHLEGEL, John Frederick, minister here (1:261), son of John Frederick and
Ursula Barbara (Arnold) Schlegel, was born Je 9, 1753 at Nazareth; he
married My 9, 1785 Anna Rosina Mack; he died My 30, 1805 and was buried Je
1, 1805. There was no issue of this union.
SCHLEY, Sophia married George Eckman.
SCHOBER, Peter (1:195), married Sophia Ambrose.
Issue: Catharine (2nd daughter), born Ja 22, 1778; died Mr 4, 1858;
married John Henry Weller.
SCHOPP, John married Eve Loy.
Issue: Levi (1:147), born Ja 3, 1833; baptized Ap 6, 1834.
Caroline Elizabeth (1:98), born My 30, 1839; baptized Ap 5, 1840.

SCHREIACK, Catharine married John Caspar Schaffner.
SCHREIBER, Martha Elizabeth married William Hall (or Gall).
SCHREIBER, Mary Ann married Simon Meredith.

SCHULER, Samuel, windlass-maker, of Lancaster (1:134) married Elizabeth Krämer (1:130); she was born in Pennsylvania, the daughter of Michael and Elizabeth Krämer, she married later Ludwig Protzmann.
SCHULTZ, Martin, chair-maker, of Mechanicstown (1:134) married Mr 26, 1822 Sabina Krieger (2:188), daughter of John Krieger, innkeeper, and Eva (Eiler); she was their eldest daughter and was born Mr 30, 1803; she died Ap 4, 1823 and was buried Ap 5, 1823.
SCHULZ, Joseph B. (or C.), married Elizabeth Anna Reynolds (or Randall).
    Issue: John Horatio (1:143), born F 28, 1831; baptized Ap 12, 1832.
        Adalina Clarissa (1:146), born F 10, 1833; baptized F 8, 1834.
        Jane Eleanor Bloomfield (1:150), born F 7, 1835; baptized Jl 19, 1836.
        Theodosia Margaretha Rebecca Anna (1:94), born O 31, 1837; baptized F 11, 1838.
SCHUMAN, Henry Frederick, M.D., married Johanna Salome Leinbach.
    Issue: Parmenio (son) (1:196), born Jl 8, 1803; baptized Jl 24, 1803.
de SCHWEINTZ, Robert married Marie _____.
    Issue: Louis Alexander (2:45), born Jl 11, 1849; baptized Ag 5, 1849.
SCOTT, Henrietta H. married William A. Corban.
SEBASTIAN, John married Maria Hummer.
    Issue: Sophia (1:211), born Ja 21, 1811; baptized F 21, 1811.
SEBASTIAN, Sarah had an illegitimate son by Henry Seiffert.
SEBASTIAN, Susanna had an illegitimate son by George Loy.
SEBASTIAN, Susanna married Joseph Merik.
SEFTON, Andrew (1:87), son of Charles and Mary Sefton; married Mr 28, 1833 Elizabeth Weller, daughter of John Jacob and Margaret (Weller) Weller.
SEFTON, Charles married Mary _____.
    Issue: Sevilla, born N 15, 1815; married Levi S. Reifschneider.
        Andrew married Elizabeth Weller.
SEIFFERT, Elizabeth married William Cover.
SEIFERT, Henry had by Sarah Sebastian an illegitimate son Henry (1:212) who was born Ag 7, 1811 and baptized D 14, 1811.
SEIFFERT (SEIFFARTH), John married Salome Schmiedt.
    Issue: Eiza (1:212), born Jl 12, 1811; baptized Ag 25, 1811.
SEIFFERT (SEIPHERT), Matthew, joiner, married Elizabeth Dorf.
    Issue: Matthew (1:199), born Mr 10, 1804; baptized Ja 13, 1805.
SEIFFERT, Sarah had an illegitimate child by Elias Drachsel.
SHANK, Mary [wife of John, according to her tombstone, Reformed cemetery at Sabillasville]; she was born Mr 15, 1776; she died Ap 16, 1865 and is buried at Sabillasville (burial date: Ap 18). (2:241).
SHARRETT, Louise (or SHADDOCK, Lucy) married George Loy.
SHAUM, Jacob D. (2:157) married D 19, 1861 Sevilla Weller.
    Issue: Amanda Catharine (2:60), born Ag 22, 1864; baptized D 25, 1864.
SHEALOR, David married Catharine _____.
    Issue: Henry Agustus (1:122), born My 13, 1826; baptized Jl 12, 1826.
SHEALOR, David (1:83) of Catoctin Furnace, son of Martin and Susanna Shealor; he was married two or more times; he married on O 28, 1827 Mary Carty.
    Issue: Thomas (1:137), born Ag 7, 1828; baptized Ag 24, 1828.
SHEALOR, David (1:85), son of Martin and Susanna Shealor, married on My 30, 1830 Sarah McLamee.
SHEARER, George Allen (2:255), born S 3, 1879; died Jl 10, 1880; buried Jl 11, 1880 at Creagerstown.
SHEETS, Sarah married George Stitely.
SHELEY, Susanna married Jesse Stump.

SHIELDS, Susanna married Michael Waldman.
SHIFF, Barbara, daughter of Michael and Anne Shiff, married John Timmons.
SHINGLEDECKER, Elizabeth J. married Levi O. Miller.

SHOOK, Henry, farmer (1:133), married Je 13, 1820 Elizabeth Wilheid,
   daughter of Conrad Wilheid, cartwright, and Anna Elizabeth (Krieger); she
   was born N 7, 1795.
   Issue: Daniel (1:120), born Ap 16, 1823; baptized Ap 29, 1823.
SHOOK, Jacob married Elizabeth Young.
   Issue: Samuel (1:136), born N 6, 1827; baptized Ja 8, 1828.
SHOOP, John married Eva Gaugh.
   Issue: George (1:150), born O 4, 1835; baptized Jl 24, 1836.
SHRINER, William E. of Frederick County (2:151) married F 19, 1850 Elizabeth
   Jane Parish of Carroll County.
   Issue: Margaret Ellen (2:119), born N 17, 1852; baptized Jl 8, 1853.
SHUFF (SCHOFF), _____ married Barbara Wilhide (1:196).
SHUFF (SCHOFF), Anna Maria married Jacob Wilhide.
SHUFF, Catharine married Cyrus Six.
SHUFF, George (2:234), died D 16, 1861, aged 84 or 85; buried at Apple's
   Church D 17, 1861.
SHUFF, Hanna married John Dwier.
SHUFF, Harriet Elizabeth married Michael Joseph Colliflower.
SHUFF, Henry.
   Issue: Edward Oliver (2:117), born F 27, 1850; baptized N 24, 1850.
SHUFF, Henry married Margaret _____.
   Issue: Millard Francis (2:125), born N 2, 1860; baptized Mr 3, 1861.
SHUFF, Jane married George Kinsey.
SHUFF (SCHOFF), Jesse married Sophia Kunz.
   Issue: Mary Anna (1:115), born Ja 22, 1820; baptized Ja 29, 1821.
      John Adam (1:146), born Ag 29, 1833; baptized F 5, 1834.
SCHUFF (SCHOFF), John married Barbara Frölich.
   Issue: Catharine (1:193), born Ja 24, 1802; baptized Ja 24, 1802.
      Elisa (1:196), born My 26, 1803; baptized Je 26, 1803.
      Carolina (1:202), born F 1, 1806; baptized Mr 30, 1806.
      Maria (1:207), born Jl 9, 1808; baptized S 18, 1808.
      Benjamin (1:210), born N 22, 1809; baptized D 31, 1809.
      John (1:212), born D 11, 1811; baptized D 17, 1811.
SHUFF, John married Elizabeth _____.
   Issue: Rosa Lee (2:66,132), born Ag 29, 1871; baptized D 3, 1871.
SHUFF (SCHOFF), Jonathan, farmer, son of _____ and Jane, married Christina
   Heller.
   Issue: Sophia (1:197), born N 23, 1803; baptized Ja 31, 1804.
      Jesse (1:213), born O 22, 1805; baptized Mr 22, 1812.
      William (1:213), born Ag 2, 1808; baptized Mr 22, 1812.
      Anna Maria (1:213), born Ag 1, 1811; baptized Mr 22, 1812.
SHUFF (SHOFF), Jonathan (1:134) married D 26, 1820 to Polly Ehrhard, who was
   married previously to _____ Matthes.
SECHRIST, Elizabeth married Samuel Wolf.
SIMES, Masse married Joseph Kums.
SIME, Mary E. (2:254), born F 14, 1839; died Ag 9, 1879 at Catoctin Furnace;
   buried at Prospect Hill Church near Lewistown Ag 10, 1879.
SIPES (SEIPS), George W. married Mary L. Eyler.
   Issue: Fannie Mesora (2:72), born Ap 27, 1879; baptized Ag 31, 1879.
SIPES, Mary (2:236), born Ap 2, 1788; died Jl 10, 1862; buried Jl 12, 1862.
SIPES, William (2:149), son of Mary Sipes (unmarried); he married Mr 31,
   1843 Maria Emilia Boller (2:288), daughter of John R. and Catharine (Reid-
   enauer) Boller; she was born D 7, 1824 and baptized Ja 13, 1825; she was a
   Communicant O 8, 1839; she died Jl 26, 1862 of consumption and was buried
   at Graceham Jl 27, 1862.

Issue: Edward Theodore (2:42), born Jl 14, 1844; baptized S 22, 1844.
Henry Alfred (2:43), born N 26, 1846; baptized F 7, 1847.
George William (2:45), born O 21, 1848; baptized F 1, 1849.

John Thomas (2:46,242), born N 6, 1850; baptized Mr. 8, 1851; died Ja 16, 1866 and buried at Graceham Ja 18.
Reuben Alison (2:47), born F 9, 1853; baptized My 15, 1853.
Amadeus Washington (2:121), born F 7, 1856; baptized My 11, 1856.
Granville Milton (2:54), born Ap 14, 1858; baptized O 16, 1859.
Mary Ellen Catharine (2:56), born D 5, 1860; baptized Mr 28, 1861.
SIX, Catharine E. married Jacob Weller.
SIX, Cyrus married Catharine Shuff.
Issue: Joanna (2:113), born Mr 9, 1845; baptized Mr 23, 1847.
Edward Oliver (2:113), born My 16, 1847; baptized Mr 23, 1847.
Mary Ellen (2:114), born O 23, 1847(?).
Elvira Isabel (2:116), baptized Ja 12, 1850.
Julian Elizabeth (2:118), born D 8, 1850; baptized Jl 6, 1851.
Joseph Scott (2:119), born F 25, 1853; baptized S 25, 1853.
George Anderson (2:123), born S 17, 1854; baptized O 7, 1858.
Samuel (2:123), born Ja 7, 1856; baptized O 7, 1858.
Ida Rebecca (2:59), born Mr 22, 1860; baptized Ja 12, 1864.
May Augusta (2:59), born My 6, 1863; baptized Ja 12, 1864.
SIX, Philip married Isabella _____.
Issue: Sarah (1:89), born Ap 18, 1816; married (1) _____ Fries and (2) Edward O. Norris.
SIX, Samuel (2:154) married F 25, 1855 Sarah Ellen Stauffer (2:228), daughter of Henry and Mary Magdalena (Krall) Stauffer); she was born Ja 4, 1835 and baptized Ap 8, 1835; shed was confirmed D 31, 1854; she died Ag 23, 1856 and was buried Ag 25, 1856.
Issue: George William Henry (2:50,228), born Ag 8, 1856; baptized Ag 31, 1856; died O 16, 1856; buried O 17, 1856.
SIX, Wilfred married Hannah Rebecca Firor.
Issue: Ann Elizabeth Savannah (2:118), born Ag 20, 1850; baptized Ja 22, 1851.
Laura Virginia (2:119), born F 22, 1853; baptized My 29, 1853.
SIX, Wilfred (2:150) married S 17, 1846(?) Magdalena Firor.
SMELTZ, John married Elizabeth Rodeneiser.
Issue: Catharine married Jacob Reed.
SMELTZER (?), Isabel married _____ Ryan.
SMITH (SCHMIDT), Abraham, farmer, son of Mathias and Anna Maria (Buchmann or Hugmann) Schmidt; he married Esther Favor (or Lefever).
Issue: Anna (1:188), born Je 8, 1799; baptized S 15, 1799.
Anna Maria (1:194), born Mr 31, 1802; baptized Je 27, 1802.
SMITH, Amanda married John Ambrose.
SMITH, Ann Maria married Jacob William Sweeney.
SMITH (SCHMIDT), Casper, in the mountains, married Christina _____; he was a Communicant O 8, 1758 (1:107); she was a Probationer O 8, 1758 (1:91) and a Communicant Jl 31, 1762 (1:107).
Issue: Juliana (1:155,225), born F 25, 1759 at 3 p.m.; baptized F 28, 1759; died Mr 7, 1759 and buried Mr 8 on the parents' farm.
Matthaeus (1:155), born Ap 29, 1760 at 4 a.m.; baptized Ap 30, 1760.
Petrus (1:157), born Je 11, 1762 at 3 p.m.; baptized Je 13, 1762.
SMITH (SCHMIDT), Catharine Barbara (1:225), died O 19, 1761, aged 18-3-2, of convulsive sickness of 8 years which became consumption; buried in the churchyard O 22, 1761.
SMITH, Charles married Elizabeth Herbaugh.
Issue: William Washington (1:138), born D 4, 1828; baptized Ap 26, 1829.
Joseph Madison (1:146), born S 8, 1833; baptized N 17, 1833.

Barbara Elizabeth (1:149), born S 17, 1835; baptized F 7, 1836.
Julian (1:101), born S 1, 1840; baptized My 16, 1841.
Catharine Melinda (1:105), born My 5, 1843; baptized O 29, 1843.
SMITH (SCHMIDT), Daniel, farmer, married (name not given).
Issue: Ezra (1:195), born F 6, 1803; baptized Ap 4, 1803.
SMITH, George (2:148,288), son of John George and Margaret (Zoller) Schmidt;
he was born Mr 26, 1821 at Lachen in the Palatinate; he was a Communicant
Maundy Thursday, 1843; he married D 14, 1841 Araminta Eigenbrod, daughter
of Christian Henry and Margaret (Eyler) Eigenbrod; she was born at Grace-
ham O 16, 1811 and was a Communicant D 4, 1825. George Smith went west.
Issue: stillborn (2:215), S or O, 1842.
Mary Margaret (2:42), born Ap 3, 1844; baptized My 26, 1844.
George Christian (2:43), born Jl 18, 1846; baptized O 25, 1846.
SMITH (SCHMITT), George Henry (2:293), born N 6, 1826 at Lititz; he was a
Communicant in 1843.
SMITH (SCHMIDT), George Jacob, single, was a Probationer O 9, 1763 (1:91).
SMITH, Jacob, farmer, married Maria Lefever (or Le Favour) (1:195); he was
the son of Matthew Smith.
Issue: Matthias (1:198), baptized Ap 29, 1804.
SMITH, John, weaver, married in 1804 Elizabeth Fröhlich (1:265), daughter of
Henry and Maria Fröhlich; she was born O 23, 1786; she was a Probationer
in 1801 and a communicant in 1805; she died Je 21, 1818 of a leg injury
which developed into consumption and was buried Je 23, 1818.
Issue: David (1:200), born Ap 2, 1805; baptized My 5, 1805.
Emanuel (1:203,262), born Ja 7, 1807; baptized F 15, 1807; died F
19, 1808 of convulsions; buried F 21, 1808.
Samuel (1:208), born F 11, 1809; baptized My 21, 1809.
Henry (1:211), born My 5, 1811; baptized Je 24, 1811.
Margaret (1:215), born S 1, 1813; baptized Ja 1, 1814.
Juliana Anna (1:219), born F 23, 1816; baptized S 22, 1816.
SMITH (SCHMIDT), John, soap-boiler (1:134; 2:215), son of John Conrad and
Maria Sybilla (Gross) Schmidt; he was born O 24, 1789 at Lachen, in Rhein-
pfalz; he married (1) on F 8, 1821 Margaret Born (2:187), daughter of
Jacob Born, farmer, and Margaret (Weller)); she was the eldest daughter and
was born Ag 9, 1791 in Frederick County; she died F 25, 1823 and was
buried F 27, 1823.
Issue: Two, of whom one daughter survived him.
Antoinette Sybilla (1:117), born N 11, 1821; baptized N 28, 1821;
she had an illegitimate son by Parmenio Renatus Harry.
SMITH (SCHMITT), John, tobacco-stripper (2:215), born O 24, 1789; died Ag
18, 1843; buried Ag 19, 1843; married (2) Catharine Elizabeth Oehme
(2:292) who was born Jl 18, 1791 at Gnadenthal; she was a Communicant Ja
24, 1807 at Lititz. Married Mr 7, 1824.
Issue: Daniel August (2:204), born N 30, 1828 at Lititz; baptized D 7,
1828; died Ap 22, 1833 of scarlet fever; buried Ap 23, 1833.
Carolina Elizabeth (2:17), born O 16, 1830; baptized O 24, 1830.
John William (2:23,294), born My 30, 1833; baptized Je 9, 1833.
son (died before the father)
son
SMITH (SCHMIDT), John, distiller and farmer (1:134) married (2) Ja 31, 1822
Maria Stauffer (2:205), daughter of Christian and Barbara (Weller) Stauf-
fer; she was born O 2, 1795; she died N 19, 1833 of dropsy and was buried
N 21, 1833.
Issue: Mary Ann (1:119), born Jl 30, 1822; baptized S 9, 1822.
Matilda (2:17), born Ag 17, 1830; baptized O 31, 1830.
son
daughter
SMITH, John (2:150) [married ca. 1848 ?] Mary Lohr.

86

Issue: John William (2:46), born Mr 24, 1849; baptized Ag 5, 1849.
    Margaret Josephine (2:46), born Ja 13, 1851; baptized D 2, 1851.
SMITH, John (2:290,294), born Mr 24, 1824 at Lachen in the Palatinate; he
    was a Communicant on Whitsunday, 1843.
SMITH (SCHMIDT), John (1:131) married Je 25, 1815 Anna Maria Willjar, daugh-
    ter of John and Anna Margaret (Protzman) Willjar, in the mountains; Anna
    Maira was born Ja 21, 1794.
SMITH (SCHMIT), John George (2:207), born Mr 9, 1798 at Lachen in the Pala-
    tinate; he married D 30, 1818 Margaret Zoller; came to America in June,
    1832; joined the congregation My 16, 1833; he died N 3, 1834, apparently
    of jaundice; buried N 5, 1834.
    Issue: (4, at least 3 sons)
        George, born Mr 26, 1821; married Araminta Eigenbrod.
SMITH (SCHMIDT), John Mattheus, farmer, married _____ Waer.
    Issue: Anna Maria (1:196), baptized Jl 23, 1803.
SMITH (SCHMIDT), Joseph married Catharina _____.
    Issue: Susanna (1:182), born O 31, 1796; baptized D 11, 1796.
SMITH, Joshua (1:88), son of Moses and Anna (Kid) Smith, married O 23, 1834
    Sophia Stokes, daughter of George and Hannah (Ambrose) Stokes.
    Issue: Margaret married George F. Eyler.
SMITH, Joshua (2:160) married O 10, 1869 Eliza Rouzer.
SMITH (SCHMIDT), Leonard, farmer, married Elizabeth Kuhn.
    Isseu: Christian (1:190), born O 8, 1800; baptized N 21, 1800.
SMITH (SCHMIDT), Margaret married Jacob First.
SMITH, Margaret Ann (2:231), born F 24, 1858; died Ag 20, 1858; buried Ag
    22, 1858 at Apple's Church.
SMITH (SCHMIDT), Margaretha married John Cookerly.
SMITH (SCHMIDT), Maria married Jacob Reitnauer.
SMITH, Martha Virginia (2:235), born Ja 25, 1856; died Mr 8, 1862; buried Mr
    10, 1862 at Mechanicstown.
SMITH (SCHMIDT), Peky married Jacobus Tanner.
SMITH, Peter married Magdalena _____.
    Issue: Magdalena married Levi Kessler.
SMITH (SCHMITT), Philip Lorenz (2:293), born Jl 24, 1826 at Lachen in the
    Palatinate; a Communicant in 1843. Went west.
SMITH (SCHMIDT), Salome married John Seiffarth.
SMITH, Sarah married John Mondshour.
SMITH (SCHMIDT), Sophia married Jacob Süss.
SMITH, Thomas E. married Julia Ann Maria Wilhide (Lutheran).
    Issue: John Clarence (2:131), born O 14, 1870; baptized Ja 8, 1871.
SMITH, William married Catharine Harbaugh.
    Issue: Charles Calvin (2:135,250), born Ag 19, 1875; baptized Ap 29, 1876;
        died My 2, 1876; buried My 3, 1876 at Mechanicstown.
SMITH (SCHMIDT), William married Elizabeth Thomas.
    Issue: Perry Elioth (1:217), born Ap 26, 1815; baptized My 18, 1815.
SMITH, Zephaniah (2:255,293), born D 19, 1814 in Frederick County; a Commun-
    icant Ap 4, 1833; died Ag 20, 1879 and was buried at Graceham Ag 22, 1879.
SNOG, Caty married Adam Butler.
SNYDER (SCHNEIDER), Abraham married Elizabeth Bauman.
    Issue: Mary Anne (1:146), born My 29, 1833; baptized S 2, 1833.
SNYDER (SCHNEIDER), Anna Elizabeth married John Frederick Becker.
SNYDER (SCHNEIDER), Catharina married George Haber.
SNYDER (SCHNEIDER), Jacob, farmer, married Dorothea Willheidt.
    Issue: Peggi (1:196), born Ag 6, 1803; baptized N 12, 1803.
        Elizabeth (1:196), born Ag 6, 1803; baptized N 12, 1803.
SNYDER (SCHNEIDER), Jacob (1:231), born in Jl, 1725 in Grünwetterspach,
    duchy of Württemberg; came to America in 1751; lived in the mountains; he
    was taken into the church 1773; first communion O 8, 1774; he died S 27,
    1778 and was buried in the churchyard S 29, 1778; he married in 1757 Maria

Magdalena Bissinger (1:263) who was born Mr 15, 1731 at Ensweingen in Württemberg; she came to America in her 21st year; she died F 13, 1810 and was buried F 15, 1810. They were the parents of 12 children.
Issue: Christian (1:230), born Ap --, 1764; died O 5, 1772; buried in the churchyard O 7, 1772.
    Anna Maria (1:164), born N 1, 1772 at 6 p.m.; baptized N 8, 1772.
    Anna Rosina (1:165,230), born Ag 24, 1774 at 8 a.m.; baptized Ag 28, 1774; died S 12, 1774; buried in the churchyard S 13, 1774.
    Barbara (1:166), born My 25, 1777; baptized Je 7, 1777.
SNYDER, Jacob & Magdalena; Probationers O 9, 1774 (1:91); she was a Communicant N 13, 1785 (1:108).
SNYDER (SNIDER), Martin (2:153) married Mr 2, 1854 Harriet Martin.
SNYDER, Susanna married Michael Colliflower.
SOUTH, Susanna.
Issue: Maria Wilhelmina (1:183), born Ja 25, 1797; baptized Ap 23, 1797.
SOUTHER, Margaret married Jonathan Meyers.
SOWERS (SAURS), John Henry married Sophia Mutschler.
Issue: Henry Gottlieb (1:151), born D 2, 1836; baptized Ja 7, 1837.
SPAULDING, Anna E. married Joseph Wilhide.
SPEAK, Sarah Elizabeth (2:238), born Ja 17, 1862; died Ag 5, 1863; buried Ag 7, 1863 at Creagerstown.
SPEARS, Harriet married Richard Ridgely.
SPENGLER, John married Margaret Lingefelder.
Issue: Elizabeth (1:199), born D 14, 1804; baptized Mr 17, 1805.
SPIES, Catharine married Gabriel Kuhn.
SPIEKER, _____ married Maria Bühler (1:259).
Issue: Johanna Regina married Daniel Greiss.
Maria Bühler later married Daniel Protzman.
STARK, William (moved away in 1844) married Catharine Boller (2:289), daughter of Philip William and Catharine (Lanius) Boller; she was born Ja 19, 1811; she was a Communicant Ap 12, 1827.
Issue: Maria Elizabeth (2:25), born D 26, 1833; baptized Mr 2, 1834.
    Araminta (2:29), born My 9, 1836; baptized Je 12, 1836.
    Susanna (2:32 says mother Susanna); born Je 12, 1838; baptized Ag 12, 1838.
    Margaret Ann (2:39), born N 25, 1840; baptized O 10, 1841.
    John Benjamin (2:41), born Ja 29, 1843; baptized Je 5, 1843.
STAUB, Anna Matilda married Abraham Goushon.
STAUB, Christian of Kriegerstown (brother of Nicholas); married Christina Lang.
Issue: Frederick (1:201), born N 25, 1805; baptized N 25, 1805.
    Thomas (1:208), born Mr 3, 1809; baptized Jl 19, 1809.
STAUB, Daniel, on the Manakusie, married Elizabeth Berg.
Issue: Salomon (1:202), born Ja 2, 1806; baptized Mr 30, 1806.
STAUB, John (1:94) was baptized My 20, 1838, when apparently over 80.
STAUB, Nicholas (1:202) (brother of Christian Staub) married Elizabeth Jansen (Camsten).
Issue: Maria (1:202), born D 25, 1805; baptized Mr 30, 1806.
    William (1:208), born S 4, 1808; baptized Jl 19, 1809.
    Ludwich (1:215), born F 2, 1811; baptized S 18, 1813.
STAUFFER, Anna Elizabeth married John Bush.
STAUFFER, Barbara married Philip Ranck.
STAUFFER, Daniel (2:144), joiner, son of John Christian and Barbara Stauffer; he was born Mr 25, 1800 in Frederick County; he married N 30, 1826 Sophia Derr.
Issue: Angelina (2:11), born Ag 23, 1827; baptized S 30, 1827.
    Cassandra Elizabeth (2:14), born F 12, 1829; baptized Mr 22, 1829.
    Jane Rebecca (2:19), born F 25, 1831; baptized My 22, 1831.

Edward Augustus (2:24), born Ap 14, 1833; baptized N 15, 1833.
Frederic Owen (1:151), born My 5, 1836; baptized S 25, 1836.
John Tilghman (2:32), born Je 27, 1838; baptized N 2, 1838.
William Henry (2:37), born Mr 4, 1840; baptized My 7, 1840.
STAUFFER, Elizabeth married John Fraley.
STAUFFER, Frederic (2:151) married Je 9, 1851 Martha Medcalfe.
Issue: Alverda Wilmina (2:118,237), born Ap 3, 1852; baptized Ag 25, 1852;
    died Ja 27, 1863; buried Ja 29, 1863 at Graceham.
    Helen Theodocia (2:52), born S 20, 1854; baptized Mr 28, 1858.
    James Napoleon (2:51), born N 30, 1856; baptized F 15, 1857.
    William Albert (2:59,241), born Mr 19, 1864; baptized Je 19, 1864;
    died Ap 18, 1865; buried Ap 19, 1865 at Graceham.
STAUFFER, George married Agnes _____.
Issue: John Ephraim (2:62), born My 12, 1867; baptized Ag 11, 1867.
STAUFFER, George E. had by Mary Jane Warner an illegitimate daughter Georgi-
    ann Eliza (2:121,239) who was born Ja 27, 1856, baptized My 24, 1856,died
    O 15, 1863, buried O 16, 1863 at Apple's Church. Mary Jane Warner later
    married _____ Dehuff.
STAUFFER, Henry (2:144,287), son of John Christian and Barbara Stauffer; he
    was born Ap 22, 1806; he was a Communicant D 4, 1825; he married S 30,
    1827 mary Magdalen Krall (2:255,287), who was born O 9, 1805; she was a
    Communicant Ap 12, 1827; she died N 19, 1879 and was buried N 20, 1879 at
    Graceham.
Issue: James Frederic (2:293; 1:136), born Ja 14, 1828 in Frederick
    County; baptized Mr 30, 1828.
    Mary Ann (1:138), born Ja ?, 1829; baptized My 17, 1829.
    Sarah Ellen (2:27), born Ja 4, 1835; baptized Ap 8, 1835; married
    Samuel Six.
STAUFFER, Jacob, weaver, married Anna Margaret Kuntz (or Kuns).
Issue: Elias (1:205), born Ap 4, 1808; baptized Ap 24, 1808.
    Joseph (1:211), born Ap 24, 1811; baptized Je 16, 1811.
    Lydia (1:216), born N 13, 1814; baptized D 13, 1815.
    William (1:116), born Ag 14, 1820; baptized Ap 10, 1821.
STAUFFER, John Christian, weaver (2:191,217,287), was born My 16, 1776 and
    was baptized O 8, 1820; he was a Communicant D, 1820; he died D 10, 1845
    (a widower) and was buried D 12, 1845; he married Barbara Weller (2:216,
    287) (or Peitzel, 1:193,197), daughter of Philip Weller and Juliana (Wott-
    ring), later the wife of Henry Peitzel; Barbara was born S 1, 1771 in
    Frederick County; she was a Communicant Mr 23, 1815; she died F 12, 1845
    and was buried F 14, 1845.
Issue: Catharine Sophia (1:212), born Mr 29, 1790; baptized O 8, 1811;
    married Henry Jans.
    Elizabeth (1:176), born Ag 31, 1792 at 11 a.m.; baptized Mr 3,
    1792; married George Colliflower.
    Maria (1:181), born O 2, 1795; baptized N 1, 1795; married John
    Smith.
    Sarah (1:185), born My 28, 1798; baptized Je 24, 1798; married
    Frederick Weller.
    Daniel (1:189), born Mr 25, 1800; baptized Ap 26, 1800; married
    Sophia Derr.
    John (1:193; 2:191), born F 6, 1802; baptized Mr 7, 1802; died F
    10, 1825 of ardent gall fever; buried F 12, 1825.
    Matilda (1:197), born Ja 22, 1804; baptized F 26, 1804; married
    John Daniel Wilhide.
    Henry (1:202), born Ap 22, 1806; baptized Je 8, 1806; married Mary
    Magdalen Krall.
    Carolina (1:207), born Ja 2, 1809; baptized F 3, 1809.
    Juliana (1:217), born Ap 21, 1815; baptized My 28, 1815; married
    John Firor.

STAUFFER, Maria had an illegitimate son by John Pittenger.
STAUFFER, Mary Ann married John Henry Fraley.
STAUP, David (1:90) married O 26, 1842 Anna Wilhite.
STEECE, Henry (1:87) married Mr 29, 1832 Susan Shaeffer.
STEM, John married Juliana Harbaugh.
    Issue: Henry Wilson (1:103), born S 19, 1842; baptized My 19, 1843.
STEM (STEMM), Catharine married William Harbaugh.
STEM (STEMM), Reuben married Susanna Stoner.
    Issue: Mary Catharine (1:145), born D 20, 1832; baptized Jl 27, 1833.
STEM, William married Susan McClane.
    Issue: William Johnson (1:101), born Ag 12, 1840; baptized Jl 10, 1842.
        Julian Elisabeth (1:101), born N 5, 1841; baptized Jl 10, 1842.
        Nancy (1:104), born F 20, 1843; baptized My 14, 1843.
STEVENSON, Joshua married Margaret _____ (2:224); she was born D 26,
    1822; she died F 23, 1854 and was buried F 25, 1854 at Stone Church,
    Mechanicstown.
STEWART, Sarah married William Hart.
STIMMEL (STIMMELL), David (2:225), born Ja 20, 1815; died Ag 2, 1854; buried
    Ag 3, 1854 at Apple's Church.
STIMMEL, John (1:83), son of Henry and Catharina Stimmel; he married S 2,
    1827 Mary Lehman, daughter of Jacob and Catharine Lehman.
STIMMEL, Margaret married Jacob Cover.
STIMMEL, William, of Mechanicstown District, married on Ja 17, 1878 Eliza-
    beth Boller (2:163).
STITELY, Anna married William Orlandus Weller.
STITELY, George married Sarah Sheets.
    Issue: William Henry Harrison (1:100), born Je 20, 1840; baptized N 29,
        1840.
STITELY, Jacob of Frederick County (2:151) married Ja 17, 1850 Barbara Ann
    Eyler, also of Frederick County.
STITELY, Susan married Solomon Eyler.
STOCKSLEGER, Amos (2:236), born My 9, 1831; died Jl 19, 1862; buried at
    Creagerstown Jl 20, 1862.
STOKES, Catharine married Samuel Weller.
STOKES, George married Hannah Ambrose.
    Issue: Sophia married Joshua Smith.
STOKES, Josuah.
    Issue: Addison Clark (2:234), born D 3, 1849; died S 22, 1861 of a fall
        from a hickory tree; buried S 22, 1861 at Mechanicstown.
STOKES, Sophia married Thomas Weller.
STOKES, Susanna married _____ Hart.
STOLL, Amanda married Thomas Gurley.
STOLL (STULL), Ann married David Weller.
STOLL (STULL), Catharine Ann married Jacob R. Mumma.
STOLL, Elizabeth married John Humerich.
STOLL (STULL), Georgiana married Abraham Lohr.
STOLL (STULL), Harriet C. married Eugene Jacob Gernand.
STOLL, John married Anne Kuhns.
    Issue: Georgiana (1:140), born Mr 10, 1830; baptized Ja 31, 1831.
STOLL (STULL), William (2:153) married Ja 2, 1855 Sarah Arthur.
STONER, Susanna married Reuben Stem.
STONER, William married Catharine Ellen Parrish.
    Issue: Martha Ellen (2:118), born My 30, 1850; baptized F 23, 1851.
        Theodore Columbus (2:118), born Jl 10, 1852; baptized O 31, 1852.
STOTZ, Maria married Samuel Süss.
STRAWSBAUGH, Nancy A. M. married Joseph N. Lohr.
STREFER, Margaret married Bernard Rinn.
STREHLE, Georg married Catharina Strehle.
    Issue: Henoch (1:209), born D 28, 1805; baptized Ag 21, 1809.

Henrietta (1:209), born F 24, 1807; baptized Ag 1, 1809.
Josua (1:209), born S 15, 1809; baptized D 13, 1809.

STRENG, John married Anne Woodring, daughter of Jacob and Barbara (Keiper) Woodring.
Issue: Maria Catharina (1:137), born Je 12, 1828; baptized Ag 3, 1828.
STUMP, Jesse married Susanna Sheley.
Issue: Morgan Eden Nelson (1:95), born S 15, 1837; baptized S 8, 1838.
SULLIVAN, John, schoolmaster, married Eliza _____.
Issue: Charles Hellebruce (1:136), born Mr 4, 1827; baptized Ja 6, 1828.
SÜSS, Benjamin, blacksmith (1:134; 2:287), son of John George Süss, farmer, and Maria Barbara (Eigenbrod); he was born Je 25, 1797 in Frederick County; he was a Communicant O 8, 1820; he married My 16, 1822 Sarah Boller (2:287), daughter of Philip William and Catharina (Lanius) Boller; she was born My 3, 1802 in Northampton County, Pennsylvania; she was a Communicant Mr 30, 1820.
Issue: Clementina Louisa (2:2,295), born Jl 28, 1823; baptized Ag 17, 1823; a Communicant O 8, 1839.
Joshua Owen (2:6,293), born Je 17, 1825; baptized Jl 24, 1825; a Communicant in 1841.
Llewellyn (2:11,294), born Ag 22, 1827; baptized S 30, 1827; a Communicant in 1843.
Emma Olivia (2:16,295), born S 1, 1829; baptized O 18, 1829; a Communicant in 1843.
Reuben Gilbert (2:20,294), born My 20, 1831; baptized Je 19, 1831; went west.
Josias Jeromus (2:23,209), born Jl 15, 1833; baptized Ag 18, 1833; died Mr 30, 1835 of measles; buried Ap 1, 1835.
Sabina Clymena (2:30), born My 19, 1837; baptized Je 18, 1837.
Josiah Benjamin (2:38), born Ag 5, 1840; baptized S 13, 1840.
William Lucas (2:40,216), born S 6, 1842; baptized O 16, 1842; died Jl 20, 1844, aged 1-10-14; buried Jl 21, 1844.
Marianne (2:42,216), born Mr 19, 1845; baptized Mr 22, 1845; died Mr 23, 1845; buried Mr 24, 1845.
SÜSS, Catharina Barbara (daughter of John George Süss and Maria Barbara, née Eigenbrod) had an illegitimate son by Anthony Leiber.
SÜSS (SIESS), Elisha or Elijah, weaver, son of Emanuel Süss, married Mr 28, 1826 Abigail Protzman, daughter of Ludwig Protzman, shoemaker, and Maria Elizabeth (Rausser); Abigail was born Ap 2, 1807 in Graceham.
Issue: Mary Henrietta (1:135), born Ap 23, 1827; baptized My 13, 1827.
Sophia Elizabeth (1:148), born Mr 14, 1835; baptized My 2, 1835.
SÜSS, Emanuel married Maria Jackson.
Issue: John (1:198), born F 5, 1804; baptized My 6, 1804.
SÜSS, Godfrey, tanner & nailsmith (2:216,287), son of John George and Catharine Süss, was born F 9, 1765 at 'Heidelberg'; he was a Communicant at Bethlehem O 1, 1785; he died Ag 14, 1844 and was buried Ag 16, 1844; he lived to see 34 grandchildren of whom 15 died before him; he married N 16, 1791 Anna Maria Krämer (2:228,287,292), daughter of Michael and Elizabeth Krämer, who was born O 31, 1769 at Lancaster, Pennsylvania; she was a Communicant S 13, 1789; she died at 12:15 p.m. on Jl 30, 1856 and was buried Jl 31, 1856; she had 38 grandchildren and 13 great-grandchildren when she died.
Issue: Elizabeth (1:176), born Mr 8, 1793 at noon; baptized Mr 10, 1793; died F 11, 1849; married George Park.
John (1:179), born D 26, 1794 at 3 a.m.; baptized D 28, 1794; married (1) Elizabeth Schuler.
Maria (1:183; 2:224,295), born D 27, 1796 at 5:30 a.m.; baptized Ja 1, 1797; a Communicant Mr 30, 182-; died Je 13, 1854; buried Je

15, 1854.

Frederick William (1:187), born Ja 18, 1799; baptized Ja 27, 1799.

Rosina (1:190), born N 27, 1800; baptized N 30, 1800; married Alexander Harbaugh.

Elias (2:293; 1:193), born Ap 18, 1802; baptized Ap 25, 1802; a Communicant O 8, 1820.

Aaron (1:199; 2:214), born O 25, 1804; baptized N 4, 1804; died F 18, 1841; buried F 20, 1841.

Rebecca (1:204), born Ap 5, 1807; baptized Ap 26, 1807; married Emanuel Gernand.

Carolina (1:208; 2:295), born My 25, 1809; baptized My 28, 1809; a Communicant D 4, 1825.

Salome (1:210), born Je 17, 1810; baptized Jl 15, 1810; married (1) William Delaplane and (2) Parmenio Renatus Harry.

Jeremiah (1:214; 2:199), born Ja 13, 1813; baptized Ja 22, 1813; died My 2, 1831 of an early abdominal injury, and was buried My 4, 1831.

Amy (1:216), born My 29, 1814; baptized Je 26, 1814; died Ja 25, 1836 of gall fever, and was buried Ja 26, 1836; she was unmarried.

SÜSS, J. George and M. Barbara; Probationers F 2, 1783 (1:92); Communicants Mr 25, 1785 (1:108); Magdalena was a Probationer (1:92).

SÜSS, Jacob married Anna Maria _____.

Issue: George (1:173b), born Jl 16, 1791 at 1 a.m.; baptized Jl 21, 1791.

SÜSS (SIESS), Jacob married Sophia Smith (1:137).

SÜSS, Jacob, mason, son of John George and Maria Barbara (Eigenbrod) Süss, married Sophia Schmidt.

Issue: Joseph Alfred (1:116), born Mr 21, 1821; baptized Ap 20, 1821.

George William (2:1,193), born F 6, 1823; baptized F 16, 1823; died Ag 8, 1827 of dysentery; buried Ag 10, 1827.

Anna Elizabeth (2:6), born Ap 17, 1825; baptized My 29, 1825.

Emeline Sophia (2:12), born Je 13, 1828; baptized Jl 27, 1828.

Robert Jacob Coleman (2:17), born Ag 18, 1830; baptized S 12, 1830.

SÜSS, John, farmer (1:134; 2:235,287), eldest son of Gottfried Süss, tanner, and Anna Maria (Kraemer); he was born D 26, 1794 in Graceham; he was a Communicant Ap 4, 1833; "a worthy member of this congregation for nearly 30 years." He died My 3, 1862 and was buried at Graceham My 5, 1862; he married Ag 12, 1821 Elizabeth Schuler (2:287), eldest daughter of Samuel Schuler, windlass-maker, and Elisabeth (Kraemer); she was born O 4, 1799 at Lancaster; she was a Communicant Je 29, 1816 at Lititz.

Issue: Joseph Augustus (2:2), born Mr 18, 1823; baptized Ap 27, 1823.

Raymond Silvester (2:6), born Je 7, 1825; baptized Jl 10, 1825; married Salome Angelica Gernand.

Clementina Elisabeth (2:10,201),born Ap 14, 1827; baptized My 20, 1827; died Ja 2, 1833; buried Ja 4, 1833; Death was caused by scarlet fever.

William Alexander (2:15,201), born Je 1, 1829; baptized Je 28, 1829; died D 29, 1832 of scarlet fever; buried D 30, 1832.

Anna Maria (2:20,296), born Ag 24, 1831; baptized O 2, 1831; died Mr 12, 1854; married William Gernand.

Jeremiah Franklin (2:27), born Ja 2, 1835; baptized Ja 10, 1835.

Orlando Leander (2:30,297), born Je 2, 1837; baptized Je 5, 1837; married Martha Anders.

Aaron Winfield (2:38,234,297), born Ag 8, 1840; baptized S 13, 1840; died Ja 16, 1862 of an internal injury sustained 4 years before; buried Ja 18, 1862.

SÜSS, John George (1:234-235) (son of peasants, Lutherans); born Ap 18, 1718 at Wertheim an der Saur, Lower Alsace; at the age of 18 he enlisted in the Prince of Darmstadt's Cavalry Grenadier Regiment in the French service,

and served 9 years, then returned home; he started for America with 2 sisters Mr 10, 1750 and arrived in Philadelphia safe Ag 24, 1750. After he paid the charges for himself and his sisters he started for Tulpehocken. There he stopped for a year, then went over the Blue Mountains, took up a tract of land and built a house before he married. When the Indian war broke out he fled to Heidelberg [Berks County] where he came to know the Moravians and became a probationer. In 1765 he bought 50 acres of land here, near our Gemeinhaus, and in October he and his family moved here. For 6 years he suffered with a heaviness in the chest. His end was so easy that he seemed to sleep away. He died D 6, 1785 after 13 days illness and was buried in the churchyard D 8, 1785. He married My 1, 1753 Maria Catharina Dock who was brought up a Lutheran (1:238-239); she came to America with some of her brothers and sisters in 1751; she was born Ja 11, 1726 in Bischweiler in Alsace; she died Ag 10, 1789 after being paralyzed on the right side a few months before, so that her mind and speech were affected. They were the parents of 4 sons and 4 daughters, of which 1 daughter died before the father and mother.
Issue: Paul, born N 11, 1758; married Maria Magdalena Beyerle.
John George, born Mr 23, 1764; married Maria Barbara Eigenbrod.
Godfrey, born F 9, 1765; married (1) Anna Maria Krämer.
Anna Maria (1:161), born F 12, 1768 in the evening; baptized F 17, 1768.
SÜSS, John George, farmer and blacksmith (1:127; 2:188); son of John George and Maria Catharina (Dock) Süss, born Mr 23, 1754 in Heidelberg (Berks County); he died O 14, 1823 and was buried O 15, 1823; 2 sons and 2 out of 18 grandchildren died before him; he married F 13, 1781 Maria Barbara Eigenbrod (2:211) (called Catharina Barbara 1:169); she was the daughter of John Yost and Eva Maria (Schörer) Eigenbrod, and was born O 1, 1758; she was a Communicant Mr 25, 1785; she died Ap 22, 1840 and was buried Ap 24, 1840; she lived to see 46 grandchildren (12 dead) and 12 great-grandchildren (1 dead).
Issue: Catharine Barbara (2:230,292), born N 29, 1781; baptized D 2, 1781; a Communicant D 4, 1802; unmarried, had an illegitimate son by Anthony Leiber; she died Ap 2, 1858; buried Ap 3, 1858 at Graceham.
George (1:170; 2:187), born D 1, 1783; baptized D 7, 1783; unmarried; blacksmith; died D 22, 1822; buried D 23, 1822.
Elizabeth (1:172), born My 25, 1785 at 4-5 a.m.; baptized My 25, 1785; died Ag 30, 1832; married (1) Abraham Fahs and (2) Conrad Wilhide.
John (1:166b,238), born O 20, 1787 at 4-5 a.m.; baptized O 21, 1787; died Ap 20, 1789 of smallpox; buried in the churchyard.
Jacob (1:170b), born Ap 21, 1790 at 1-2 a.m.; baptized My 2, 1790; married Sophia Schmidt.
Anna Maria (1:175b), born N 29, 1792 at 9 p.m.; baptized D 2, 1792; married Frederick Wampler.
Samuel (1:180), born My 16, 1795 at 9 a.m.; baptized Je 7, 1795; married Maria Stotz.
Benjamin (1:184), born Je 25, 1797; baptized Jl 9, 1797; married Sarah Boller.
Daniel (1:188), born N 18, 1799; baptized N 24, 1799.
SÜSS (SEAS), Mary E. married Frederick Augustus Wilman.
SÜSS (SIESS), Orlandes (son of John and Elizabeth (Schuler) Süss) married Martha Anders.
Issue: Infant son (2:236), born Ag 26, 1862; baptized -- --, ----; died S 8, 1862; buried S 9 at Graceham.
Anderson Ellsworth (2:59), born Ap 25, 1864; baptized O 9, 1864.
Caroline Virginia (2:62,243), born F 13, 1867; baptized Ag 8, 1867; died F 13, 1867 [sic] and buried at Graceham.

93

Orpha Jane (2:63), born N 23, 1868; baptized D 9, 1868.

John Joseph (2:72), born N 23, 1874; baptized My 23, 1880.

SÜSS, Paul (1:127; 2:206), son of Johann Georg and Catharina Süss, was born N 11, 1758 at 'Heidelberg', Pennsylvania; he died Je 25, 1834 of a cough of many years; buried Je 27, 1834; he married O 4, 1787 Maria Magdalena Beyerle (2:217,292), eldest daughter of Jacob Beyerle (Lutheran elder here); she was born S 26, 1771 at Lancaster County, Pennsylvania; she was a Communicant Ag 13, 1800; she died D 8, 1845 and was buried D 10, 1845. There was no issue.

SÜSS, Raymond Sylvester (2:152,293), son of John and Elizabeth (Schuler) Süss or Seiss; he was born Je 7, 1825; he was a Communicant on Whitsunday 1843; he married Mr 23, 1852 Salome Angelica Gernand, daughter of John Jacob and Anna Theodora (Becker) Gernand; she was born O 15, 1827 and baptized N 11, 1827.
Issue: William Allen (2:47,224), born D 21, 1852; baptized F 20, 1853; died Je 11, 1854 and was buried Je 12, 1854.
Addison Harvey (2:49), born O 4, 1854; baptized N 26, 1854.
Milton Howard (2:51), born S 7, 1856; baptized S 24, 1856.
Franklin Hayes (2:53), born F 27, 1858; baptized O 28, 1858.

SÜSS (SIESS), Samuel (1:180; 2:229), son of John George and Maria Barbara (Eigenbrod) Süss; he was born My 16, 1795 and baptized Je 1, 1795; he died My 10, 1857 and was buried My 11, 1857 at Graceham; he married Maria Stotz (2:248) who was born Je 12, 1798; she died Ja 25, 1875 and was buried Ja 27, 1875 at Graceham.
Issue: Eliza Jane (1:118; 2:255), born Ja 2, 1822; baptized My 26, 1822; died N 5, 1879; buried N 7, 1879 at Graceham; married _____ Clabaugh.
Arthur Benjamin (1:120), born N 30, 1823; baptized Ap 4, 1824.
Arnold Richard (1:122), born Ja 31, 1826; baptized Mr 26, 1826.
John Addison (1:137), born Jl 5, 1828; baptized Ag 24, 1828.
Hugh Timothy (1:143), born Mr 10, 1831; baptized Ap 22, 1832.
Samuel Sidney (1:145), born Mr 12, 1833; baptized Ag 11, 1833.
Catharine Maria (1:150; 2:214), born Ag 13, 1835; baptized Ag 14, 1836; died Mr 26, 1842; buried Mr 28, 1842.
Joseph Leander Franklin (1:95), born Ap 5, 1838; baptized Je 10, 1838.
George Johnson (1:100), born S 19, 1840; baptized N 8, 1840.
Ellen Louisa (1:104), born Ja 29, 1843; baptized Je 4, 1843.

SÜSSMANN, Elizabeth, single (1:91), was a Probationer Mr 6, 1764 and a Communicant D 6, 1766.

SiSSMANN (SÜSSMAN), Engelhart (1:237) married in 1741 Maria Catharina Dielforter; she was born Mr 15, 1715 at Gernborn, in Zweibrücken; she came to America in 1749; he died in Germany; she married (2) Jacob Lochman; she died Ja 13, 1788.
Issue: two daughters, who came to America with the mother in 1749.

SWEENEY, Anna Maria married John Edward Engel.

SWEENEY (SWENNEY), Israel married Anna Maria Wilheid.
Issue: Thomas Blackford (1:144), born Jl 20, 1832; baptized Ja --, 1833.
Jacob William (1:149), born S 28, 1835; baptized D 26, 1835.

SWEENEY (SWEENY), Jacob William married Ann Maria Smith.
Issue: George Daniel (2:130), born O 13, 1869; baptized Ja 16, 1870.

SWITZER, Jonas married Anne Isabella _____.
Issue: Deborah (1:87), married Zebulon Groff.

TANNER, Jacobus married Peky Schmidt.
Issue: William (1:208), born D 28, 1808; baptized Je 25, 1809.

THOMAS, Elizabeth married William Smith.

THOMAS, Susanna married John Ogle.

TIMMONS, John (1:86), son of Peter and Elizabeth Timmons, married D 9, 1830

Barbara Shiff, daughter of Michael and Anne Shiff.
TOONE, Robert married Sarah _____.
Issue: Samuel (1:157), born Mr 29, 1763; baptized My 1, ----.

TORNING, Thomas had by Elizabeth Wittmer an illegitimate daughter Elizabeth
Lavina (1:221) who was born O 2, 1817 and baptized Ap 17, 1818.
TRAINER, Thomas.
Issue: James (1:121), born Jl 23, 1824; baptized D 8, 1824.
TREBE, Peggi married James Berry.
TRIBER, Thomas married Maria Zimmermann, daughter of _____ and Maria Catha-
rina.
Issue: Maria Catharina (1:203), born Ap 22, 1806; baptized N 2, 1806.
TROXEL, Abraham married Isabella _____.
Issue: William Henry (2:129), born Ja 12, 1866; baptized N 4, 1866.
TROXEL, Charlotte married George Wolf.
TROXEL, David (1:85), son of John Troxel, married Ag 31, 1830 Juliana Fieser
(2:241); she was born N 9, 1809; she died Ag 5, 1865 and was buried at
Apple's Church Ag 6.
TROXEL, Elias married Sarah _____.
Issue: Mary Ann or Mary Ellen married William Little.
TROXEL, Emanuel (2:250), died Ap 15, 1876 in Washington County; buried Ap
16, 1876 at Apple's Church.
TROXEL, John married Elizabeth Dodero.
Issue: Maria (1:86) married Jacob Biggs.
TROXEL, John (2:230), born D 23, 1773; died S 17, 1857; buried S 18, 1857 at
Apple's Church; he married Elizabeth Young (2:228) who was aborn Je 8,
1774; died D 4, 1856; buried D 6, 1856 at Apple's Church.
TROXEL, John married Susanna Rebecca Hesser.
Issue: Abraham Alexander (2:58), born N 16, 1860; baptized S 12, 1862.
George William (2:121), born N 23, 1854; baptized My 27, 1855.
TROXEL, Lewis married _____ Barton.
Issue: Julia Sabina (2:136), born Mr 17, 1880; baptized Jl 17, 1880.
TROXEL, Margaret Savilla married Edward Boller.
TROXEL, Samuel J. married Sophia Elizabeth Colliflower, daughter of Michael
Joseph and Harriet Elizabeth (Shuff) Colliflower.
Issue: Clarence Joseph (2:64,246), born Jl 6, 1870; baptized O 22, 1870;
died Mr 3, 1871, aged 0-7-25; buried at Graceham Mr 5, 1871.
Robert Lee (2:66), born O 12, 1871; baptized D 3, 1871.
Addie Bruce (dau.) (2:67), born F 4, 1873; baptized Jl 20, 1873.
Morris Luther (2:68), born Mr 17, 1875; baptized Jl 11, 1875.
Alva Franklin (2:70), born Ap 8, 1877; baptized Ag 31, 1877.
Florence Ellen (2:72), born Ap 18, 1879; baptized My 19, 1880.
Zeppa Grace (2:73), born O 23, 1880; baptized Ja 19, 1881.
TROXEL, Sarah married Tobias Newcomer.
TSHUDY, Salome married Samuel Renatus Heubener.

UMBACH, John married Christine Bippus.
Issue: John George (1:152), born F 4, 1837; baptized Mr 12, 1837.
UTTLY, Ssamuel, minister (1:227), born Ja 6, 1722 at Leedes-Parish, York-
shire, England; baptized in the Church of England; married F 10, 1766
Elizabeth Kremser; he died at 3:30 a.m. Mr 10, 1771, aged 49-2-3.

"Ich fuhlts von Jugend auf des Hlds gnadenzüge, in meinem 16. Jahr
gerieth ich in grosse Verlegenheit über meinem Gang nahm mir auch Vor ein
Gott wohl gefälliges leben zu führen, aber vergebens, ich wurde muthlos,
u. gag alles auf, bis ich nach einiger Zeit durch einen gewissen [Mann?]
der sich vor andern besonders bey mir distinguirte, von neuen in Verlegenheit kam u. den Vorsaz fasste, darnach zutrachten, wodurch mein Herz
getröstet u. zur Tuhe gelangen möchte, weil ich es aber durch eigene Kraft

suchte zu erhalten u. mich dabey gewann, wurde ich bald müde, u. war doch
dabey in meinem Gewissen verdammt, dass ich glaubte, die Gnaden Thüre wäre
für mich Verschlossen, u. ich von Gott verworfen, in diesen Jammervollen
zustand verblieb ich bis 1738. Da ich Mr. Ingham predigen hörte, u.
dadurch hinlängl. über zeugt wurde. Es wäre noch Gnade auch für mich;
fasste also wieder neuen Muth, u. wurde durch die Predigten dieses Manns
immermehr von der Liebe Jesu zu Sündern überzeugt, mein Herz wurde nach u.
nach lichte (achte?), u. die Neigung zur Sünde u. die Lust zur Welt ver-
schwand.   Ich war aber noch nicht vest gegründet, u. wurde wieder in
allerley umstände ein geflochten, die nur mein Christenthum wieder Zweifelhaft machten.   In dieser Ungewissheit blieb ich, bis Br. Petrus Ao
1741. hir anfing das Evangelium zu Predigen. Seine Worte Drungen wie ein
Feuer in meine Seele ein, ich lernte mich als ein armer Sünder kennen, u.
zugl. wo das Mittel für meine Krankheit zu finden sey. u. hatte Hoffnung
dass der Heiland mich noch seines Verdienstes Theilhaftig machen werde,
als ich nun von meinen Vermeinten Guten ganz entblöst Vor ihm im Staub
gebeugt worden, nahete Er sich zu mir, offenbarte sich meinen Herzen als
mein Versöhner, befreyete mich von allen Zweifel, wusch mich in seinen
Blute u. liess mich friede vor seinen Augen finden, so dass kein Umstand
mir diese Gnade bis auf diesen Tag hat Zweifelhaft machen können. Ao 1742
kamen mehr Geschw. nach Yorkshire, u. das gab Gelegenheyt, dass auch ich
in unsrere Conexion kam, u. ich sehnte mich nach näheren Gemeinschaft mit
den Brüdern, ich schrieb deswegen einen Brief, u. wurde 3 Tage darauf am
8t. Dec. 1743 in die Gemeine aufgenommen, wobey mirs unaussprechl. wohl
war, u. war zugl. versichert dass was da, mit mir auf Erden vorgekommen,
auch in Himmel geschehen wäre 1744 genoss ich mit der gemein; so wir
überhaupt in meinem Leben das H. Abm. zum ersten mal. mein Herz wurde
dabey mit einer unbeschreiblichen Gottes Kraft durch drungen u war versichert, dass ich Jesu Fleisch gegessen u. sein Blut getruncken hier; u.
denn zu Folge auch in lebendiges Glied an seinem Leibe d. 13. Nov. 1745
zog ich in die Gemeine nach Fullneck d. 16. Dec. kam ich unter die Stunden
[Beter?] d. 20t. Mart. 1746 wurde ich zum Arbeiter unter den led. Brn.
eingesegnet. d. 20t. Jul. 47 zog ich zum Dienst derselben, nach Gumersal
u. wohnte daselbst mit vielen Vergnügen.   Ao. 48 wurde ich mit 19 andern
Brn. in den Chor Bund eingerichtet.   1752 ging ich als Arbeiter der led.
Br. nach Dublin bis d. 20t. Aug. 54. wieder nach Gumersal versetzt wurde.
Ao 55 wurde Acoluth.   1756 kam ich nach Wiltshire zur Bedienung der dasi-
gen led. Br. u. Assistent im Predigen.   1761 wohnte ich der led. Br.
Confer. in Lindsey-house mit bey u. kehrte wieder nach Wiltshire zurük.
Von Oct. 1762 bis d. 26. Aug. 65 war ich in Fulnek als gehülfte bey dem
led. Br. Chor u. genoss gar Viele Segen für mein Herz. in Aug. 65 reiste
ich meinen Ruf zu folge con hier ab u. langte in Sept. in Shuth an, all-
hier hatte das Vergnügen eine Besuch in etl. Schlesischen gemeinen zu
thun, u. wurde am 10t. Febr. 1766 mit der led. Schw. Elisabeth Kremser
verheurathet u. am. 10t. Mertz zum Diacono der Br. Kirche ordinirt.
Worauf d. 12t. unsere Abreise auf den uns bestimmten Posten in Antigoa
erfolgt. d. 22 Apr. kammen wir inLondon, u. d. 6 July. glückl. in St.
Johns auf Antigoa an. Sie waren beyde mit einander am Dienst des Evangelii
unter den Negroes daselbst, bis d. 29. Nov. 1768. Am 7 Jan. 69 kamen sie
in behtlehem an, allwo er der Oeconomie auf seiner Profession gedient, bis
sie ihren Ruf zu folgen das Gemeinlein hier in Manakosy mit dem Wort u
Seelen Pflege zu bedienen, umgang u. zengnis war ihnen zum Segen.   Er war
also hier 9 Wochen gesund u. 9 Wochen krank, bis am 10t. Mart. früh um
halb 4 Uhr. der Sabbath der Glieder bey ihm eintrat, u. er in Jesu Arm u.
Schoos sanft u. seelig entschlief, seines Alters 49 Jahr 2 monat u. 3
Tage."

VALENTINE, David (1:85) married F 19, 1829 Margaret Crum.
VALENTINE, Elizabeth married Joseph Ogle.

VALENTINE, George (2:149) married Mr 27, 1845 Susanna Harbaugh.

VALENTINE, John (2:147) married D 28, 1837 Lavinia Harbaugh (2:237,288), daughter of John and Elisabeth (Koch) Harbaugh; she was born Ja 17, 1810; she was a Communicant D 4, 1825; she died My 10, 1863 and was buried at Graceham My 12, 1863.
Issue: Josephine Maryann (2:33), born Ja 12, 1839; baptized My 19, 1839.
    Susanna Elisabeth (2:38,214), born N 2, 1840; baptized N 28, 1840; died D 1, 1840 and was buried D 2, 1840.
    Margaret Ann Eliza (2:39), born O 20, 1841; baptized F 19, 1842.
VALENTINE, Solomon married Magdalena Beierle.
Issue: George Wesley (1:135), born My 18, 1827; baptized My 19, 1827.
    Magdalen Elisabeth (1:141), born Ap 14, 1831; baptized Je 12, 1831.
VALENTINE, Theodore married Mary Catharine _____.
Issue: Augusta Virginia Isabella (2:219), born Ja 21, 1850; died Mr 11, 1850; buried at Apple's Church Mr 13, 1850.
VAN VLECK, Sarah married The Reverend Nicholas Henry Eberhard.
VERTRIES, Hartmann (1:231), born O 15, 1716 at Fussgenheim in the Palatinate; came to America with his parents in his youth; he married F 10, 1744 (wife's name not given); he and his wife went to Bethlehem in 1747, were received in the church there Ja 19, 1748, first communion S 7, 1748; came here in 1764 to live on land given him by his father; he died D 28, 1778 and was buried in the churchyard D 20, 1778.
VOGEL, Juliana married Thomas C. Ramsburg.

WAER, _____ married John Matheus Schmidt.
WAGGEMAN, Richard married Anna Maria Miller.
Issue: Lycurgus Franklin (2:116), born Ag 23, 1849; baptized O 17, 1849.
    Lucretia Frances (2:116), born Ag 23, 1849; baptized O 17, 1849.
WALDMAN, Michael, "an old Revolutionary soldier" (1:84) married My 15, 1828 Mary Petty.
WALDMAN, Michael married Susanna Shields.
Issue: William Henry (1:152), born Mr 25, 1837; baptized My 28, 1837.
    Zephanah (1:96), born N 18, 1838; baptized Mr 10, 1839.
WALDMAN, Peter married Nancy Ann Long.
Issue: William Augustus (1:99), born Ja 19, 1840; baptized Ag 9, 1840.
WALKER, John married Elizabeth _____.
Issue: Eliza (1:85) married Solomon Frailey.
WALTER, Aloysius (2:160) married F 4, 1869 Flora Mozelle Dorsey, daughter of Owen Dorsey; she was born Jl 8, 1850 and baptized Mr 25, 1866.
WALTERS, Sarah Ann Elizabeth married Joseph Alfred Gernand.
WALTMAN, [Michael] (the hero of the Revolution).
Issue: Mary (1:83) married Ellis Eldridge.
    Thomas
WALTMAN (WALKMAN), Michael, laborer, married Polly Betty (Petty).
Issue: Margaret (1:94), born Ap 15, 1802; baptized Jl 25, 1802.
    Peter (1:210), born Je 15, 1810; baptized N 18, 1810.
WAMPLER, Frederick (1:131), born in Maryland; married My 24, 1814 Anna Maria Siess [sic], daughter of John George and Maria Barbara (Eigenbrod) Süss; she was born N 29, 1792 in Maryland, and was baptized D 2, 1792.
Issue: Sabina (1:217), born Mr 22, 1815; baptized My 19, 1815.
    Daniel (1:222), born D 23, 1818; baptized F 28, 1819.
WARD, William, foreman on Mr. Bruce's plantation, married Elizabeth Miller.
Issue: Sally (1:194), born Jl 26 [1799?]; baptized Je 19, 1802.
    Mary (1:194), born Je 5, 1801; baptized Je 19, 1802.
WARENFELTS, Urias married Susanna _____.
Issue: Lily Ida Susanna (2:241); died Ag 10, 1865; aged 2-9-23; buried at

97

Apple's Church Ag 12, 1865.
WARN, Susan married Thompson Anderson.
WARNER, Henry (2:154) married Je 14, 1855 Hannah Wireman.
WARNER, Maria married The Reverend Carl Gottlieb Blech.
WARNER, Mary Jane had an illegitimate daughter by George E. Stauffer.
WARNER, Mary Jane married _____ Dehuff.
WARNING, _____ married _____ McDonald.
WEARE, Thomas, laborer, married Catharine Fuller.
    Issue: Sarah (1:190), born O 5, 1798; baptized Ag 1, 1800.
WEBB, Catharine S. V. married Ephraim Gilbert.
WEBB, Charles Henry (2:242), died F 25, 1866, aged 1-11-8; buried at
    Mechanicstown F 25, 1866.
WEBER, George married Elizabeth _____.
    Issue: Jacob (1:157), born Je 19, 1762; baptized Jl 25, 1762.
        daughter (1:225), born Ap 4, 1764; died Ap 4, 1764.
        Catharine (1:159), born Je 9, 1765; baptized Je 16, 1765.
WEDEL, George, miller (1:131) married Mr 5, 1816 Rosina Born, daughter of
    Jacob and Anna Margaret (Weller) Born; she was born D 9, 1798; she was
    baptized D 16, 1798; she was a Communicant Mr 30, 1828; she died N 14,
    1830 of a rheumatic condition, a type of consumption and dropsy; she was
    buried N 16, 1830.
    Issue: Samuel Washington (1:219), born S 19, 1816; baptized D 15, 1816;
        confirmed Palm Sunday, 1841; died F 24, 1842 and was buried F 25,
        1842.
        Joseph Hiram (1:114), born S 30, 1820; baptized D 10, 1820.
        Sarah Anna (1:221), born Jl 16, 1818; baptized S 27, 1818.
WEDELL, George married Mary Ann _____.
    Issue: Mary Catharine married John Hahn.
WEDDEL, Mary Ann married William Woollard.
WEDDELL, Henry (2:150) married N 11, 1847 Susan Brown.
    Issue: Amy Alice (2:115), born Ag 18, 1848; baptized My 13, 1849.
        Joseph Amadeus (2:117), born O 15, 1849; baptized Ag 29, 1850.
        Julia Savannah (2:120), born Ag 5, 1853; baptized Ja 31, 1854.
WEDDEL, Isaac married Margaret or Rebecca Wilhide (Willheid).
    Issue: Catharine Anna (1:113), born Mr 13, 1820; baptized Jl 2, 1820.
        Harriet (1:136), born Ja 24, 1828; baptized Mr 2, 1828.
WEDDLE, Frederick William married Mary Ann Garver.
    Issue: Cassandra Elizabeth (1:105), born O 3, 1842; baptized Je 18, 1843.
WEDDLE, Margaret (2:221), born in Virginia; died Ja 27, 1852, aged about 55
    years; buried Ja 28, 1852.
WEDDLE, Samuel married Ann _____.
    Issue: Alice Virginia (2:221), born My 15, 1851; died Ag 4, 1851; buried
        Ag 5, 1851 at Apple's Church.
WEGELE, John, farmer, in the mountains, married Catharine Gnädig.
    Issue: James Thomas (1:116), born Ap 1, 1821; baptized Jl 1, 1821.
WEICHSEL, Henry W. married Angelina Cryan.
    Issue: John Henry (2:112), born Ja 3, 1845; baptized Ja 11, 1845.
WEIHL, William married Catharine _____.
    Issue: Daniel (1:219), born Ag 25, 1816; baptized O 20, 1816.
WEKER, Samuel married Anna Kotter (later the wife of John Groschong).
    Issue: Rebecca (1:207), born F 26, 1805; baptized Mr 16, 1805.
WELLER, _____ married Ephraim Crouse.
WELLER, Agnes had an illegitimate daughter by Joseph Wollard.
WELLER, Agnes C. married Jago Colliflower.
WELLER, Ann had an illegitimate son Julius Addison (2:122,232) who was born
    O 3, 1854, baptized S 16, 1856, died Ag 27, 1859 and was buried at Grace-
    ham Ag 28, 1859.
WELLER, Ann Rebecca married George Reidnauer.
WELLER, Ann Theresa married Henry Wilhide.

WELLER, Anna Margaret (Harbach), wife of John Jacob, Jr.; she was a Probationer Jl 19, 1767 (1:91); they both communed O 7, 1769 (1:108).
WELLER, Barbara Ann Rebecca married Stephen G. Ramsburg.
WELLER, Calvin Levi (2:294), son of John and Deborah (Krieger) Weller, born O 8, 1834; he married Emily Virginia _____.
Issue: Samuel Mortimer (2:124), born Je 3, 1860; baptized F 27, 1861.
    Harvey Madura (2:135), born F 23, 1877; baptized Je 17, 1877.
WELLER, Daniel married Catharine Willheid (1:113).
WELLER, David (2:145,290,291), son of Daniel and Catharine (Wilheid) Weller was born Je 8, 1807; a Communicant D 4, 1824; died Mr 22, 1875 and was buried in Hill Cemetery, Mechanicstown Mr 23, 1875; he married Mr 11, 1830 Maria Matilda Harbaugh (2:291), daughter of Christian and Maria Magdalena (Firor) Harbaugh; she was born Ja 2, 1809 and was baptized Ja 14, 1809; she died 1837.
Issue: Anna Rebecca (2:19), born Mr 13, 1831; baptized Mr 23, 1831.
    Augustus Alexander (2:22), born Ag 2, 1832; baptized S 7, 1832.
    Clemens Leander (2:25,206), born Ap 28, 1834; baptized Je 7, 1834; died Je 9, 1834; buried Je 10, 1834.
    Josiah Parmenio (2:27), born Je 24, 1835; baptized Jl 1, 1835.
    Elmyra Elizabeth (2:31), born O 26, 1837; baptized D 18, 1837.
WELLER, David (2:149,290), son of Daniel and Catharine (Wilhide) Weller, was born Je 8, 1807 in Frederick County; he married (2) on Mr 27, 1845 Ann Stull.
WELLER, Elias married Margaret Krieger (1:151).
WELLER, Elias (1:130; 2:238), son of John Jacob and Anna Margaret (Harbaugh) Weller, was born S 12, 1786 in Maryland; he was a Communicant for 56 years; he died Ag 3, 1863 and was buried at Graceham Ag 5, 1863; he married Je 4, 1811 Rosina Krieger, daughter of Lorenz and Anna Maria (Harbaugh) Krieger; she was born F 13, 1783 in Maryland; she died Ja 12, 1818 of complete debilitation and was buried Ja 14, 1818.
Issue: Carolina (1:213), born F 24, 1812; baptized Mr 30, 1818; died D 29, 1852; married Jacob Wilhide.
    Uriah (1:215; 2:236,293), born D 14, 1813; baptized D 26, 1813; a Communicant Ap 4, 1833; died Je 30, 1862; buried at Graceham Jl 1, 1862.
    Lydia Anna (1:218,265), born Mr 18, 1816; baptized Ap 10, 1816; died Je 4, 1817 of an eruption (Ausschlag) on head which developed into fever; buried Je 6, 1817.
WELLER, Elias, farmer (1:132; 2:238,288), son of John Jacob and Anna Margaret (Harbaugh) Weller, was born S 12, 1786 in Frederick County; a Communicant N 28, 1807; he died Ag 3, 1863 and was buried Ag 5, 1863 at Graceham; he married (2) on O 18, 1818 Maria Margaret Krieger, daughter of Lorenz and Anna Maria (Harbaugh) Krieger (2:232); she was born My 16, 1787 in Frederick County; she was baptized My 20, 1787; she was a Communicant Ag 13, 1808; she died Ap 5, 1859 of Apoplexy suddenly, and was buried Ap 7, 1859 at Graceham.
Issue: Anna Theresia (1:111; 2:250,292), born My 1, 1819; baptized My 30, 1819; a Communicant Ap 12, 1838; died unmarried Ja 7, 1876; buried Ja 9, 1876 at Graceham.
    James Alexander (1:116; 2:293), born Ap 26, 1821; baptized Je 11, 1821; moved to Lititz. Communicant in 1841.
    Anna Maria Caecilia (2:3,202), born Jl 5, 1823; baptized Ag 29, 1823; died F 3, 1833 of scarlet fever; buried F 4.
    Lewis Henry (2:6,293), born My 15, 1825; baptized Je 19, 1825; Communicant in 1841. Went west.
    Martin Jacob (2:11,201-202), born Ag 19, 1827; baptized S 30, 1827; died Ja 7, 1833 of cold fever; buried Ja 8, 1833.
    Martha Matilda (2:18,202), born N 3, 1830; baptized D 26, 1830; died F 20, 1833 of scarlet fever; buried F 21, 1833.

WELLER, Elias (C.) (2:148,288), son of Daniel and Catharine (Wilhide) Weller, was born Jl 26, 1809; a Communicant Ap 4, 1833; he married Ap 30, 1839 Deborah Geisbert (2:249) who was born Jl 10, 1820; she died D 16, 1875 very suddenly, and was buried at Chewsville, Maryland D 18, 1875.
Issue: Mary Ann Melissa (2:38), born Je 4, 1841; baptized S 5, 1841.
    Margaret Ann (2:41,222), born N 22, 1842; baptized Mr 26, 1843; died My 10, 1853; buried My 11, 1853.
    Joanna Catharine (2:42), born Ap 22, 1845; baptized Jl 27, 1845.
    Charles Abraham (2:45), born Ag 28, 1846; baptized S 16, 1846.
    Julia Ann Elizabeth (2:114), born Mr 24, 1848.
    John Daniel (2:45), born Ap 11, 1849; baptized My 27, 1849.
    Maria Ellen (2:46), born Ja 14, 1851; baptized D 11, 1851.
    Martin Henry (2:47), born Ja 3, 1853; baptized Ap 28, 1853.
    Michael Amadeus (2:49), born Mr 8, 1854; baptized Je 11, 1854.
    George Elias (2:51), born My 18, 1857; baptized Ag 30, 1857.
    Victoria Amanda Deborah (2:54), born N 25, 1858; baptized Je 14, 1859.
    William McClellan (2:57), born Mr 22, 1861; baptized Je 3, 1862.
    Elsidora Ada (2:64), born D 14, 1868; baptized O 9, 1870.
WELLER, Elizabeth, wife, Probationer O 8, 1758 (1:91).
WELLER, Elizabeth, wife of Jacob, Sr., was a Communicant S 16, 1759 (1:107).
WELLER, Elmira married Daniel [David?] L. Wilhide.
WELLER, Ephraim Elias (2:234), son of John and Deborah (Krieger) Weller, wasborn N 13, 1836; a Communicant D 31, 1854; died Ag 19, 1861 of dysentery; buried at Mechanicstown Ag 20, 1861.
WELLER, Frederick (1:131; 2:288), son of John Jacob and Anna Margaret (Harbaugh) Weller, was born D 21, 1789 in Frederick County; a Communicant N 28, 1807; married D 13, 1814 Sarah Stauffer (2:233,288), daughter of John Christian and Barbara (Weller) Stauffer; she was born My 28, 1798 in Frederick County; and was baptized Je 24, 1798; she joined the church O 8, 1817; she died S 18, 1860 of stomach cramps and was buried S 19, 1860 at Graceham.
Issue: Maria Anna (1:218), born Ap 9, 1816; baptized Ap 10, 1816; a Communicant in 1841; died My 17, 1854; married Levi Krieger.
    Elizabeth (1:111), born Mr 19, 1819; baptized My 2, 1819; died Ap 13, 1857; buried Ap 14, 1857; married James Krieger.
    William Henry (1:115; 2:293), born F 28, 1821; baptized Ap 15, 1821.
    John Levi (2:2), born Je 17, 1823; baptized Jl 20, 1823.
    Catharina Theresia (2:7), born S 17, 1825; baptized S 27, 1825; married Comenius Rondthaler.
    Lydia Anna (2:10,203), born My 16, 1827; baptized Je 9, 1827; died Mr 31, 1833 of scarlet fever; buried Ap 1, 1833.
    Joseph Augustus (2:13,293), born Ja 9, 1829; baptized Ja 20, 1829.
    Edward Frederick (2:18,294), born Ja 5, 1831; baptized F 4, 1831.
    Sophia Frederica (2:22), born S 15, 1832; baptized O 1, 1832.
    Barbara Anne Rebecca (2:28), born Jl 8, 1835; baptized Ag 16, 1835.
WELLER, Georg married Catharine Huber (1:205).
WELLER, George (1:130,266), son of John Jacob, widower, and Anna Margaret (Herbach); he was born Ag 5, 1783; baptized Ag 10, 1783; died F 2, 1820; buried F 3, 1820; he was married Jl 5, 1807 at Jacob Weller's house in the new town to Catharine Huber (1:265), daughter of John Jacob and Susanna (Harbaugh) Huber; she was born O 23, 1787 in Frederick County and was abaptized O 28, 1787; she was a Probationer Ap 18, 1808 and a Communicant N 26, 1808; she died N 10, 1817 of consumption and was buried N 11, 1817.
Issue: Nathanael (1:206), born Jl 5, 1808; baptized Jl 10, 1808; died Jl 17, 1833 and is buried at Graceham; married Maria Busch.
    Juliana Margaret (1:220; 2:206), born F 26, 1817; baptized Mr 16, 1817; died Mr 23, 1834 of consumption; buried Mr 25, 1834.

WELLER, Henry married Catharine Schober (1:189).
WELLER, Isaac (2:255,288), son of John Daniel and Catharine (Wilhide) Weller, was born Ap 8, 1815; a Communicant Ap 12, 1835; died Ag 11, 1880 and was buried at Graceham Ag 13, 1880; he married Rebecca Elizabeth Harbaugh (2:288), daughter of Christian and Maria Magdalena (Firor) Harbaugh; she was born D 21, 1818; she was a Communicant Ap 12, 1835.
Issue: Catharine Amanda (1:97), born N 2, 1838; baptized Mr 24, 1839.
    Isabella Sophia (2:37), born Jl 19, 1840; baptized Ag 30, 1840.
    Sevilla Magdalene (2:40), born S 17, 1842; baptized D 25, 1842.
    Daniel Edward (2:42,220), born Ja 17, 1845; baptized Mr 23, 1845; died S 22, 1850; buried S 23, 1850.
    Zachariah Winfield (2:44,220), born Ap 11, 1847; baptized Je 27, 1847; died S 17, 1850; buried S 18, 1850.
    William Orlandus (2:45), born My 15, 1849; baptized My 27, 1849.
    Sarah Elizabeth (2:47), born Ja --, 1852; baptized Ap 18, 1852.
    William Washington (2:50), born O 14, 1855; baptized Ja 19, 1856.
WELLER, Isabella married John Carson.
WELLER, Jacob (2:151) married S 5, 1850 Catharine E. Six.
WELLER, Jacob, Sr., was a Communicant O 8, 1758 (1:107).
WELLER, Jacob (1:242-243) son of Daniel Weller, was born S 16, 1704 at Dietenshausen; he married in 1726 Anna Margaret Koehn who died at Skippack, of the dropsy; he came to America 1737, arriving at Philadelphia in the fall of that year; thence they went to look up his friends, particularly John Peitzel, which led him into the Crice Creek settlement. Thence the family came here in 1742, and he was present at our first communion. As his years advanced he retired and spent most of his time reading the Holy Scriptures and other edifying books, praying for the welfare of his children and grandchildren, and was a beloved and venerable patriarch, of exemplary career. He was healthy all his life until the 27th of April, when he became completely helpless. He died My 8, 1794 and was buried My 10. His wife, who was very ill this spring, was able to take care of him, for which he was very happy and grateful.
WELLER, Jacob (1:242-243), son of Daniel Weller (Reformed), was born S 16, 1704 at Dietenshausen in Berleburg; he died My 8, 1794 and was interred in the burial ground in his orchard; he married (2) in Mr, 1738 at Crice Creek, Maria Barbara Wilhide ("a blessed vessel"); she had previously been the wife of _____ Vieruhr; she died Jl 17, 1754.
Issue: Philip (1:125,162) married Juliana Wotring.
    John Jacob (1:162) married (1) Magdalena Krieger and (2) Anna Margaret Herbach.
    John (1:126,165) married Maria Barbara Krieger.
    Elizabeth Juliana, born Ap 16, 1744; died D 26, 1795; married John Gump.
    son (died before the father)
    daughter (died before the father)
WELLER, Jacob (1:242-243), son of Daniel Weller, was born S 16, 1704 and died My 8, 1794; he married (3) Ag 13, 1755 Anna Elizabeth Krieger (1:253-254) whose father was a citizen of Bettelhausen; she was born in 1719 at Bettelhausen in Wittgenstein; she died Ap 2, 1800 and was buried Ap 4, 1800.
Issue: daughter, died in infancy
WELLER, James married Mary _____.
Issue: Eleanor Adelaide (2:56), born Ja 3, 1861; baptized Mr 10, 1861.
WELLER, John (2:145,288), son of Daniel and Catharine (Wilhide) Weller, was born D 8, 1805; a Communicant Ap 15, 1824; he died Ag 10, 1869 and was buried Ag 11, 1869; he married Ja 15, 1829 Deborah Krieger (1:205; 2:288), daughter of John Jacob and Maria Catharine (Bush) Krieger; she was born D 29, 1807 and was baptized Ja 24, 1808; she was a Communicant Ag 13, 1823.
Issue: Simon Augustus (2:15) born Jl 19, 1829; baptized Ag 23, 1829;

married Anna Barbara Brown.
Frances Ellen (2:18), born F 18, 1831; baptized Mr 23, 1831; married Ephraim Groshon.
Calvin Levi (2:26), born O 8, 1834; baptized N 28, 1834; married Emily Virginia _____.
Ephraim Elias (2:29), born N 13, 1836; baptized D 25, 1836; died Ag 19, 1861; married ? .
Agnes Marion (2:32), born S 19, 1838; baptized N 25, 1838.
Savannah Catharine (2:39), born S 12, 1841; baptized O 24, 1841; married Martin Augustus Williar.

WELLER, John, farmer (1:126,259), son of John Weller, farmer and Maria Barbara (Wilheld); he was born Ag 27, 1747 in Graceham; he died Ag 18, 1802 and was buried Ag 19, 1802; he married Ap 19, 1768 Maria Barbara Krieger (1:78), daughter of Lorenz Krieger, farmer and Maria Elisabeth (Hahn); she was born My 10, 1747 near Graceham; she died Je 15, 1820 and was buried Je 16. She lived to see 13 grandchildren and 6 great-grandchildren.
Issue: Anna Margaret (1:161,258), born at 1 p.m. Ag 18, 1769; baptized Ag 20, 1769; died S 1, 1800; buried S 3; married Jacob Born.
Anna Elizabeth (1:165), born at 8 a.m. Ap 22, 1774; baptized Ap 24, 1774.
John Henry (1:167), born Ag 1, 1778; baptized Ag 2, 1778; married Catharine Schober.
John Renatus (1:168,232), born S 4, 1781 in the evening; baptized S 9, 1781; died S 24, 1781 and was buried in the churchyard S 25, 1781.
John Daniel (1:169), born D 2, 1782; baptized D 8, 1782.

WELLER, John of Eyler's Valley (1:90) married Ap 30, 1842 Mary A. Eiler.
Issue: William Corsey (2:238), born F 26, 1858; died Jl 11, 1863; buried Jl 12 at Eyler Valley Chapel.

WELLER, John C. (2:151) married Ag 29, 1850 Amy Brown.

WELLER, Johann Daniel, farmer (1:129; 2:214), son of John and Maria Barbara (Krieger) Weller was born D 2, 1782 in Frederick County; he lived to see 14 grandchildren - 1 of them dead; he died Mr 2 1842 and was buried Mr 4; he married O 1, 1803 Catharine Wilhide (2:241,292), daughter of Frederick Wilhide, who was born Ap 26, 1787 or 1781 in Frederick County; she was a Communicant D 5, 1819; she died Jl 11, 1865 and was buried Jl 12 at Graceham.
Issue: John (1:201), born D 8, 1805; baptized D 15, 1805; died Ag 10, 1869; married Deborah Krieger.
David (1:204), born Je 8, 1807; baptized Je 21, 1807; married Maria Matilda Harbaugh.
Elias (1:209), born Jl 26, 1809; baptized Ag 13, 1809; married Deborah Geisbert.
Anna Rebecca (1:214,264), born S 22, 1812; baptized N 15, 1812; died F 20, 1813 of convulsions; buried F 22, 1813.
Isaac (1:217), born Ap 8, 1815; baptized My 14, 1815; married Rebecca Elizabeth Harbaugh.

WELLER, John Henry, farmer (1:128; 2:196), first son of John Weller, farmer, and Maria Barbara (Krieger); he was born in Frederick County Mr 21, 1778; he died O 21, 1829 of mania a potu; he was buried O 23, 1829; he married Je 18, 1799 Catharine Schober (2:230), second daughter of Peter Schober, farmer, and Sophia (Ambrose); she was born Ja 22, 1778 in Frederick County; she died Mr 4, 1858 and was buried at Apple's Church Mr 5, 1858.
Issue: None

WELLER, John Jacob, junior, joiner (1:162,265), son of Johann Jacob Weller (of Jacob) and Anna Margaretha (Herbach); he was born Fl 4, 1770 at 8 p.m. at Graceham, and was baptized Jl 8, 1770; he died My 26, 1818 of consumption and was buried My 27, 1818; he married Catharina Leonhardt (her name

not given 1:176,178,183 - only his).
Issue: Margaret (1:176,242), born Ja 3, 1793 at noon; baptized Ja 18,
   1793; died Je 21, 1793; buried Je 22, 1793.
Elisabeth (1:178,244), born My 7, 1794 at 9 p.m.; baptized My 15,
   1794; died F 2, 1795; buried F 4 in the churchyard.
Joseph (1:180,245), born S 20, 1795 in the evening; baptized S 21,
   1795; died S 21, 1795; buried S 22, 1795 in the churchyard.
Thomas (1:183), born My 27, 1797 at 10 a.m.; baptized Je 1, 1797.
Samuel (1:186), born Ja 1, 1799; baptized Ja 11, 1799.
Maria (1:191), born F 5, 1801; baptized F 15, 1801.
William (1:195), born Mr 20, 1803; baptized Ap 1, 1803.
Benjamin (1:199,263), born F 5, 1805; baptized F 23, 1805; died N
   1, 1810 of throat swelling; buried N 2, 1810.
Rosina (1:203), born Mr 3, 1807; baptized Mr 15, 1807.
Jonathan (1:207), born Mr 6, 1809; baptized Mr 26, 1809.
WELLER, John Jacob, blacksmith (1:129), eldest son of John Jacob and Anna
   (Krall) Weller; he was born in Frederick County; he married O 14, 1800
   Margaret Weller who was born O 22, 1780; she was the 4th daughter of John
   Jacob Weller (related to the husband) and Anna Margaret (Harbaugh).
Issue: John (1:194), born S 5, 1802; baptized S 8, 1802.
Anna Rebecca (1:219), born Jl 3, 1816; baptized Jl 28, 1816.
Elizabeth married Andrew Sefton.
WELLER, John Jacob (1:125,245-246,262), eldest son and first child of Jacob
   and Maria Barbara (Wilhide) Weller; his last 8 years he suffered with a
   bad leg then his body became swollen and he had difficulty in breathing,
   finally stitches developed in the side; he died My 27, 1809, aged 70-0-6;
   he was buried My 29, 1809; he married Jl 13, 1762 Magdalena Krieger
   (1:226), eldest daughter and first child of Lorentz and Maria Elizabeth
   (Hahn) Krieger; she died D 28, 1765 at the age of 22-8-0, from the effects
   of child-birth; she was buried D 30, 1765 in the churchyard.
Issue: Maria Elizabeth (1:157), born Je 1, 1763 at 2 a.m.; baptized Je 1,
   1763; married _____ Reedy, of Lititz.
Maria Barbara (1:159), born N 12, 1765;1 baptized N 17, 1765;
   married Johan Willheit.
WELLER, John Jacob (1:125,262), son of Jacob and Maria Barbara (Willheid)
   Weller, died My 27, 1809 at the age of 70-0-6; he married S 23, 1766 (as
   his second wife) Anna Margaret Harbaugh, daughter of George and Catharine
   (Williar) Harbaugh; she was born Jl 21, 1749 at Crice Creek; she died Ap
   11, 1795 of a cough and was buried in the churchyard Ap 12, 1795.
Issue: Anna Catharine (1:161), born Ap 27, 1768 towards midnight; baptized
   My 1, 1768; married John Adam Gernand.
John Jacob (1:162,265), born Jl 4, 1770 at 8 p.m.; baptized Jl 8,
   1770; died My 26, 1818; buried My 27, 1818; married Catharina
   Leonhardt.
Anna Maria (1:164,241), born O 31, 1772 at 2 a.m.; baptized N 1,
   1772; died Jl 1, 1792; buried in the churchyard Jl 2, 1792. The
   cause of death was consumption.
*John [see next page] (1:165,257-258), born Ag 27, 1775 at 7 p.m.;
   baptized S 3, 1775; died Je 5, 1800; buried Je 7 at Hagerstown;
   unmarried. Probationer 1799; Communicant 1800.
Anna Margaret (1:167,231), born Ap 18, 1778; baptized Ap 19, 1778;
   died Jl 4, 1779 of dysentery; buried Jl 6, 1779 in the churchyard.
Anna Margaret (1:168), born O 22, 1780 in the early morning;
   baptized O 23, 1780; married John Jacob Weller.
Geârge (1:170), born Ag 5, 1783; baptized Ag 10, 1783; died F 2,
   1820; married Catharine Huber.
Elias (1:174), born S 12, 1786 at 1 p.m.; baptized S 17, 1786;
   married (1) Rosina Krieger and (2) Maria Margaret Krieger.

Frederick (6th son) (1:170b), born D 21, 1789 at 6 p.m.; baptized D
    27, 1789; married Sarah Stauffer.
WELLER, John Jacob and Magdalena were Probationers O 8, 1764 (1:91).
WELLER, Jonathan married Elizabeth Baumgärtner.
Issue: Catharine Eva (2:26), born My 4, 1834; baptized Ag 31, 1834.
*WELLER, John (son of John Jacob and Anna Margaret (Harbaugh) Weller), born
    Ag 27, 1775 - died Je 5, 1800; suffered an injury similar to a pneumato-
    cele many years ago, which caused him and his father much concern; went to
    Hagerstown for an operation, which did more harm than good. He had a
    second operation on My 11, 1800; however, it was accompanied with greater
    pain than the first one, and in a short time fatal symptoms, including
    facial convulsions, appeared.
WELLER, Joseph (1:85), son of Jacob and Rebecca Weller, married Mr 30, 1830
    Matilda Rifesnider, daughter of John and Catharina Riefsnider.
WELLER, Mary married Charles Eyler.
WELLER, Mary married Richard Paget.
WELLER, Mary Ellen (2:239), born N 23, 1844; died Mr 13, 1864; buried Mr 15,
    1864 at Graceham.
WELLER, Nathanael, shoemaker in Mechanicstown, (2:145,204), son of George
    and Catharina (Huber) Weller, was born Jl 5, 1808 and was baptized Jl 10,
    1808; he died Jl 17, 1833 of consumption and was buried Jl 19, 1833; he
    married Ap 10, 1828 Maria Bush, daughter of George and Elisabeth (Crall)
    Bush.
Issue: Horatio Nelson (2:15), born Je 9, 1829; baptized Jl 15, 1829.
    George Alexander Hamilton (2:19,199) born Mr 20, 1831; baptized My
        15, 1831; died Jl 6, 1831 of convulsions; buried Jl 8, 1831.
    Harriet Angelica (2:23,203), born O 3, 1832; baptized Ja 27, 1833;
        died Mr 15, 1833 of scarlet fever; buried Mr 17, 1833.
WELLER, Philip, blacksmith, (1:125,231), 2nd son of Jacob and Maria Barbara
    (Wilhide) Weller, was born Je 12, 1742; he was received in the church O
    22, 1766 and took communion O 7, 1769; he was epileptic, and seven years
    ago during a seizure fell on a redhot plough-share, causing a severe burn
    which never healed.   At times he was insane; in lucid periods he was
    exceedingly patient.   (Here the text adds, with apparent irrelevance,
    'klein u[nd] sünderhaft' (small and sinful). He died O 7, 1779 and was
    buried O 9, 1779 in the churchyard; he married S 30, 1766 Juliana Wottring
    (1:260), eldest daughter of John Daniel and Anna Maria (Rebmann) Wottring,
    who was born Ag 24, 1746 in York County, Pennsylvania; she married (2)
    Henry Peitsel; she died S 10, 1803 and was buried S 11, 1803.
Issue: Elizabeth (1:160), born Ag 1, 1767 about 10 a.m.; baptized Ag 2,
        1767.
    Jacob (1:161), born N 14, 1768 in the evening; baptized N 20, 1768.
    Daniel (1:162), born Ap 4, 1770 at 3 p.m.; baptized Ap 13, 1770.
    Barbara (2:216;1:163), born S 1, 1771 at 11:30 p.m.; baptized S 8,
        1771; died F 12, 1845; buried F 14, 1845; married John Christian
        Stauffer.
WELLER, Rosanna had an illegitimate son Martin Daniel (1:151), born Je 22,
    1839; baptized N 22, 1836 [sic].
WELLER, Phil & Juliana; Probationers O 12, 1766 (1:91), Communicants O 7,
    1769 (1:108); she was readmitted after being excluded 4 years, Mr 25, 1785
    (1:108).
WELLER, Samuel (1:89), son of Christian Weller, married Mr 7, 1839 Catharine
    Stokes.
WELLER, Sarah E. married James H. Frailey.
WELLER, Sevilla married Jacob D. Shaum.
WELLER, Simon Augustus (2:294), son of John and Deborah (Krieger) Weller,
    wasborn Jl 19, 1829; married Anna Barbara Brown.
Issue: Laura Elizabeth (2:48), born F 11, 1854; baptized My 30, 1854.

William Theodore (2:50), born Je 20, 1855; baptized O 7, 1855.
Emma Deborah (2:52,236), born Ap 2, 1858; baptized My 23, 1858; died N 17, 1862; buried at Graceham N 19, 1862.
Alfred Cyrus (2:55), born Ja 3, 1861; baptized F 27, 1861.
Ephraim McClellan (2:57), born Je 30, 1862; baptized Ag 24, 1862.
Charles Joseph (2:61), born S 22, 1865; baptized Ap 1, 1866.
Addison Oliver (2:63,244), born F 13, 1868; baptized My 31, 1868; died N 28, 1868; buried N 29, at Graceham.
Lottie Nevada (2:67), born S 14, 1873; baptized D 7, 1873.
WELLER, Thomas married Sophia Stokes.
Issue: Joel (2:2), born N 7, 1822; baptized Ap 27, 1823.
Marianna Maria (2:4), born Je 28, 1824; baptized S 5, 1824.
Rosina (2:8), born F 10, 1826; baptized Jl 16, 1826.
Sophia Catharina (2:11), born Ag 15, 1827; baptized S 23, 1827.
Samuel David (2:15), born Ap 16, 1829; baptized Jl 12, 1829.
Arnold Jacob (2:20,219), born Ap 3, 1831; baptized Jl 17, 1831; died F 19, 1850; buried F 21, 1850 at Mechanicstown.
Elizabeth Louisa (2:24), born Je 21, 1833; baptized S 1, 1833.
Susanna Barbara (2:29), born O 7, 1836; baptized N 22, 1836.
Francis Thomas (2:33), born Jl 23, 1838; baptized F 6, 1839.
WELLER, William married Mary Dixon.
Issue: Besse Pearl (2:72,255), born O 20, 1879; baptized N 25, 1879; died N 25, 1879; buried N 27, 1879 at Graceham.
WELLER, William Henry married Mary Franklin.
Issue: John Thomas (2:119), born Ap 10, 1852; baptized Mr 13, 1853.
WELLER, William Joseph had by Peggy Ann Platt an illegitimate daughter Angeline (1:97; 2:211), who was born Ja 18, 1829 and baptized Jl 26, 1839; said Angeline died Jl 31, 1839 and was buried Ag 1, 1839.
WELLER, William Orlandus, son of Isaac and Rebecca Elizabeth (Harbaugh) Weller, was born My 15, 1849; he married Anna Stitely.
Issue: Charles Clifton (2:68), born O 5, 1874; baptized D 20, 1874.
Cordelia Gertrude (2:70), born F 21, 1877; baptized Je 17, 1877.
Roy Edgar (2:72), born D 12, 1879; baptized Mr 28, 1880.
WELTY, Frances married John Nipple.
WELTY, Jacob H. (Reformed) of near Graceham (2:162), son of John and Mary (Gesey) Welty, married at the age of 25 years on Ap 16, 1872 A. Catherine Gesey (21 years of age when married), daughter of Daniel and Elizabeth (Bowus) Geesey [sic].
WELTY, John (1:90) married Ag 15, 1842 Polly Geesey
Issue: Jacob H. married A. Catherine Gesey.
WERFELS, Magdalena married John Firor.
(WESNER?), Elizabeth married Frederick Miller.
WHITMORE, Annie L. married James T. Rosensteel.
WILDER, Mary married Henry Wilhide.
WIERMAN, Joseph F. (2:150,242), was born in 1822; married D 25, 1849 Sophia E. Wilhide; he died N 4, 1865 and was buried at Mechanicstown N 5, 1865.
WIERMAN (WIREMAN), William A. (2:152), married Ag 26, 1852 Rebecca Eiron.
Issue: Thomas Michael (2:49), born Mr 11, 1855; baptized Ap 15, 1855.
Elizabeth Alice (2:51), born N 19, 1856; baptized Ja 1, 1857.
William Henry Alexander (2:53), born Jl 29, 1858; baptized O 17, 1858.
Mary Louise (2:55,232), born Ja 28, 1860; baptized Ap 8, 1860; died Ja 28, 1860 [sic]; buried My 4, 1860.
WILE, George (1:88) married Hannah Brandenburg, daughter of Samuel and Magdalen Brandenburg; he died before Mr 28, 1834 when his widow remarried; her second husband being George Colliflower.
Issue: Peter (1:88) married Rebecca Beierle.
WILE, Peter (1:88), son of George and Hannah (Brandenburg) Wile, married O 2, 1836 Rebecca Beierle, daughter of John George and Susan (Bauer)

Beierle.
WILEN, Louisa married Henry Dustman.
WILES, _____ married Catharine Domer (1:147).
WILES, Frederick B. (1:90) married D 26, 1839 Mary Lamison.
WILES, Jacob B. married Elizabeth Wilhite.
Issue: Cornelia Ann Melinda (1:147), born S 14, 1834; baptized O 2, 1834.
    Maria Minerva (1:150), born Je 30, 1836; baptized Ag 7, 1836.
    Tearman Tilghman (1:94), born Ap 29, 1838; baptized Je 3, 1838.
    Catharine Elisabeth (1:100), born Ja 24, 1841; baptized Ja 26,
       1841.
    Sophia Delila (1:106), born N 5, 1843; baptized Ja 1, 1844.
    Hannah Martha (2:114), born Mr 5, 1848; baptized Jl 30, 1848.
    Lilia Regina (2:118), born Mr 28, 1851; baptized My 18, 1851.
WILES, Sophia Jane married Charles Hewit.
WILHIDE, Amadeus Christian, son of John and Mary Magdalene (Harbaugh)
    Wilhide, was born Ap 5, 1854; he married Laura Gaugh (whose first husband
    was _____ McKiney ?).
Issue: Addie Cordelia (2:135), born Ja 15, 1877; baptized S 25, 1877.
    Ernest Luther (2:136), born Mr 22, 1879; baptized My 13, 1880.
WILHIDE, Anna married David Staub.
WILHIDE, Anna Maria married Israel Sweeney.
WILHIDE, Arnold married Isabel Wilhide.
Issue: Fannie Key (2:133), born Ja 15, 1874; baptized N 2, 1874.
WILHIDE, Barbara married George Herman, Jr.
WILHIDE (WILHEIT), Benjamin married Barbara Knauff (1:94).
WILHIDE (WILHEID), Benjamin, farmer, (2:144,246), son of Frederick and
    Catharina (Peistel) Wilhide, was born Ap 21, 1802 in Frederick County;
    hedied Jl 21, 1871 and was buried at Stone Church in Mechanicstown on Jl
    23, 1871; he married My 30, 1826 Mary Barbara Knouff, daughter of Henry
    and Mary Ann (Wile) Knouff; she was born My 18, 1798 at Middletown Valley,
    Maryland.
Issue: Josephine Aurelia (2:10,295), born Je 5, 1827; baptized Jl 14,
       1827; a Communicant·O 9, 1842; married Benjamin Franklin Herbert.
    Benjamin Wilson (2:13,203), born N 1, 1828; baptized Ja 25, 1829;
       died Mr 19, 1833 of scarlet fever; buried Mr 20, 1833.
    Mary Ann Louisa (2:18,296), born Ja 8, 1831 in Frederick County;
       baptized F 20, 1831.
    Catharine Ellen (2:23,296), born Ja 8, 1833; baptized Mr 24, 1833.
    Susanna Exilia (2:26,296), born N 10, 1834; baptized D 28, 1834.
    Washington Alexander (2:30), born D 30, 1836; baptized Mr 12, 1837.
    Arnold Randolph (2:34), born Je 28, 1839; baptized S 15, 1839.
    Frederick Nelson (2:40), born Mr 15, 1842; baptized S 4, 1842.
WILHIDE, Caroline married Theodore Nathanael Eyler.
WILHIDE, Charles Zachariah Taylor, son of Joseph and Sarah (Eyler) Wilhide,
    was born Ja 13, 1847.
Issue: Joseph (2:253), died N 11, 1877, aged 1-7-27; buried N 12, 1877 at
    Mechanicstown.
WILHIDE (WILHEIT), Conrad, wagoner (2:204), born in Frederick County N 18,
    1769; he died Ap 28, 1833 of consumption of the stomach and was buried Ap
    30, 1833; he married (1) Anna Elizabeth Krieger (1:264), daughter of
    Lorenz and Anna Maria (Harbaugh) Krieger; she was born N 13, 1775; she
    died Ap 10, 1814 of consumption, and was buried Ap 12, 1814.
Issue: Maria (1:178), born Ja 2, 1794 at 2 a.m.; baptized F 20, 1794.
    Elizabeth (1:181), born N 7, 1795; baptized N 8, 1795; married
       Henry Shook.
    Sarah (1:184), born Je 21, 1797; baptized Ag 13, 1797.
    John Daniel (1:187), born Ap 10, 1799; baptized My 13, 1799;
       married Matilda Stauffer.
    Joseph (1:200), born Ap 30, 1805; baptized Je 9, 1805; married

Sarah Eyler.
Lydia (1:206; 2:188), born My 20, 1808; baptized Jl 30, 1808; died
  Ag 30, 1823; buried S 1, 1823.
William (1:210), born Mr 18, 1810; baptized My 20, 1810; married
  Harriet Dorsey.
Ezra (1:215), born Ag 11, 1813; baptized N 14, 1813; died in 1847;
  married (1) Mary Ann Hummer and (2) Susan Hummer.
David married Elizabeth Christina Moser.
WILHIDE (WILHEID), Conrad, farmer, (1:131; 2:204), born in Frederick County
  N 18, 1769; died Ap 28, 1833 of consumption of the stomach and was buried
  Ap 30, 1833; he married (2) on D 18, 1814 Elizabeth Süss (formerly the
  wife of Abraham Fahs), (1:131,129; 2:200), daughter of Johann Georg Süss
  and Maria Barbara (Eigenbrod); she was born in Frederick County My 25,
  1785; she died Ag 30, 1832 in childbed, and was buried Ag 31, 1832.
Issue: Phoebe Anna (1:218), born Ag 15, 1815; baptized O 8, 1815; married
  George Washington Foreman.
  Carolina (1:220,265), born Je 6, 1817; baptized Jl 20, 1817; died
    Mr 4, 1818 of diarrhoea and vomiting, causing internal convul-
    sions; buried Mr 6, 1818.
  Zephaniah (1:222), born Ja 5, 1819; baptized F 18, 1819.
  Andrew (1:117; 2:190), born O 12, 1821; baptized Ja 1, 1822; died
    My 1, 1824 of convulsions; buried My 2, 1824.
  George (2:4,190), born Ag 12, 1824; baptized Ag 28, 1824; died S
    22, 1824; buried S 22, 1824.
  Frederick (2:4,293), born Ag 12, 1824; baptized Ag 28, 1824.
  Theresa Catharina (2:8,296), born Jl 8, 1826 in Frederick County;
    baptized Ag 27, 1826.
  Elias (2:22,201), born Ag 4, 1832; baptized Ag 27, 1832; died Ag
    31, 1832; buried S 1, 1832.
WILHIDE, Conrad married Harriet E. Wolf (Reformed).
Issue: Alice Virginia (2:125), born Ap 4, 1861; baptized Ag 4, 1861.
  Cornelius Alexander (2:128), born Ja 13, 1864; baptized O 26, 1864.
  William Columbus (2:129), born S 9, 1866; baptized O 8, 1866.
  John Franklin (2:130), born Mr 6, 1869; baptized Jl 30, 1869.
WILHIDE, Daniel (2:38,158,240,297), son of John Daniel and Matilda
  (Stauffer) Wilhide, was born F 13, 1840; he married F 19, 1863 Susan
  Elizabeth Wolfe; he died Jl 8, 1864 and was buried at Stone Church in
  Mechanicstown on Jl 9, 1864.
Issue: Martha Ellen (2:127), born N 15, 1863; baptized My 18, 1864.
WILHIDE, Daniel L. (2:159) married D 18, 1866 Elmira Weller.
WILHIDE (WILHEIT), David married Elizabeth Moser (1:95).
WILHIDE (WILHEID), David (2:143), son of Conrad and Anna Elizabeth (Krieger)
  Wilhide; he was born in Frederick County; a Communicant O 8, 1830; he
  married S 30, 1824 Elizabeth Christina Moser (2:289), daughter of Leonard
  and Elizabeth (Schenkler) Moser; she was born S 7, 1805 in Frederick
  County, and a Communicant O 8, 1830.
Issue: Joseph Alfred (2:5), born F 26, 1825; baptized Ap 17, 1825.
David Leonard (2:10), born Je 4, 1827; baptized Je 16, 1827; married Jane
  Ellen Wilhide.
  Sophia Elisabeth (2:14), born Mr 7, 1829; baptized Ap 12, 1829.
  Parmenio Cyrus (2:19), born F 26, 1831; baptized Ap 3, 1831.
  Otšo Cornelius (2:24), born Ag 28, 1833; baptized O 8, 1833;
    married (1) Margaret L. Matthews and (2) Margaret Ann Eyler.
  Elias Nelson (2:28,297), born O 12, 1835; baptized N 22, 1835.
  Maria Margaret (2:32,298), born My 19, 1838; baptized Jl 22, 1838.
  Sarah Matilda (2:37), born F 28, 1840; baptized My 7, 1840.
  Caroline Ellen (2:112), born Mr 17, 1844; baptized Mr 29, 1845.
WILHIDE, David Leonard (2:152), son of David and Elizabeth Christina (Moser)
  Wilhide, born Je 4, 1827; baptized Je 16, 1827; married Ap 14, 1851 Jane

Ellen Wilhide (2:245), daughter of John Daniel and Matilda (Stauffer) Wilhide; she was born Mr 30, 1831; she died S 19, 1869, aged 38-5-19; buried S 20, 1869 at Stone Church in Mechanicstown.
Issue: Ephraim Miles (2:233), born Ag 12, 1858; died F 24, 1861; buried F 25, 1861 at Mechanicstown.
    Joseph Milton (2:128,242), born Ja 29, 1865; baptized Jl 4, 1866; died Jl 9, 1866; buried Jl 10, 1866 at Mechanicstown.
WILHIDE, Dorothea married Jacob Snyder.
WILHIDE, Edward Owen (2:294), son of John Daniel and Matilda (Stauffer) Wilhide, was born F 17, 1835; he married Prudence Agnes Eyler, daughter of Jonas Nathaniel and Sophia Theresa (Moser) Eyler; she was born Ap 11, 1842.
Issue: Anna Urilla (2:126), born N 26, 1862; baptized Ap 3, 1863.
    William Harvey (2:129), born Jl 26, 1866; baptized Je 21, 1867.
    Sophia Elizabeth (2:130), born S 13, 1868; baptized My 13, 1869.
    Josiah Theodore (2:133), born S 16, 1872; baptized Mr 24, 1875.
    James Edward (2:136), born N 17, 1877; baptized Ag 15, 1878.
WILHIDE, Elizabeth married Jacob B. Wiles.
WILHIDE, Ellen Catharine married George Freshman.
WILHIDE (WILHEIT), Ezra, son of Conrad and Anna Elizabeth (Krieger) Wilhide, was born Ag 11, 1813; baptized N 14, 1813; died in 1847; he married Mary Ann Hummer who was born D 3, 1817; she died My 21, 1841 and was buried My 23, 1841. (2:214)
Issue: John Levi (1:95), born O 28, 1837; baptized Jl 22, 1838.
    Sarah Ann Elizabeth (1:98), born D 5, 1839; baptized Ap 5, 1840.
WILHIDE (WILHITE), Ezra (1:90; 2:217), son of Conrad and Anna Elizabeth (Krieger) Wilhide, was born Ag 11, 1813 and was baptized N 14, 1813; he was confirmed on his deathbed; died in 1847; he married N 19, 1842 Susan Hummer (2:218) (1:104 says Susan Ann Hammer); she was born F 13, 1820; she died Jl 21, 1847 and was buried Jl 22, 1847.
Issue: Niles Mortimer (1:104), born F 3, 1843; baptized Je 5, 1843.
    Ezra (2:112), born O 11, 1844; baptized My 11, 1845.
    Jane Isabella (2:43), born Ja 3, 1847; baptized Je 21, 1847.
WILHIDE (WILLHEID), Frederick, farmer, was born Ap 13, 1777; a Communicant Ag 12, 1821; he married in 1800 Catharina Peitzel (2:210), born Jl 10, 1781; a Communicant My 29, 1819; died My 8, 1836 of dropsy and she was buried My 10, 1836; she lived to see eight grandchildren.
Issue: Son, stillborn My 2, 1800; buried My 3, 1800 (1:258).
    Benjamin (1:193), born Ap 21, 1802; baptized My 9, 1802; married Mary Barbara Knouff.
    Sybilla (1:198), born Mr 31, 1804; baptized Jl 1, 1804; [died D 2, 1886]; married John Jacob Gernand.
    Maria (1:201; 2:295), born D 23, 1805; baptized Ja 5, 1806; a Communicant Ag 13, 1823.
    Joseph (1:205), born D 21, 1807; baptized Mr 26, 1808.
    Elizabeth (1:210), born F 9, 1810; baptized My 6, 1810.
    Henry (1:213), born Mr 7, 1812; baptized My 10, 1812; married Catharine Delfy.
    Horatio (1:78,216) born D 25, 1814 in Frederick County; baptized Ja 20, 1815; died Ag 16, 1820 of diarrhea.
    Jacobus Frederick (1:220), born F 2, 1817; baptized F 16, 1817; married Margaret Zoller.
    John William (1:119; 2:207), born Jl 27, 1822; baptized S 8, 1822; died N 16, 1834 of sore throat; buried N 18.
WILHIDE, Frederick.
Issue: Catharine, born Ap 26, 1781 or 1787; married John Daniel Weller.
WILHIDE, Frederick.
Issue: Anna Maria married John Rodeneiser.
WILHIDE, Frederick married F 22, 1849 Elizabeth Matthews (she was previously

married to _____ Robinson.
WILHIDE, Hannah married William Morehead.
WILHIDE, Henry married Catharine Morgenstern.
Issue: Anna Maria (1:207), born Ja 18, 1809; baptized Ja 30, 1809; died F
1, 1809.
WILHIDE, Henry married Ann Theresa Weller.
Issue: Mary Ellen (2:112), born N 23, 1844; baptized F 25, 1845.
WILHIDE, Henry (2:148), son of Frederick and Catharina (Peitzel) Wilhide,
was born Mr 7, 1812; he married Mr 21, 1839 Catharine Delfy (or Delphy).
Issue: William Nelson (1:100), born N 8, 1840; baptized Ap 11, 1841;
married Maggie Graham.
Isabella Marcella (1:103), born N 28, 1842; baptized Ja 25, 1843.
Jacob Edward (1:110), born Mr 14, 1844; baptized S 8, 1844.
Joseph Wilson (2:115), born Ja 19, 1849; baptized Jl 1, 1849.
George Franklin (2:120), born D 1, 1853; baptized S 24, 1854.
WILHIDE, Henry, son of Polly Wilhide, married Mary Wilder.
Issue: Charles Oliver (2:116), born Ag 8, 1849; baptized Ap 5, 1850.
Leanora Jane (2:126), born Mr 8, 1863; baptized O 31, 1863.
WILHIDE, Ida S., married George W. Harding.
WILHIDE, Isabel married Arnold Wilhide.
WILHIDE (WILLHEIDT), Jacob, farmer and shoemaker, married Anna Maria Schoff
(1:191).
Issue: Johanna (1:183), born N 2, 1796; baptized Ja 29, 1797.
Solomon (1:186), baptized D 16, 1798.
Sophia (1:259), died Ag 5, 1802; buried Ag 6, 1802.
Eliza (1:195); baptized F 20, 1803.
Dorgas (1:200), born Mr 7, 1805; baptized Je 9, 1805.
Rebecca (1:202), born Mr 7, 1806; baptized Je 15, 1806.
Anna Maria (1:208,262), born Ja 7, 1809; baptized Ap 16, 1809; died
Ap 20, 1809 of convulsions; buried Ap 22, 1809 in the churchyard.
Thomas (1:211), born Je 15, 1810; baptized N 28, 1810.
Maria (1:214), born Ja 29, 1813; baptized Ap 11, 1813.
WILHIDE, Jacob married Caroline Weller (2:221,290), daughter of Elias and
Rosina (Krieger) Weller; she was born F 24, 1812; she was a Communicant O
8, 1830; died D 29, 1852 at Eyler's Valley and her age was 40-10-4; she
was buried D 30, 1852.
Issue: Anna Maria (1:100), born Ja 5, 1841; baptized F 14, 1841; married
William D. Hankey.
WILHIDE (WILLHEID), Jacob had by Magdalena (née Moser) Melony an illegit-
imate son Jacob (1:218) who was born Ap 26, 1815 and who was baptized Jl
14, 1815.
WILHIDE (WILLHEID), Jacob had by Maria Protzman an illegitimate son John
(1:211) who was born O 3, 1810 and who was baptized Ap 3, 1811.
WILHIDE (WILLHEID), Jacob married Rebecca Late.
Issue: Jacob (1:112), born N 11, 1819; baptized Ja 17, 1820.
WILHIDE (WILHEIT), Jacobus Frederick (1:220; 2:148), son of Frederick and
Catharina (Peitzel) Wilhide; he was born F 2, 1817; baptized F 16, 1817;
married S 4, 1838 (as his second wife) Margaret Zoller (2:207,288),
daughter of John and Magdalena (Dewald) Zoller; she was born in Je, 1798
in the Palatinate; she was previously married to Johann Georg Schmidt.
Issue: Sarah Caroline (2:34), born D 20, 1839; baptized Mr 8, 1840.
WILHIDE, James.
Issue: George Washington (2:117), born Ja 26, 1846; baptized Jl 21, 1850.
Mary Catharine (2:117), born Mr 18, 1850; baptized Jl 21, 1850.
WILHIDE (WILHEID), John, junior, farmer (1:130; 2:247), son of John and
Maria Barbara (Weller) Wilhide; he was born O 30, 1789 in Maryland; died
Ja 10, 1873; buried Ja 12, 1873 at Graceham; he married S 3, 1811 Maria
Born (2:196), daughter of Jacob and Anna Margaret (Weller) Born; she was
born Ja 6, 1793 in Maryland; she died F 24, 1830 from the results of a

difficult confinement, and was buried F 26, 1830.
Issue: Mariane (1:213), born My 17, 1812; baptized Je 14, 1812.
Daniel (1:215), born S 9, 1813; baptized O 3, 1813.
Carolina (1:80,219), born N 11, 1816 at Graceham; baptized D 15, 1816; died O 7, 1821; buried O 9, 1821.
Samuel Jacob (1:222), born N 3, 1818; baptized D 5, 1818.
William Henry (1:114; 2:187), born O 13, 1820 near Graceham; baptized N 26, 1820; died F 25, 1823; buried F 27, 1823.
John Alexander (2:2,293), born Ap 26, 1823; baptized Je 22, 1823.
Elizabeth Olivia (2:7), born Mr 4, 1826; baptized Ap 18, 1826.
John Henry Washington (2:16,294), born Ja 2, 1830; baptized Mr 21, 1830; married Susan Miller.
WILHIDE (WILLHEIT), John married Barbara Weller (1:186).
WILHIDE (WILHEID), John and Barbara were Probationers My 20, 1792, and Communicants Mr 29, 1794 (1:92).
WILHIDE, John married Maria Eyler (1:152).
WILHIDE, (WILHEID), John (2:146,287), son of John and Maria Barbara (Weller) Wilhide, was born O 30, 1789; a Communicant Ag 13, 1818; he married Ja 30, 1831 (as his second wife) Maria Barbara Eyler (2:245), daughter of Jonas and Anna Regina Eller; she was born Ja 17, 1789; she was a Communicant Ag 13, 1816; she died My 9, 1869 and was buried at Graceham My 11, 1869. She had previously been married to Daniel Krieger.
WILHIDE (WILLHEID), John, Lutheran, farmer, (1:127,2:190), was born S 30, 1762; died Ap 29, 1824; buried My 1, 1824; 15 of his 20 grandchildren survived him; he married F 1, 1785 Maria Barbara Weller, Moravian (2:199), 2nd daughter of John Jacob and Magdalena (Krieger) Weller; she was born N 12, 1765 and was baptized N 17, 1765; she died S 4, 1831 of dropsy and complete emaciation, and was buried S 5, 1831.
Issue: Maria Elizabeth (1:173), born O 11, 1785 at 2 a.m.; baptized O 17, 1785; married _____ Zöller.
Maria Magdalena (1:166b), born O 28, 1830; married Christian Martin.
John (1:169b; 2:247), born O 30, 1789 towards evening; baptized N 1, 1789; died Ja 10, 1873 and buried at Graceham Ja 12, 1873.
Samuel (1:175b), born Ap 4, 1792 at 6 p.m.; baptized Ap 8, 1792; married Susanna Müller.
Maria Barbara (1:180), born S 10, 1795 at 11 p.m.; baptized S 20, 1795.
Matilda (1:200), born Ap 9, 1805; baptized Ap 21, 1805.
WILHIDE, John, near Hunting Creek (2:149), married Ag 20, 1846 Mary Magdalene Harbaugh (2:290), daughter of Christian and Maria Magdalena (Firor) Harbaugh; she was born D 3, 1823; she was a Communicant O 8, 1839.
Issue: Lemuel Luther (2:114), born Jl 3, 1847; baptized O 3, 1847; married Celestia Anna Esterline.
Clementina Elizabeth (2:44,231), born Ag 5, 1848; baptized O 15, 1848; died Ja 26, 1859; buried at Graceham Ja 27, 1859.
Amadeus Christian (2:49), born Ap 5, 1854; baptized Je 25, 1854; married Laura Gaugh.
Lewis Henry (2:52,230), born Mr 5, 1858; baptized Mr 20, 1858; died Mr 25, 1858; buried at Graceham Mr 26, 1858.
WILHIDE (WILHEID), John Daniel (2:143,245,287,291), son of Conrad and Anna Elizabeth (Krieger) Wilhide, was born in Frederick County Ap 10, 1799; baptized My 13, 1799; a Communicant D 4, 1825; died F 15, 1870 and was buried at Graceham F 16, 1870; he married Ja 26, 1826 Matilda Stauffer (2:216,287), daughter of Christian and Barbara (Weller) Stauffer; she was born Ja 22, 1804 in Frederick County; a Communicant O 8, 1820; she died Je 2, 1845 and was buried Je 4, 1845; 9 children survived her.
Issue: John William (2:8,293), born My 21, 1826; baptized Jl 13, 1826.
Carolina (2:11,295), born O 29, 1827 in Frederick County; baptized

D 25, 1827.

Conrad Alexander (2:14,293), born Ap 11, 1829; baptized Je 14, 1829.

Jane Ellen (2:19,296), born Mr 30, 1831 in Frederick County; baptized My 22, 1831; married David Leonard Wilhide.

Simon (2:22), born D 13, 1832; baptized Ja 8, 1833; married Catharine E. Willard.

Edward Owen (2:27), born F 17, 1835; baptized Mr 25, 1835; married Prudence Agnes Eyler.

Maria Elizabeth (2:33), born F 6, 1838; baptized F 9, 1838.

Sarah Anna (2:33,211), born F 6, 1838; baptized F 9, 1838; died D 20, 1839; buried D 22, 1839.

Daniel (2:38), born F 13, 1840; baptized F 22, 1840; died Jl 8, 1864; married Susan Elizabeth Wolfe.

Martin Henry (2:41,297), born Je 13, 1843; baptized Jl 17, 1843.

WILHIDE, John H. (2:164) married Catherine M. Pryor D --, 1880.

WILHIDE, John Henry Washington (2:151), son of John and Maria (Born) Wilhide, was born Ja 2, 1830 and was baptized Mr 21, 1830; he married Ag 15, 1850 Susan Miller of Catoctin.

WILHIDE, Joseph of Mechanicstown (1:84; 2:145,287), son of Conrad and Anna Elisabeth (Krieger) Wilhide, was born Ap 30, 1805; he was a Communicant Ap 4, 1833; he married Ja 10, 1828 Sarah Eyler (2:249), daughter of Jacob and Rebecca (Luckenbach) Eyler, who was born Mr 12, 1809; she was a Communicant Ap 4, 1833; she died O 27, 1875 and was buried at Mechanicstown Cemetery on O 28, 1875.

Issue: Augustus Henry (2:13,201), born O 10, 1828; baptized D 21, 1828; died Ja 6, 1833 of scarlet fever; buried Ja 7.

Ephraim Miles (2:21,294); born S 15, 1831; baptized Ja 22, 1832.

Robert Leander (2:25), born Mr 31, 1834; baptized My 11, 1834; married Augusta Ann Grimes.

Maria Louisa (2:29,217), born Mr 16, 1836; baptized My 15, 1836; died N 1, 1846; buried N 2, 1846.

Juliana Ellen (2:31,298), born F 3, 1838; baptized My 13, 1838; married John Lewis Willman.

Catharine Elizabeth (2:39,217), born S 1, 1841; baptized N 21, 1841; died Ag 29, 1845; buried Ag 30, 1845.

Harriet Eliza (2:42), born D 12, 1844; baptized Mr 29, 1845.

Charles Zachariah Taylor (2:44), born Ja 13, 1847.

WILHIDE, Joseph (2:163) and Anna E. Spaulding, both of Mechanicstown, were married on D 20, 1876.

WILHIDE, Joseph Alfred, son of David and Elizabeth Christina (Moser) Wilhide, had by Susanna Moser, daughter of Anna Catharine Herzog, an illegitimate son Alfred (2:119,223), who was born Je 13, 1852 and baptized Ja 30, 1853; the son Alfred died Ja 28, 1854 and was buried Ja 30, 1854 at Apple's Church.

WILHIDE, Josiah married Julia Freeze.

Issue: Harry Wilson (2:134), born Ja 20, 1872; baptized Ja 23, 1876.

Susan Catharine (2:134), born O 28, 1873; baptized Ja 23, 1876.

George Washington (2:134), born ----; baptized Ja 23, 1876.

WILHIDE, Julia Ann Maria married Thomas E. Smith.

WILHIDE, Lemuel L. (no church), son of John and Mary Magdalena (Harbaugh) Wilhide, married Celestia Anna Esterline (Winebrennerian).

Issue: Julia Myrtle (2:132), born N 7, 1871; baptized Jl 28, 1872.

John Graceham (2:134), born O 25, 1874; baptized Ag 10, 1875.

WILHIDE, Lem'l.

Issue: Clesen L. (2:256), born D 23, 1878; died N 22, 1880; buried N 23, 1880 at Graceham.

WILHIDE, Margaret married Henry Fröhlich.

111

WILHIDE, Margaret (or Rebecca) married Isaac Weddel.

WILHIDE, Maria Barbara married (1) _____ Firor (Vieruhr) and (2) Jacob Weller.

WILHIDE, Mary Ann married Andrew Reidenour.

WILHIDE, Mary M. married Joseph E. Eyler.

WILHIDE, Otto Cornelius (2:154), son of David and Elizabeth Christina (Moser) Wilhide, was born Ag 28, 1833; baptized O 8, 1833; married Jl 24, 1856 Margaret L. Matthews.

WILHIDE, Otto Cornelius (2:155), son of David and Elizabeth Christina (Moser) Wilhide, married Ap 14, 1859 Margaret Ann Eyler.

WILHIDE, Robert Leander (2:294), son of Joseph and Sarah (Eyler) Wilhide, was born Mr 31, 1834; he married Augusta Ann Grimes.
Issue: Claudia (2:122), born Jl 17, 1857; baptized Ag 4, 1857.
  Charles Albert (2:128), born S 15, 1865; baptized My 8, 1866.

WILHIDE, Samuel (2:157) married Ap 1, 1862 Mary Catharine Ferney.
Issue: William Albert (2:126), born O 5, 1862; baptized Mr 12, 1863.

WILHIDE, Samuel (1:131), son of John and Maria Barbara (Weller) Wilhide, was born Ap 4, 1792 in Frederick County; he married Je 19, 1814 Susanna Müller who was also born in Frederick County.
Issue: Sabina (1:216), born Ag 28, 1814; baptized O 16, 1814.

WILHIDE, Samuel Jacob (1:89), son of John and Mary (Born) Wilhide, was born N 3, 1818; he married S 1, 1839 Ann Koontz.

WILHIDE, Sarah M., married George Miller.

WILHIDE, Sopohia E., married Joseph F. Wireman.

WILHIDE, Simon (2:157,294), son of John Daniel and Matilda (Stauffer) Wilhide, was born D 13, 1832 and was baptized Ja 8, 1833; he married Mr 9, 1862 Catharine E. Williard.

WILHIDE, Solomon, son of Jacob and Anna Maria (Schoff) Wilhide, was baptized D 16, 1798; he married Susanna Lehman.
Issue: Solomon (1:136), born F 20, 1828; baptized Mr 17, 1828.
  Susanna (1:140), born Mr 18, 1830; baptized O 29, 1830.
  Jacob (1:140), born Mr 18, 1830; baptized O 31, 1830.

WILHIDE, William (2:147), son of Conrad and Ann Elizabeth (Krieger) Wilhide, was born Mr 18, 1810 and was baptized My 20, 1810; he married D 24, 1833 Harriet Dorsey, daughter of Michael and Elizabeth Dorsey.
Issue: John Webster (1:103), born D 16, 1840; baptized Ja 25, 1843.
  William (1:130), born N 14, 1841; baptized Ja 25, 1843.

WILHIDE, William Nelson (2:160), son of Henry and Catharine (Delfy) Wilhide, was born N 8, 1840; he married My 21, 1868 Maggie Graham.

WILLIAMS, _____
Issue: Cassandra (1:170b), born Ja 5, 1789; baptized Ja 30, 1790.

WILLIAR, Amanda Caroline (2:114), born Ja 16, 1846; baptized Ag 15, 1847.

WILLIAR (WILJAHR), Andrew, junior, tanner, in the mountains, son of Andrew and Margaret (Harbaugh) Williar, was born Je 1, 1786; he married Anna Barbara Römer (or Römann).
Issue: Maria Catharine (1:217), born D 2, 1814; baptized F 12, 1815.
  Henry Römann (1:219), born O 6, 1816; baptized D 1, 1816.
  William Alexander (1:222), born N 6, 1818; baptized D 25, 1818.
  George Peters (1:118), born Ja 4, 1822; baptized Ap 5, 1822.
  Margaretha Anna (2:4), born Ap 6, 1824; baptized Je 20, 1824.

WILLIAR (WILLARD, WILJAR), Andrew (2:193), son of Peter and Magdalena Elizabeth (Schlim) Williar, was born Mr 21, 1758 in Frederick County; he died Ag 5, 1827 of liver trouble and was buried Ag 6, 1827; he married (1) Margaret Harbaugh (1:266), daughter of George and Catharine (Williar) Harbaugh; she was born O 11, 1761; she died Ap 24, 1819 of pains and swellings in the extremities, and was buried Ap 25, 1819; she lived to see 11 grandchildren. The marriage of Andrew Williar and Margaret Harbaugh took place in 1781.

112

Issue: Michael (1:154), born Jl 15, 1782; married Catharina Haber.
Margaret (1:170), born S 11, 1783; baptized S 15, 1783; died O 28, 1861; married Frederick Eyler.
Gertrude (1:171; 2:146), born N 10, 1784; baptized N 15, 1784; died Je 11, 1835; married (1) Jacob Reidenauer and (2) Philip William Boller.
Andrew (1:174), born Je 1, 1786 at 4-5 a.m.; baptized Je 1, 1786; married Anna Barbara Röhmann.
Elizabeth (1:166b), born O 14, 1787 at 4 p.m.; baptized O 15, 1787; died Ap 11, 1822; married John Jacob Gernand.
John Henry (1:168b,238), born Mr 5, 1789 before noon; baptized Mr 10, 1789; died Mr 21, 1789 of smallpox and was buried in the churchyard.
Adam (1:171b), born S 26, 1790 towards evening; baptized S 27, 1790.
Renatus (1:175b), born My 6, 1792 at 6 p.m.; baptized My 27, 1792.
John (1:262,178), born Jl 17, 1793 at 6 a.m.; baptized Ag 11, 1793; died Jl 2, 1808 and was buried Jl 3, 1808; he was trying to close a second story window when he was struck by lightning, which also ignited some chips lying around him and charred (beschädigt) his body.
Charles (1:179), born Ap 13, 1795 at 10 p.m.; baptized My 24, 1795; married Elizabeth Ricksecker.
Son (1:185,251), born Ja 6, 1798; died Ja 7, 1798; buried Ja 9, 1798 in the churchyard.
Daughter (1:254), born Mr 21, 1800; died Mr 28, 1800; buried Mr 30, 1800.
WILLIAR (WILLIARD, WILJAHR), Andrew, senior, farmer (1:132; 2:193), son of Peter and Magdalena Elizabeth (Schlim) Williar; he was born My 21, 1758 in Maryland and lived in the mountains; he married (2) on Ag 5, 1819 Rebecca Protzman (2:221,289), daughter of Ludwig and Maria Elizabeth (Rauser) Protzman; she was born O 26, 1789 at Graceham; she married (2) Frederic Favorite; she died N 7, 1852.
Issue: Lewis Emanuel (1:113), born My 30, 1820; baptized Je 18, 1820.
Son, unbaptized (1:80), born F 20, 1822; died F 20, 1822 of convulsions.
WILLIAR, Catharine (1:260) died S 25, 1803, aged 54-4-0; buried S 27, 1803.
WILLIAR, Andrew and Margaret were Probationers My 25, 1785 (1:91), and Communicants N 13, 1785 (1:108).
WILLIAR, Anna Maria married John Gump.
WILLIAR, Barbara married Jacob Reitnauer.
WILLIAR (WILLIARD), Catharine married William Fröhlich.
WILLIAR (WILLIARD), Catharine E. married Simon Wilhide.
WILLIAR, Cecilia Ann married George Williar.
WILLIARD, Charles of Harbaugh's Valley married Margaret Ann Williard.
Issue: Amanda Caroline (1:105), born Ap 2, 1843; baptized Ag 15, 1843.
Margaret Ann (2:113), born Jl 25, 1847; baptized F 18, 1847.
WILLIAR (WILLIARD), Charles married Sarah Favorite.
Issue: Delila Catharine (1:102), born O 19, 1842; baptized D 4, 1842.
WILLIAR (WILLIARD, WILLJAR), Charles, farmer in the valley (1:133), son of Andrew and Margaret (Harbaugh) Williar, was born Ap 13, 1795 in Frederick County; he married S 30, 1819 Elizabeth Rickescker (2:207), daughter of Henry (schoolmaster) and Catharina (Miller) Ricksecker; she was born Ja 22, 1798 in Frederick County; she died Ag 9, 1834 in childbed and was buried Ag 10, 1834.
Issue: Augustus Henry (1:115), born D 13, 1820; baptized Ja 14, 1821.
Cecelia Ann (2:1), born D 21, 1822; baptized Mr 13, 1825.
Hiram Alexander (2:5), born N 26, 1824; baptized Mr 13, 1825.
John Adam (2:9), born Ap 21, 1827; baptized My 13, 1827; married

Rebecca Charlotte Eyler.
Comenius Frederick (2:17), born F 21, 1830; baptized My 1, 1830.
Mary Catharine (2:21,204), born My 25, 1832; baptized My 25, 1832;
died My 11, 1833 of convulsions; buried My 12, 1833.
Cornelia Elisabeth (2:26,207), born My 31, 1834; baptized Je 29,
1834; died Ag 15, 1834 of cholera infantum; buried Ag 16, 1834.
WILLIAR (WILLIARD, WILLJAR), Elias, farmer, in the mountains (2:191), son of
John and Anna Margaret (Protzman) Williar; he was baptized N 6, 1780 in
Frederick County; he died N 29, 1824; he was buried N 30, 1824; he married
D 6, 1808 Anna (or Nancy) Eyler.
Issue: Ezra (1:209), born Je 27, 1809; baptized Ag 10, 1809.
Zephaniah Eyler (1:211), born F 20, 1811; baptized Je 18, 1811.
Lorenz Eyler (1:214), born N 16, 1812; baptized D 22, 1812.
Maria (1:217), born Jl 5, 1814; baptized Ap 28, 1815.
Margaret Anna (1:219), born F 9, 1816; baptized My 23, 1816.
Elizabeth (1:221), born D 3, 1817; baptized Ap 26, 1818.
Levina (1:222), born Mr 20, 1819; baptized Ap 18, 1819.
Hannah (1:115), born N 8, 1820; baptized Ja 14, 1821.
Adam (1:119), born My 21, 1822; baptized S 15, 1822.
Eleanora Susanna (2:6), born Je 19, 1825; baptized S 7, 1825.
WILLIAR, Elizabeth Magdalena, wife of Peter was a Probationer O 8, 1758
(1:91) and a Communicant Jl 29, 1759 (1:107); Peter was a Communicant O 8,
1758 (1:107).
WILLIAR (WILLIARD), Ezra married Elizabeth Lemmerson.
Issue: Richard Elias Lammerson (1:94), born Ja 15, 1838; baptized F 11,
1838.
Martha Ann Elizabeth (1:99), born Je 26, 1840; baptized Ag 9, 1840.
Laura Jane Melinda (1:102), born O 20, 1842; baptized D 4, 1842.
Valentine Zephaniah (1:102), born O 20, 1842; baptized D 4, 1842.
Amanda Emma Jane (2:112), born N 10, 1844; baptized Ja 11, 1845.
Catharine Adeline (2:116), born D 26, 1849; baptized Ag 4,
1849.[sic]
WILLIAR (WILLIARD), George married Cecilia Ann Williar.
Issue: Martin Henry (1:103), born D (27?), 1842; baptized Ja 16, 1843.
Mary Ellen (2:113), born S 3, 1845; baptized N 19, 1845.
Columbus (2:114), born F 24, 1848; baptized N 24, 1848.
WILLIAR, Israel of Sabillasville (2:147), son of John and Sarah (McLane)
Williar, married S 21, 1834 Lavinia Eyler (2:289), daughter of George and
Elsie Anna (Kaufman) Eyler; she was born Ja 6, 1812; she was a Communicant
O 8, 1830.
Issue: Samuel (2:28), born Jl 11, 1835; baptized Ag 22, 1835.
Josiah (2:29), born N 21, 1836; baptized Ja 8, 1837.
David Franklin (2:32), born N 22, 1838; baptized Ja 13, 1839.
Anna Margaret (1:100), born D 20, 1840; baptized Ja 24, 1841.
George Washington (1:103), born N 20, 1842; baptized F 19, 1843.
Mary Amanda (2:112), born F 6, 1845; baptized Mr 30, 1845.
Beatus (2:217), died in 1846 or 1847.
Cornelius Augustus (2:114), born Jl 3, 1848; baptized Ag 15, 1848.
John Frederick (2:46), born Ag 19, 1850; baptized My 2, 1851.
James Calvin (2:119), born Jl 24, 1853; baptized S 18, 1853.
WILLIAR (WILLIARD, VIELLIEARD), Jacob (1:225), died at 4 p.m. on Je 5, 1764
after 11 days illness of smallpox, aged 21-4-8; buried Je 7, 1764, in the
churchyard.
WILLIAR, Jacob married Ann Reinhold.
Issue: Josephine (2:121), born N 29, 1854; baptized Je 4, 1855.
WILLIAR, Jacob married Elizabeth Krieger. (1:95,150).
WILLIAR (WILLIARD), John married Elizabeth Null.
Issue: Margaret Ann (1:101), born F 14, 1840; baptized My 16, 1841.
Catharine Elizabeth (1:105), born F (12?), 1842; baptized Ag 16,

1843.
WILLIARD (WILLIART), John, in the mountains (1:126,263), 4th son of Peter and Elizabeth Magdalena (Schlim) Williar, was born My 24, 1753; he lost his health through the use of strong drink, and died S 29, 1810; he was buried S 30, 1810; he married My 26, 1775 Anna Margaret Protzman (2:215), daughter of Lorentz and Maria Elizabeth (Häns) Protzman; she was born Ja 11, 1754 in Frederick County; she was a Communicant Ja 22, 1781; she died Mr 3, 1844 and was buried Mr 6, 1844.
Issue: John (1:166), born F 11, 1776 early in the morning; baptized F 12, 1776; married (1) Sarah McClain and (2) Rachel Manahan.
John Jacob (1:167), born D 20, 1777 during the morning; baptized D 22, 1777; married Elizabeth Krieger.
Elias (1:168), born N 6, 1780; baptized N 14, 1780; married Anna Eyler.
Peter (1:171), born Ja 30, 1784; baptized Ap 22, 1784; married Elizabeth Müller.
Lorenz (1:174), born My 27, 1786; baptized Je 6, 1786; died Je 3, 1855; married Catharine Miller.
Daniel (2:215;1:169b), born Je 17, 1789 at 3-4 a.m.; baptized Je 23, 1789; died Mr 4, 1844; buried Mr 6, 1844.
Aaron (1:172b), born Ap 7, 1791 at 5-6 p.m.; baptized Ap 17, 1791.
Anna Maria (1:178), born Ja 21, 1794; baptized Mr 2, 1794; married John Smith.
Elizabeth (1:247,184), born N 13, 1797; baptized N 20, 1797; died D 9, 1797; buried D 10, 1797.
WILLIAR (WILLIARD, WILJAHR), John (1:81), son of John and Anna Margaret (Protzman), was born F 11, 1776 on the mountain; he died Ap 11, 1822 and was buried Ap 12 in our churchyard, where his relations were, at his request; he married (1) Sarah (or Sally) McClain (Mieklen, etc.), (1:263), daughter of Joseph and Susanna McClain; the date of this marriage is unknown, as he withdrew from the church; she died F 17, 1812, aged 20-4-0, and was buried F 18, 1812 in the churchyard; they were married 3 years.
Issue: Eliza (1:210), born N 17, 1809; baptized Ja 5, 1810; married Daniel Robeson.
Israel (1:212), born Je 21, 1811; baptized O 9, 1811; married Lavinia Eyler.
WILLIAR (WILLIARD, WILJAHR), John (1:81), son of John and Anna Margaret (Protzman), Williar, was born F 11, 1776; he died Ap 11, 1822 and was buried Ap 12; he married (2) Rachel (1:217 says Regina) Manaham.
Issue: Anna Maria (1:217), born My 7, 1815; baptized Je 25, 1815.
WILLIAR, John and Margaret were Probationers O 7, 1781 (1:91); they were Communicants Ja 22, 1785 (1:108).
WILLIAR (WILLIARD), John Adam (2:9,154), son of Charles and Elizabeth (Ricksecker) Williar, was born Ap 21, 1827; he married Ja 29, 1856 Rebecca Charlotte Eyler, daughter of John and Rebecca (Harbaugh) Eyler, who was born N 27, 1828 and baptized F 1, 1829.
Issue: Ella Ketura (2:122), born O 15, 1856; baptized S 6, 1857.
Sarah Jane (2:123), born F 21, 1858; baptized O 9, 1858.
Mary Susan (2:238), born D 26, 1862; died Ag 1, 1863 and was buried Ag 2 at Mechanicstown Stone Church Cemetery.
Harry Milton (2:128), born Ap 21, 1866; baptized Jl 2, 1866.
John Franklin (2:130), born Mr 23, 1869; baptized S 1, 1869.
WILLIAR (WILIARD), John Jacob (2:146,288), son of John and Anna Margaret (Protzman) Williar, was born D 20, 1777; he was a Communicant Ap 11, 1805; he married Ja 22, 1832 Elizabeth Krieger (2:288), daughter of Henry and Sophia (Protzman) Krieger, who was born S 8, 1811; she was a Communicant Ap 12, 1827.

Issue: George Frederick (2:22), born Ag 29, 1832; baptized S 15, 1832.
  Beatus (2:211), born Ja 10, 1838; died F 3, 1838 and buried F 4,
    1838.
  Romanus Exeverius (2:33), born Ap 7, 1839; baptized Ap 18, 1839.
  Martin Augustus (2:38), born My 5, 1841; baptized My 16, 1841;
    Savannah C. Weller became his wife.
  Margaret Ellen (2:40,215), born N 28, 1842; baptized Ja 11, 1843;
    died Ja 26, 1843, aged 0-2-2; buried Ja 27.
  Cornelia Elizabeth (2:42,216), born Ja 22, 1844; baptized F 15,
    1844; died My 23 1844, aged 0-4-1; buried My 24.
  Beatus (2:216), born (1845?); died (1845?).
  Sarah Alice (2:44), born Ag 1, 1846.
WILLIAR, John Jacob married Margaret Anna (née Williar). (1:94).
WILLIAR (WILLIARD, WILLJAR), Lorentz, farmer & mason (1:131,174; 2:226),
  resided in the mountains; he was the son of John and Anna Margaret (Protz-
  man) Williar, and was aborn My 27, 1786 in Frederick County; he was bap-
  tized Je 6, 1786; he died Je 3, 1855 and was buried Je 4, 1855 in Har-
  baugh's Valley; he married Mr 25, 1813 Catharine Miller who was born in
  Frederick County; she was a Communicant O 8, 1830.
Issue: Anna Maria (1:216), born S 23, 1813; baptized Je 19, 1814; married
    Hezekiah Robeson.
  John Müller (1:218), born O 22, 1815; baptized F 8, 1816.
  Catharina (1:221), born D 29, 1817; baptized Je 21, 1818.
  Charles Henry (1:112), born F 19, 1820; baptized My 14, 1820.
  Alfred Protzman (1:118), born Mr 10, 1822; baptized Ap 9, 1822.
  Joel Peter (2:5), born D 1, 1824; baptized F 24, 1825.
  Jacob Frederick (2:9), born F 18, 1827; baptized My 13, 1827.
  Anna Rebekka (2:16,205-206), born Jl 27, 1829; baptized O 11, 1829;
    died D 26, 1833; buried D 27, 1833.
  Harriet Jane (2:21,204), born Mr 10, 1832; baptized Ap 29, 1832;
    died Ag 4, 1833; buried Ag 5, 1833.
  Reuben Lorenz (1:152), born O 14, 1836; baptized F 4, 1837.
WILLIAR, _____ married Maria Elizabeth _____ (1:227); she was born about
  1682 at Erlebach, Oberamt Kaiserslautern, Churpfalz; she died a widow
  "alte Mutter" on O 14, 1770 at 11 p.m., and was buried O 16, 1770.
WILLIAR (WILLIARD), Margaret Ann married Charles Williard (Williar).
WILLIAR, Martin Augustus of Mechanicstown (2:38,158), son of John Jacob and
  Elizabeth (Krieger) Williar, was born My 5, 1841 and was baptized My 16,
  1841; he married on Ap 21 or 22, 1864 Savannah Catharine Weller of Mechan-
  icstown, daughter of John and Deborah (Krieger) Weller; she was born S 12,
  1841.
Issue: Effie Deborah (2:61), born S 23, 1866; baptized Ja 20, 1867.
  Allen John Jacob (2:65), born Je 2, 1871; baptized S 24, 1871.
WILLIAR, Mary Ann married _____ Deberry.
WILLIAR (WILLIARD, WILLJAR), Michael (1:130), son of Andrew and Margaret
  (Harbaugh) Williar; he married Ag 30, 1808 Catharina Haber who was born in
  Frederick County, the daughter of George and Catharina (Schneider) Haber.
WILLIAR (WILLIARD), Michael; baptized at Millerstown [Fairfield]; he married
  Mary (or Catharine) Roeder.
Issue: Margaret Catharine (1:138), born My 18, 1829; baptized Je 21, 1829.
  Michael Joseph (1:142), born Ap 27, 1831; baptized N 13, 1831.
  Andrew Adam (1:147), born Je 20, 1834; baptized Ag 24, 1834.
  William Washington (1:152), born Jl 18, 1837; baptized S 17, 1837.
WILLIAR (WILLIARD, VILLIARD, VIELLIEARD), Peter (1:243), born in 1714 at
  Erlebach near Kaiserslautern; came to America in 1744; brought up Re-
  formed; died Jl 28, 1794 and was buried Jl 29; he married in 1742 Magda-
  lena Elizabeth Schlim (1:241); she was born in 1722 at Allsenbrück, 4
  hours from Kaiserslautern in the Palatinate; she was brought up in the
  Reformed Church; she died Ja 19, 1792 and was buried Ja 21. She lived to

116

see 31 grandchildren; they were the parents of ten children, 2 sons and 1 daughter died before him and her; he married twice; he lived to see 36 grandchildren.

Issue: John (4th son), born My 24, 1753; died S 29, 1810; married Anna Margaret Protzman.
    Andrew, born Mr 21, 1758; died Ag 5, 1827; married (1) Margaret Harbaugh and (2) Rebecca Protzman.
    Maria Elizabeth (1:156), born S 18, 1760 at 8 a.m.; baptized S 22, 1760; died S 28, 1824; married Christian Harbaugh.
    Julianna (1:157), born Je 2, 1763 at 7 a.m.; baptized Je 5, 1763; married Tobias _____.
    Philip married Catharine Ritter.
WILLIAR (WILLIARD, WILLJAR), Peter (1:131), son of John and Margaret (Protzman) Williar, was born in Frederick County; he married on Je 11, 1812 Elizabeth Müller who was born in Frederick County.
Issue: Araminta (1:214), born S 20, 1812; baptized D 22, 1812; married Tobias Fahs.
    Catharina (1:216), born D 22, 1813; baptized Je 19, 1814.
    Eliza Anna (1:220), born D 25, 1816; baptized Ap 20, 1817; Samuel Harbaugh was her husband.
    David (1:111), born Je 26, 1819; baptized S 5, 1819.
    George (1:117), born Ja 24, 1821; baptized S 9, 1821.
    Susanna (2:5), born N 27, 1824; baptized F 24, 1825.
    Anne Maria (1:135), born Je 30, 1827; baptized N 4, 1827.
WILLIAR (WILLIARD), Philip, farmer and weaver, in the mountains; son of Peter and Magdalena Elizabeth (Schlim) Williar; he married Catharine Ritter; both were Probationers My 25, 1785 (1:91) and borh were Communicants N 13, 1785 (1:108).
Issue: Elizabeth (1:169,234), born F 14, 1782; baptized F 22, 1782; died N 13, 1785; buried N 17, 1785.
    Philip (1:171), born Mr 9, 1784; baptized Ap 22, 1784.
    John (1:173), born F 5, 1786 at 11 p.m.; baptized F 6, 1786.
    Barbara (1:167b), born Je 25, 1788; baptized Je 29, 1788.
    Frederick (1:171b), born S 15, 1790 at noon; baptized S 27, 1790.
    Joseph (1:176,242), born N 30, 1792 at 3 a.m.; baptized Ja 1, 1793; died S 18, 1793 of a prevalent neck sickness; buried S 19, 1793 in the churchyard.
    Catharine (1:179), born Ag 9, 1794 at 10 a.m.; baptized N 16, 1794.
    Esther (1:183), born F 8, 1797; baptized Je 25, 1797.
    Joseph (1:187), born F 13, 1799; baptized My 27, 1799.
    Judith (1:192), born Jl 6, 1801; baptized O 18, 1801.
WILLIAR (WILLIARD), Zephaniah married Sarah A. _____.
Issue: Margaret Serena Emma Jane (2:70), born N 19, 1876; baptized Mr 25, 1877.
WILMAN, Anna Kunigunda married (1) _____ Miller and (2) Peter Hirschel.
WILMAN, Frederick Augustus (2:40), son of John and Charlotte (Harbaugh) Wilman, was born Jl 26, 1842; baptized S 4, 1842; married Mary E. Seas.
Issue: Mary Jeanette (2:131), born O 6, 1870; baptized Jl 2, 1871.
    John Elijah Harbaugh (2:67), born Mr 23, 1872; baptized O 19, 1873.
    Martha Ella (2:68), born S 15, 1874; baptized Ap 19, 1875.
    Belva Elizabeth (2:70), born O 13, 1876; baptized F 14, 1877.
    Robert Luther (2:71), born N 14, 1878; baptized Ag 19, 1879.
WILMAN, John (2:146,288), born S 4, 1791 at Herzogshausen in Darmstadt; confirmed 1805; joined this church My 22, 1836; died Ap 20, 1849 and was buried Ap 22 in a private graveyard near Sabillasville; he married My 28, 1833 Charlotte Harbaugh (2:288,292), daughter of Christian and Maria Elizabeth (Williar) Harbaugh, who was born Je 21, 1800; she was a Communicant Mr 30, 1820. They were the parents of 6 children, 2 of whom died

before he did.
Issue: John Lewis (2:27), born Ap 20, 1835; baptized Ap 20, 1835; married
    Julian Ellen Wilhide.
  Henry Otto (2:30), born N 21, 1836; baptized Ja 8, 1837.
  Julius Theodore (2:32), born N 5, 1838; baptized D 16, 1838.
  Frederick Augustus (2:40), born Jl 26, 1842; baptized S 4, 1842;
    married Mary E. Seas.
WILLMAN, John Lewis (2:155,294), son of John and Charlotte (Harbaugh) Will-
  man, was aborn Ap 20, 1835; baptized Ap 20, 1835; married F 4, 1857 Julian
  Ellen Wilhide, daughter of Joseph and Sarah (Eyler) Wilhide; she was born
  F 3, 1838 and was baptized My 13, 1838.
  Issue: Charles Louis (2:126), born Ap 10, 1863; baptized F 14, 1864.
WILSON, Isaac, blacksmith, married Polly Wowly.
  Issue: Joseph (1:197), born N --, 1803; baptized D 11, 1803.
WILSON, John married Sarah Jane Cunningham.
  Issue: John (1:136), born Ap 3, 1828; baptized Ap 27, 1828.
  Anne Maria (1:84), married Daniel Eckman.
WILSON, Priscilla married John Biggs.
WINTERS, George Harvey (2:153), son of Mary Ann; he married O 18, 1853
  Theresa Eyler, daughter of George and Elsie Nancy (Kauffman) Eyler; she
  was born Je 16, 1826 and was baptized S 17, 1826.
  Issue: Mary Catharine (2:120), born Ag 4, 1854; baptized Ag 14, 1854.
  Clara Susan (2:124), born D 28, 1858; baptized Mr 23, 1859.
  Harvey Grant (2:127), born Ap 23, 1864; baptized O 2, 1864.
WIREMAN, Hannah married Henry Warner.
WISE, Jacob, widower (1:84), son of Andrew and Barbara Wise, married Ap 16,
  1828 Jane (Patterson) Eckman, daughter of John and Ann Patterson.
WITMER, Ann married Jeremiah Harbaugh.
WITMER, Benjamin married Catharine Henning.
  Issue: Benjamin Simon (1:144), born Jl 14, 1830; baptized O 29, 1832.
WITMER (WHITMORE), Benjamin married Elizabeth _____.
  Issue: Virginia Catharine (2:127), born Mr 21, 1857; baptized Ap 23, 1864.
  Mary Frances (2:127), born Jl 11, 1859; baptized Ap 23, 1864.
  Portia Elizabeth (2:127), born Je 9, 1861; baptized Ap 23, 1864.
  Emma Jane (2:127), born S 29, 1863; baptized Ap 23, 1864.
WITMER, Christina (Teany Ann), born O 14, 1813; baptized -- --, ----; died O
  5, 1863; buried D 6, 1863 at Hawk's Church (2:239).
WITMER, Elias Hamilton (2:247), born F 18, 1847; died N 5, 1848; buried N 6,
  1848 at Stone Church in Mechanicstown.
WITMER, George Reuben married Mary Jane Newcomer.
  Issue: George Reuben (2:136), born S 20, 1878; baptized F 2, 1879.
WITMER, Greenbury (1:87) married S 4, 1832 Catharine Favorite, daughter of
  Frederick Favorite.
WITMER (WHITMER), Jacob married Susanna Coonz.
  Issue: Parmenio (1:110), born Ag 30, 1844; baptized O 27, 1844.
WITMER, Jeremiah married Hannah _____.
  Issue: Emma Jane (2:123,231), born F 26, 1857; baptized Ag 25, 1858; died
    Ag 27, 1858; buried Ag 28 at Apple's Church.
WITMER, John married _____ Kober.
  Issue: David (1:260), died S 1, 1804; buried S 2, 1804.
WITMER, Joseph (1:88), son of Christian and Elizabeth Witmer, married My 10,
  1835 Anne Catharine Eigenbrod, daughter of John and Susanna (Sänger)
  Eigenbrod.
WITMER, Mahlon of Mechanicstown (2:162 [insert]), married Ja 16, 1873 Anna
  Creeger of Mechanicstown, daughter of James Creeger (Krieger) and Eliza-
  beth (Weller).
  Issue: Joseph Randall (2:67), born N 20, 1873; baptized N 20, 1874.
  Charles Howard (2:69), born -- --, ----; baptized Mr 12, 1876.
  Catharine Elizabeth (2:71), born F 17, 1878; baptized S 1, 1878.

Mahlon Roy (2:72), born Ja 2, 1880; baptized My 9, 1880.
WITMER, William married Sabina _____.
Issue: Mary Elizabeth (2:134), born Ag 13, 1875; baptized O 24, 1875.
WITTMER, Elizabeth had an illegitimate daughter by Thomas Torning.
WOHLFAHRT, John, shoemaker & farmer, married Elizabeth Leonhart.
Issue: William (1:197), born N 4, 1803; baptized D 18, 1803.
Thomas (1:206), born N 16, 1806; baptized My 19, 1808.
Maria (1:209), born Ag 27, 1809; baptized N 12, 1809.
Benjamin (1:211), born My 31, 1811; baptized Je 9, 1811.
WOLF, Emilia married Jacob Flautt.
WOLF, Eva Catharine married John Charles Roesler.
WOLF, George married Charlotte Troxel.
Issue: Virginia Charlotte (1:110), born Ja 27, 1844; baptized O 20, 1844.
WOLF, Harriet E. married Conrad Wilhide.
WOLF, Jacob (2:225), born Je 11, 1829; died Ja 18, 1855; buried Ja 19, 1855
at Mechanicstown.
WOLF, Margaret married Moses Gorlz.
WOLF, Samuel married Elizabeth Sichrist.
Issue: Anna Eliza (1:142), born Jl 17, 1831; baptized S 18, 1831.
WOLF, Sophia (2:242), born Ag 30, 1805; died F 24, 1866; buried F 25, 1866
at Mechanicstown.
WOLF (WOLFE), Susan Elizabeth married Daniel Wilhide.
WOLF, Willhelm Adam married Elisabetha _____.
Issue: Anna Elisabetha (1:155), born Je 7, 1759 at 10 p.m.; baptized Je
10, 1759.
Johann Daniel (1:156), born Mr 26, 1761; baptized Mr 29, 1761.
Anna Catharina (1:158), born Je 23, 1763 at 3 p.m.; baptized Je 26,
1763.
Gottlieb (1:159), born My 9, 1765 at 7-8 p.m.; baptized My 12,
1765.
WOLF (WOLFE), William (2:58,239), born Ag 24, 1831; baptized O 21, 1863;
died O 31, 1863 and buried N 1, 1863 in Mechanicstown.
WOLF, William and Anna Elizabeth were Probationers Je 17, 1764 (1:91).
WOLFART, Lydia Anna married Leonard Moser.
WOODRING, Anna married Jonathan Crawford.
WOODRING, Catharine had illegitimate daughter by Henry Layton.
WOODRING, Jacob, tailor, married Barbara Keiper (or Käuber).
Issue: Anne married John Streng.
George (1:260), died O 8, 1804; buried O 9, 1804.
Barbara (1:78), born F 15, 1804 in Northampton County, Pennsyl-
vania; baptized in the Reformed Church F 31 [sic], 1804; died of
dysentery Jl 29, 1820.
Jacob (1:202), born F 4, 1806, baptized Mr 2, 1806.
Aaron (1:205), born Ja 22, 1808; baptized F 21, 1808.
Wilhelmina (1:210), born Ap 21, 1810; baptized My 13, 1810.
Maria Elizabeth (1:213), born Ap 6, 1812; baptized Ap 19, 1812.
Lucretia (1:216), born S 23, 1814; baptized O 16, 1814.
Augustina (1:220), born Ap 17, 1817; baptized Ap 27, 1817.
WOODRING (WOTTRING), John; married; a Probationer O 9, 1763 (1:91); a Communicant D 8, 1764 (1:107).
WOODRING (WOTTRING), John, Junior (1:232), son of John Daniel Wottring
(1:167); John, junior, was born Ja 2, 1741; he came to know the Moravians
in York in his youth; a Probationer O 9, 1763; a Communicant D 8, 1764; he
died N 16, 1779 after being sick about 3 weeks; lost sight and hearing
towards the end; buried N 18, 1779 in the churchyard; he married in S,
1763 Elizabeth Glatt of Heidelberg (1:232); she was born N 7, 1742; she
became a member at Heidelberg, in Pennsylvania, before her marriage; she
died D 14, 1779 after an illness of 4 weeks; she was buried in the churchyard D 16, 1779.

Issue: John Daniel (1:158), born Ag 2, 1764 early in the morning; baptized
Ag 5, 1764.
Maria Elizabeth (1:160,232), born Ag 25, 1766 at 10 p.m.; baptized
Ag 31, 1766; died Ja 16, 1780; buried Ja 18 in the churchyard.
Philip (1:161), born N 16, 1768 in the morning; baptized N 20,
1768; married Elizabeth Boller.
John (1:162), born Mr 8, 1771 at 11 p.m.; baptized Mr 13, 1771.
Jacob (1:164), born -- 6, 1773 at 5 p.m.; baptized -- 7, 1773.
Barbara (1:166), born Ap 17, 1776 in the evening; baptized Ap 21,
1776.
Magdalena (1:167,233), born Ag 31, 1778; baptized S 6, 1778; died O
1, 1781; buried O 3, 1781.
WOODRING (WOTTRING), John Daniel (1:235-236), born Je 24, 1711 at Hellerigen
in Lorraine. When 17 he was recruited in a regiment of dragoons in the
French service, deserted and returned home to his parents who were then
living in Alsace. He came to Pennsylvania with his wife and 3 children in
1739; 5 weeks later his wife and 2 children died. After living at Germantown for 4 years he removed to a place on the Conewago 9 miles from York;
here he married his second wife in 1744 and here he was converted by
Lischy's preaching; they joined the church at York. In 1760 they came
here. By his first wife he had 3 children, of whom 1 daughter survived
him. His second marriage took place in 1744 in York County, Pennsylvania,
to Anna Maria Rebmann who was born Ja 9, 1715 at Gehrsdorf, Lower Alsace;
she was brought up Reformed; came to America 1739; she died N 20, 1786;
she became blind a year before; shortly before she died she had an eye
operation at Frederick, which brought on a fatal illness; she died after
she returned home and was buried in the churchyard; he [John Daniel] died
of dropsy Ap 15, 1786 and was buried in the churchyard Ap 17, 1786. There
were 4 sons and 8 daughters of this marriage, of which 5 daughters survived him. One of these: Juliana, born Ag 24, 1746 and died S 10, 1803,
married (1) Philip Weller and (2) Henry Peizel.
WOODRING (WOTTRING), Maria Salome, single, was a Probationer Je 17, 1764
(1:91).
WOODRING (WOTTRING), Philip, carpenter and millwright (1:130,200,261), son
of John and Elizabeth (Glatt) Woodring; he was born N 16, 1768 at Grace-
ham; he died Ja 7, 1805 and was buried Ja 10, 1805; he married Elizabeth
Boller; she married (2) John Harbaugh of Muskingum.
Issue: Louisa Wilhelmina (1:188), born F 1, 1800; baptized F 9, 1800.
Benjamin (1:191,262), born Ap 22, 1801; baptized Ap 25, 1801; died
Ja 23, 1807 of a fall; buried Ja 25, 1807.
Elizabeth (1:261).
Maria (1:261).
Philip William (1:200), born Jl 9, 1805; baptized O 6, 1805.
WOOLLARD (WOLLARD), Joseph had by Agnes Weller an illegitimate daughter Katy
Keyser (2:126,240) who was born Ag 8, 1862 and baptized O 2, 1862; she
died Jl 26, 1864 and was buried Jl 27 at Graceham.
WOOLARD, William (1:88) married Ap 4, 1837 Mary Ann Weddle.
WORTHINGTON, Caroline Martha (2:220), born N 21, 1848 at Mechanicstown; ied
F 9, 1851 and was buried F 10, 1851.
WORTHINGTON, Charles (1:86), son of Walter and Sarah (Hood) Worthington,
married My 3, 1831 Elvira Hart, daughter of William and Sarah (Stewart)
Hart.
Issue: Henry Clay (1:97), born S 12, 1838(?); baptized Jl 1, 1839.
WOWLY, Polly married Isaac Wilson.
WÜNSCH, Jacob, joiner (1:129), son of Christian Wünsch of Emmaus, was born
Ag 25, 1778 at Emmaus, Northampton County; he married Ap 3, 1803 Maria
Barbara Protzman (1:199 says Polly Protzman); she was the daughter of
Daniel and Gertrude (Baumgärtner) Protzman, and was born S 16, 1781 in
Frederick County.

Issue: Edward (1:197,260), born Ja 5, 1804; baptized Ja 5, 1804; died Ja 6, 1804; buried Ja 8, 1804.
   Jonathan (1:199), born D --, 1804; baptized Ja 11, 1805.

YINGLING, John married Anna Osler.
Issue: George Carrol (2:133), born Ap 8, 1873; baptized Je 8, 1875.
YOUNG, Elizabeth married Jacob Shook.
YOUNG, Elizabeth married John Troxel.
YOUNG, Ezra (2:153) married S 21, 1854 Sabina Boller.
Issue: Thaddeus Irwin (2:237), born Ap 11, 1859; died Ja 16, 1863; buried Ja 17, 1863 at Apple's Church.
   Henry Milton (2:56,239), born Jl 17, 1861; baptized S 20, 1861; died D 28, 1863; buried D 30, 1863 at Apple's Church.
   Mark Calvin (2:59), born My 7, 1864; baptized S 11, 1864.
YOUNG, Frederic married Lydia Bauersachs.
Issue: Amadeus Frederic (1:144; 2:201), born O 22, 1832; baptized N 30, 1832; died D 8, 1832; buried D 9, 1832.
   Leander Anastasius (2:206), born D 22, 1833; died Jl 9, 1834; buried Jl 11, 1834.
YOUNG, Peter, miller, married Catharine Martz.
Issue: Margaret (1:114), born Ag 22, 1820; baptized D 19, 1820.
YOUNG, Peter married Maria Sophia Eigenbrod, daughter of John Yost and Eva Maria (Scherer) Eigenbrod; she was born Je 2, 1771 and was baptized Je 9, 1771.
Issue: Benjamin (1:171b), baptized Ag 23, 1790.
   Maria (1:194), born N 25, 1799; baptized Ag 1, 1802.
YOUNG, Philip married Nancy Benner.
Issue: Martha Ann, born O 10, 1817; married Henry Harbaugh.

ZAHM, Johann Michael, minister, married ____ _____.
Issue: Matthaeus (1:155), born Ag 1, 1759 at 2 p.m.; baptized Ag 5, 1759.
ZELER, Maranda married Octavius Agusutus Krieger.
ZENTMEYER, Sarah married Abraham Krieger.
ZENTZ, Franklin D. (2:165) and Ellen E. Boller, both of near Mechanicstown, were married Ja 27, 1881. She was the daughter of Israel Boller.
ZIEGLER, Rachel Theresa married John Henry Buchmeyer.
ZIMMERMAN, George married Elizabeth Patterson.
Issue: John Patterson (1:192), born S 16, 1801; baptized Ja 10, 1802.
   Maria Caty (1:198), baptized Jl 1, 1804.
ZIMMERMAN, John P. married Sophia Eichelberger.
Issue: Anne Elizabeth (1:143), born Ap 5, 1832; baptized Je 30, 1832.
ZIMMERMAN, Maria, daughter of Maria Catharina, married Thomas Triber.
ZIMMERMAN, Michael, farmer, married Lilli Patterson.
Issue: Anna (1:192), born N 15, 1801; baptized Ja 10, 1802.
ZÖLLER, ____ married Maria Elizabeth Wilhide (Willheith), daughter of John and Maria Barbara (Weller) Wilhide; she left the church a few weeks before her death because of her marriage and attendant circumstances; she died Je 1, 1807 and was buried Je 2 in the churchyard. (1:262)
ZOLLER, Francis married Magdalena Lang.
Issue: William Abraham (2:22), born N 12, 1832; baptized D 25, 1832.
   Sophia Emilia (2:25), born F 8, 1834; baptized Ap 20, 1834.
   George Frederick (1:151), born O 7, 1837; baptized N 27, 1837.
ZÖLLER, John married Lydia _____.
Issue: Maria Anna (1:219), born D 27, 1815; baptized O 20, 1816.
ZOLLER, John married Magdalena Dewald.
Issue: Margaret, born Je --, 1798; married Jacobus Frederick Wilhide.
ZOLLINGER, Barbara married Reuben Carlly.
ZOLLINGER, George, farmer, in the mountains, son of ____ and Sevilla (Machhold) Zollinger (1:136); he married Catharine Meyer, daughter of ____ and

Catharine (Maus) Meyer.
Issue: Margaret Sivilla (1:114), born S 4, 1820; baptized D 15, 1820.
Susanna Angelica (1:120), born Je 3, 1823; baptized Jl 27, 1823.
Lewis Augustus (1:121), born Ag 30, 1825; baptized N 9, 1825.
Mary Catharine (1:136), born N 25, 1827; baptized Je 15, 1828.
Anne Elizabeth (1:140), born Ap 3, 1830; baptized S 19, 1830.
Eleonora Francisca (1:150), born Mr 27, 1835; baptized Mr 6, 1836.
Benton George (1:96), born Ap 30, 1838; baptized D 16, 1838.

Some Negro Baptisms

Hanna, no dates [baptized Jl, 1799 ?] (1:187).

Thomas, Slave of James Ogel, Esquire, baptized S 1, 1799 (1:188).

Jenny, daughter of Samuel Hercules and Rachel (slave of James Johnson) baptized S 27, 1801 (1:192).

Clemens, son of Polly (slave of James Johnson), born Je, 1801, baptized S 27, 1801 (1:192).

Thomas, son of Stout and Hanna, about 8 months old, baptized S 27, 1801. (1:192).

Charlotta, daughter of Clemens (slave of Mr. Kee) and Pricilla (slave of Mr. Bruce) born S --, ---- and baptized Ja 24, 1802 (1:192).

Nancy and Rahel (twins), daughters of Helmgrood and Haga (slaves of John Krieger, Sr.) born N, 1801, baptized Je 19, 1802 (1:194).

Child of John (slave of Mr. Elder) and Sara (slave of Mrs. Thomas Ogle) baptized D 27, 1802 (1:195).

Maria, daughter of Petty (slave of Mr. Johnson) baptized Ja 30, 1803 (1:195).

David, son of Clemens (slave of Baker Johnson) and Jenny (slave of Mrs. Ogle) baptized N 13, 1803 (1:197).

Caty, daughter of Sammy and Susanna (slaves of Mr. Johnson) baptized Ap 3, 1803 (1:195).

Georg, son of George Luby and Jane (slave of Mrs. Kuhn) baptized My 29, 1803 (1:196).

Naemi, daughter of Adam and Rahel (slave of Mrs. Dudrow) baptized My 29, 1803 (1:196).

Joseph, negro man (Mr. Thomas Beatty's) baptized Mr 16, 1804 (1:198).

Priscilla, daughter of Jacob Buttler (slave of Mr. Elder) and Sara (slave of Mrs. Thomas Ogle) baptized Ap 15, 1805 (1:200).

Mary, daughter of Hillery (slave of Eichelberger) and Hanna (Mulatto of Kuhn) born F --, 1804, baptized Ap 22, 1804 (1:198).

Priscilla and Allen, children of Clem (slave of Mr. Johnson) and Jane (slave of Mr. Ogle) born Mr 1, 1805, baptized Je 9, 1805 (1:200).

Louis, son of Micaesy and Liendy, born O 23, 1805, baptized D 1, 1805 (1:201).

Hennrich, son of John and Sarah (slaves of Mr. Wolf), born Ag --, 1809, baptized Je 10, 1810 (1:210).

Cicely, child of Clem (slave of Mr. Johnson) and Schiny (slave of Mrs. Ogle) baptized S 23, 1808 (1:207).

Maria, daughter of Moser Kahle and Marie, born Ja 4, 1809, baptized Mr 16, 1809 (1:207).

Ely, child of Clem and Jane (slaves of Mrs. Ogle), born Ag 2, 1809, baptized Ag 28, 1811 (1:212).

Charlotta, daughter of Clem and Jane (slaves of Mrs. Ogle), born 1811, baptized O 9, 1814 (1:216).

Catharina, daughter of John Sasnip and Sarah, born Ap 2, 1815, baptized O 13, 1816 (1:219).

Aron, son of George and Lindy (slaves of Mrs. Ogle), born 1810, baptized O 9, 1814 (1:216).

George, son of George and Lindy (slaves of Mrs. Ogle), born 1811, baptized O 9, 1814 (1:216).

Susanna, daughter of George and Lindy (slaves of Mrs. Ogle), born 1814, baptized O 9, 1814 (1:216).

Anna Barbarah, daughter of Hennrich and Rudy, born Ap, 1818, baptized Ag 2, 1818 (1:221).

Anna Eliza, daughter of Jacob and Eleonora (slaves of Mr. Greis), born Ap. 1818, baptized N 8, 1818 (1:222).

Sally, daughter of Samuel and Maria, born S 19, 1818; baptized D 27, 1818 (1:222).

Joshua Armstrong, slave of Dr. W. Zimmerman (2:219), died Mr 24, 1850, aged 16 years; buried Mr 25; funeral sermon at Creegarstown Ap 7, 1850.

James Herbert, son of Otho Ferguson and Anna Maria, born My 21, 1851, baptized Je 15, 1851 (2:118).

Josephine, daughter of Otho Ferguson and Anna Maria, born Ap 16, 1853, baptized My 29, 1853 (2:119).

BITZENBERGER, Margaret; died My 7, 1870, buried Mr 8, aged about 56; nearly white; '"poor but honest"...industrious in and out-door man's labor'. Buried at Stone Church, Mechanicstown (2:245).

Sophia Jane Luby & Rebecca Ann, twin daughters of Mrs. Stanton, near Owens Creek; baptized Ja 8, 1850 (2:116).

Leonard Young (slave of H. A. Brien) married Sarah Jackson (also slave of H. A. Brien) on S 15, 1839.

Richard Richardson, free negro (1:88), son of Richard and Hagar Richardson, married D 29, 1833 Mary Stantling, free negro, daughter of John and Elizabeth Stantling.

Jeremiah Sims, slave of Mr. Zollinger in Harbaugh Valley (1:84), married S 21, 1828 Mary Tuckum, also slave of Mr. Zollinger.

John Stantling married Elizabeth _____.
Issue: Mary (free negro) married Richard Richardson.

Jacob Williamson (or Williams) and Anna _____ (both slaves of Thomas Ogle, later of Lorenz Krieger) were married.
Issue: Anna (1:175), born Mr 11, 1787 at 11-12 a.m.; baptized Je 2, 1787.
    Sarah (1:169b), born Jl 8, 1789; baptized Ag 6, 1789.
    Benjamin (1:172b), born Ap 3, 1791; baptized Ap 14, 1791.

Samuel Cookerly had by Sarah Sarris (mulatto) an illegitimate son Samuel (1:147) who was born Mr 30, 1834 and baptized My 11, 1834.

Harriet Dorsey, single, negro.
Issue: George Henry (1:94), born O 11, 1837; baptized Ja 7, 1838.

William _____ married Barbara _____ (negroes).
Issue: Heinrich (1:173b), born Ja 23, 1791; baptized Jl 24, 1791.

Alexander Howard married Daphne _____.
Issue: James Warren Hulett (2:222), died Mr 4, 1853; his age was five months and 3 days; buried at Mechanicstown Mr 5, 1853.

Samuel Cookerly married Ja 9, 1866 Mary Elizabeth Patterson (colored) (2:159).

John Lee married Jl 10, 1859 Elisabeth Hill (colored) (2:156).

Lewis Hill (free negro) married Mr 12, 1857 Jane Milberry (slave of Charles Stevens) (2:155).

Henry Thomas Clark (1:89) married O 28, 1838 Catharine Sudrics.

Edward Campbell, colored, married Sarah _____ (slave of George Herman).
Issue: Emily Jane (1:99), born Je 7, 1839; baptized Jl 26, 1840.

Alfred Fedricks (slave of George Zimmerman) married Ja 8, 1850 Mary Catharine Zimmerman (free mulatto) (2:150).

William Grex, negro, had by Sarah _____ (slave of George Herman) an illegitimate daughter Martha Ellen (1:99) who was born My 1, 1835 and baptized Jl 26, 1840.

Gabriel Ball married Sally _____.

Issue: Aaron (1:181), born Ja 17, 1796; baptized My 1, 1796.
Jacob Smith and Ann Fry (slaves of Elias Goushon) were married on Ag 3, 1828 (1:84).

Clemens _____ (slave of Mr. Johnson) married Sarah _____ (slave of Mr. Biggs).
    Issue: Darcas (1:186), born N 16, 1798; baptized Ja 9, 1799.
        Henry (1:186), born N 16, 1798; baptized Ja 9, 1799.
Mr. Johnson's slave married Sara (slave of Mr. Devilbiss).
    Issue: Samuel (1:188), baptized N 3, 1799.
        Rahel (1:188), baptized N 3, 1799.
John _____ (slave of Mr. Elder) married Sarah (slave of Mrs. Ogle).
    Issue: George (1:187), born Je 22, 1799; baptized Jl 14, 1799.
Jonathan _____ (slave of Mr. Kuhn) married Serene _____.
    Issue: Eleonora (1:121), born Je 12, 1825; baptized Jl 10, 1825.
Harry Norris (slave of Mr. Smith, in the valley) married Anna (slave of Andreas Wiljahr).
    Issue: Mary Ann (1:120), born Ja 4, 1824, baptized My 10, 1824.
Hilary Norris (1:83) (slave of Mr. Zimmerman) married Sereno Luby (slave of Mr. Kuhn), on Ag 26, 1827.
    Issue: Mary Jane (1:138), born Je 30, 1828; baptized Jl 12, 1829.
George McKinney married Sarah _____.
    Issue: John Alexander (1:135), born Ap 4, 1827; baptized Jl 28, 1827; Sponsor: Patty McKinney.
Lewis Lowny (slave of Benjamin Neidig) married Ag 29, 1844 Sarah Bell (slave of J. B. Stimmel).
Daniel Bean (slave of R. C. Brien) married O 25, 1829 Anne Williams (slave of same) (1:85).
Henry Bright (slave of Mrs. Catharine Biggs) married My 22, 1836 Harriet Richardson, free mulatto (1:88).
John Briscoe (slave of Mr. Head) married O 19, 1829 Hetty Sedwicks (slave of Mr. Zimmerman) (1:85).

www.ingramcontent.com/pod-product-compliance
Lightning Source LLC
Chambersburg PA
CBHW052217270326

41931CB00011B/2385